DATE DUE

MAY 2 9 1996	

GOING

NEGATIVE

THE FREE PRESS

NEW YORK LONDON TORONTO SYDNEY TOKYO SINGAPORE

GOING

NEGATIVE

HOW ATTACK ADS SHRINK AND POLARIZE
THE ELECTORATE

STEPHEN ANSOLABEHERE
SHANTO IYENGAR

The Free Press
A Division of Simon & Schuster Inc.
1230 Avenue of the Americas
New York, N.Y. 10020

Printed in the United States of America

printing number

2 3 4 5 6 7 8 9 10

Library of Congress Cataloging-in-Publication Data

Ansolabehere, Stephen.
    Going negative : how political advertisements shrink and polarize
the electorate / Stephen Ansolabehere, Shanto Iyengar.
        p.   cm.
    Includes bibliographical references and index.
    ISBN 0-684-82284-9
    1. Advertising, Political.   2. Advertising, Political—United
States.   3. Electioneering—United States.   4. Negativism.
I. Iyengar, Shanto.   II. Title.
JF2112.A4A57   1996
324.7'3'0973—dc20   95-563
                                                                CIP

Text design by Carla Bolte

CONTENTS

ACKNOWLEDGMENTS

This project grew, innocently enough, out of an afternoon chat over coffee in the fall of 1989. We were stumped by the presidential election of the previous year. Most political scientists claimed that George Bush was fated to win—the economy was strong, the nation was at peace. Most popular accounts claimed that George Bush had earned his victory through the masterful use of television advertising. We both felt that the reality lay somewhere in between. But where? How much could people actually learn from just a thirty-second message? Can candidates really win using just television advertisements? We began with a modest study of the subject in 1990, which raised as many questions as it answered, and decided to expand the basic ideas of that project to a much larger scale in 1992 and 1993. Six campaigns and 3,500 interviews later, this book is the result of that investigation.

Along the way we enjoyed considerable support—institutional, intellectual, and personal. We owe a major debt to the John and Mary R. Markle Foundation and to Lloyd Morrisett, president of that foundation, for their financial support of our research. Additional support was provided by the National Science Foundation. The University of California at Los Angeles contributed to this research in numerous ways. Of particular note, Kumar Patel, Vice-Chancellor for Research at UCLA, offered additional financial assistance, Madelyn De Maria managed the accounts and other paperwork for our grants, and Myra Sanders, of the UCLA Law Library, facilitated our research of the NEXIS and DATATIMES archives for Chapter 5. Peter Kubaska at

M.I.T. helped prepare the final manuscript. Stephen Ansolabehere extends a special note of thanks to the Hoover Institution, especially Tom Henriksen of the National Fellows program, for providing a year off from teaching to write this book.

This research would not have been possible without the superb assistance provided by many UCLA graduate and undergraduate students. Special thanks go to Adam Simon, Nicolas Valentino, and Sharmaine Vidanage. In addition, we would like to acknowledge the contribution of Kelly Carlin, Travis Dixon, Diana Estrada, Terri Hall, Mikel Healy, Clark Hoover, Bonnie Lemon, Victoria Mitchell, Erin O'Neal, Jaime Reyes, Jr., Raza Syed, and Nancy Wistrick. We are also grateful to Jeremy Anderson, who was the voice in all of our experimental advertisements. Mark Mellman and David Hill provided an invaluable reality check for Chapter 5.

Many colleagues and friends have commented on our research along the way. We would like to thank the participants at numerous conferences and seminars where we have discussed our findings. John Petrocik and Samuel Popkin deserve a special note of thanks for their very helpful comments. Finally, Bruce Nichols of the Free Press was an invaluable guide throughout the writing of this book.

Above all, we wish to thank our wives, Laurie Gould and Ellen Robb, for their unending patience and continued encouragement. It is to them that we dedicate this book.

GOING

1

THE NEW POLITICAL FAULT LINE

Once upon a time, this country divided itself neatly along party lines. Most people voted; those who did not tended to be poorer, less well-educated, and more apathetic, but still party loyal. The line between participants and nonparticipants was a fault line of sorts, but it was not terribly worrisome. Civic duty ideally would involve everyone, but, even falling short of the ideal, we were at least expressing our national will in our elections. Television has changed all that. Now, we are split by a new division: between loyalists and apathetics. On the one hand, media propaganda can often shore up loyalists to vote for their traditional party; on the other hand, that same propaganda is increasingly peeling off a band of citizens who turn from independence to apathy, even antipathy, toward our political institutions.

Pollsters and political scientists first noticed this new fault line in 1964. The number of people who proclaimed themselves independent of traditional party labels rose sharply in the mid-1960s. At the same time, candidates embraced television as a new means of independent communication with the voters.[1] Politicians no longer needed the legions of party workers to get their messages across; they could effectively establish personal connections with their constituents using television advertising. In addition, there arose a new class of campaign manager—the media consultant, who typically had worked on Madison Avenue and viewed selling politics much like selling any other product. By the end of the 1960s, media consultants had filled the shoes left vacant by the then-extinct ward healers and precinct captains. Within the political parties, chaos reigned. The old-style politicos in both the Democratic and Republican parties battled and lost to a new regime of populists and progressives, who opened up the parties' nominating process to all comers. By most accounts, these reforms did even greater harm to the parties, shamelessly opening schisms that in earlier years were smoothed over behind closed doors.[2]

At the time many observers mistakenly saw in the combination of televised political advertising and the nonpartisan voter the advent of a new age in America. Television advertising was to have produced a new kind of independent politician, not beholden to special interests and not part of the problems that voters increasingly associated with Washington. That day has not dawned. To be sure, the ranks of Independent voters have swollen since 1964, and television advertising is now the mainstay of contemporary political campaigns.[3] The political parties, however, remain ascendent in elections and in government. Despite an occasional Independent candidacy and the rise of the personal electoral followings of many candidates, electoral competition is still between Republicans and Democrats.[4] What is more, government, especially Congress, has become even more polarized and partisan than ever. The parties in Congress represent two increasingly cohesive and extreme positions.

The electorate has reacted with frustration and anger. In recent years, the political pulsetakers have registered record lows in political participation, record highs in public cynicism and alienation, and record rates of disapproval of the House of Representatives, the institution designed to represent the public will.

The single biggest cause of the new, ugly regime is the proliferation of negative political advertising on tv. Our argument is that a new synthesis in American politics has failed to emerge precisely because of the ways that partisans and nonpartisans react to televised political messages. Like product advertising, successful political advertising reflects people's beliefs, experiences, and preferences. One consequence of this simple axiom is that political campaigns reinforce the loyalties of partisans. Nonpartisans, by contrast, usually tune out political advertising. They find politicians, politics, and government distasteful; political advertising simply sounds like more of the same. Only negative messages resonate with such attitudes. As political campaigns have become more hostile over the last two decades, nonpartisans have heard plenty to reinforce their low opinions of politics. Unfortunately, negative campaigning only reinforces the nonpartisans' disillusionment and convinces them not to participate in a tainted process. As a result, nonpartisans have not become the electoral force that they might have. Instead, political advertising has produced a party renaissance, even though partisans are an increasingly unrepresentative segment of the public.

The evidence for this argument is drawn from a four-year study of how political advertisements affect the informedness, preferences, and participatory ethos of the electorate. The results of that study and its implications for American politics are retold in this book.

OUT, DAMNED SPOT

Political advertising is everywhere. In the past, every two years, like clockwork, the American public would be bombarded for a few weeks with televised campaign advertisements; now, with advertising increasingly being brought to bear on such major legislation as trade agreements and health care, it is hard to avoid contact with paid political advertising. The amounts of money spent on political advertising are staggering: hundreds of millions of dollars are poured into what has become the main means of political communication in the United States.[5]

To most of us, the phenomenon is as troubling as it is familiar. We deplore the extravagant expense; we mistrust the factual accuracy of the claims made by both sides; we question the motives of those who created the advertisements; and, through them, we come to distrust those who choose to make their careers in public service. Public regard for politicians has sunk to an all-time low; by wide margins, Americans believe that governmental institutions inflict more harm than good on their collective well-being. On the one hand, this is very much the era of the "permanent campaign," in which television advertising has become an essential tool in the perpetual battle for public opinion. On the other hand, the more the campaign rages, the less we seem to respect and like *any* of its contestants, or even the contest itself.

Consider just three well-known advertisements from recent elections, which together highlight the problem and controversy of political advertising.

"Willie Horton"

In early September 1988, President Bush was running even in the polls with Democratic nominee and Massachusetts Governor Mike Dukakis, when the Bush campaign and their surrogates aired the now-infamous "revolving door" advertisements to suggest that Massachusetts criminals went to prison only to be immediately released. In one particular version, the script and visuals featured a black convicted murderer, Willie Horton, who, while on a weekend furlough from a Massachusetts prison, kidnapped and raped a white woman. The advertisement implied that Governor Dukakis favored lenient treatment of hardened criminals ("Dukakis not only opposes the death penalty, he allowed first-degree murderers to have weekend passes . . ."), while Vice-President Bush favored the death penalty. The Dukakis campaign did not respond with a rebuttal advertisement. Shortly after this advertisement began playing (and recirculating in endless news reports), President Bush surged ahead of Governor Dukakis in the polls; this shift in public opinion was widely attributed to the effectiveness of the Horton advertisement.

The advertisement itself was factually misleading in several respects: it suggested that many of the furloughed convicts committed kidnap and rape (in fact, Horton was the only one who did), it failed to provide any baseline information for evaluating the overall success of the Massachusetts furlough program under Dukakis, and it implied that Governor Dukakis himself was the architect of the Massachusetts furlough program (which, in fact, he inherited from his Republican predecessor). Last, but not least, the advertisement also appealed to voters' racial prejudice and stereotypes by highlighting (both in the visuals and in the text) a black perpetrator and a white victim.

"Gays on Parade"

In the 1992 presidential campaign, President Bush was challenged for the Republican nomination by conservative commentator Patrick Buchanan. The Buchanan campaign produced an advertisement linking President Bush with the National Endowment for the Arts. Against the backdrop of scantily clad men parading down the streets of San Francisco, the announcer claimed that "the Bush Administration has invested our tax dollars in pornographic and blasphemous art. . . ." The advertisement went on to link NEA-sponsored works with homosexuality and child abuse.

Like the Horton advertisement, Buchanan's attempt to smear Bush was misleading in several respects. First, viewers were given no information about the share of the NEA budget allocated to controversial projects and artists, much less about the size of the NEA budget as a whole, and second, the scenes portraying gay men were taken from a film funded by the Reagan administration. Moreover, since budgets are set by acts of Congress, Bush's control over NEA funding was, at best, limited. He could have issued a veto to protest an NEA line item, but he would then have imperilled all other items, and Congress could always override the veto.

The advertisement received widespread attention and comment. While Buchanan failed to wrest the nomination from Bush, his "staying power" in the primaries did force the party to grant him a prime-time speaking slot at their convention; he used his time to hammer at conservative themes of "family values," projecting an image of the Republican party that was considerably to the right of most voters. Many viewers were so repelled by the convention that it was thought to have contributed to Bush's defeat in the general election.

"Forged from Tragedy"

In the California gubernatorial campaign of 1990, the Democratic nomination was contested by former San Francisco Mayor Dianne Feinstein (now a U.S. Senator) and California Attorney General John van de Kamp. Three months before the June primary, Feinstein's prospects appeared slim. She trailed her opponent badly in the polls, her campaign was in disarray, and she had been "fired" by her campaign manager (San Francisco consultant Clinton Reilly).

Until, that is, voters across the entire state were repeatedly exposed to a campaign advertisement. The advertisement began with the playing of ominous music and the flashing of the date November 27, 1978, on the screen. Black-and-white pictures of a disorganized press conference appeared, accompanied by sounds of confusion and emotional distress. Cutting through the noise, Feinstein's voice rang out authoritatively: "Both Mayor Moscone and Supervisor Harvey Milk have been shot and killed."

While the advertisement did go on to mention that Feinstein backs the death penalty and is prochoice, it was the turmoil and drama of the opening moments that captured the viewers' attention. The advertisement suggested that Ms. Feinstein had remained calm and collected (other women are heard screaming in the background) despite the extreme stress of the situation.

The murders of Mayor Moscone and Supervisor Milk, however tragic, were of limited relevance to Feinstein's bid to be Governor of California. The fact that Feinstein was witness to a grisly double murder is hardly a "qualification" for elective office. (Needless to say, the advertisement did not mention that her primary opponent had extensive experience as a prosecuting attorney and had probably witnessed a lot more blood and guts on the job.)

The Feinstein advertisement was considered a "hit." In the weeks that followed, Feinstein's candidacy was rejuvenated; she climbed to a substantial lead in the polls and went on to defeat van de Kamp handily in the primary.[6]

Why, exactly, are advertisements like these troubling? Do they distort public debate by presenting emotional and symbolic appeals, misleading soundbites, and superficial treatment of policy issues? Perhaps—but perhaps not. If voters acquire relevant and useful information from the barrage of televised advertisements, then it is hard to argue that advertising manipulates us through outright falsehood.

Does advertising distort the "truth" by portraying only a narrow range of issues selected by each candidate? Do advertisements thus still manage to manipulate voters with truths rather than lies, by inducing them to vote against their interests? This is a common charge, even though it would seem to insult voters' abilities to think for themselves. And what about the connection between politicians and voters?

Does the extensive use of broadcast advertising increase or decrease the responsiveness and accountability of elected officials? Do advertisements motivate people to vote, or do they instead increase general feelings of disillusionment with the political process?

These questions are frequently raised in public debate, and media experts of all political stripes have weighed in with endless analysis and commentary. The standard criticisms fall into two basic categories. First, and most often, critics decry the superficiality and lack of informational content of contemporary campaign discourse, which typically consists of thirty-second "spot" advertisements. Campaign themes such as "Morning in America," "the Revolving Door," "the Man from Hope," or "Forged from Tragedy" have been derided for failing to provide any significant information to voters about matters of public policy. Most observers accept as a given that the very nature of broadcast advertising—brief snippets of imagery, slogans, and musical jingles—elevates entertainment over substantive treatment of important problems. In effect, they say, advertising and deliberation are incompatible. Candidates whose advertising campaigns are more visual, dramatic, and eye-catching (i.e., less substantive) are thought to enjoy a significant electoral advantage over candidates who campaign on their policy expertise and problem-solving experience.

In addition to shallowness and superficiality, campaign advertising has also been criticized as being manipulative. Political analysts charge that misleading and deceptive appeals attempt to persuade voters to support a candidate or cause that they would reject if the issues were more clearly or comprehensively presented. According to these critics, since political speech enjoys broad First Amendment protection, the potential for distortion and deception is limited only by the marketplace. It is often thought to be rampant.

It is certainly true that political advertisers often depict events out of context, present misleading information, paint exaggerated or Manichaean portraits of the sponsor, and hurl unsubstantiated allegations at the opposition. "Truth in advertising," it is safe to say, is not a touchstone of campaign consultants and strategists. In one case, which appears to have involved a stunning display of manipulative intent, the tobacco industry urged California voters to sign a petition to place a referendum item concerning "statewide" regulation of smoking in public areas on the ballot. Many antismoking Californians mistakenly signed the petition thinking that they were supporting a measure to further restrict smoking. In fact, the measure would have *undercut* tough local antismoking ordinances. (Despite the efforts of the tobacco lobby, the measure was defeated in 1994.) Similarly, the 1988 Bush presidential campaign aired an advertisement describing the polluted state of Boston Harbor. By implying that Massachusetts Governor Dukakis had failed to address environmental degradation in his own state, this message attempted to minimize the stark contrast between the candidates on this particular issue. In fact, Dukakis's record on environmental issues had earned him the endorsement of environmental organizations; Bush's record in public office was marked by consistent opposition to the objectives of the environmental movement.

Some media observers have also suggested that fear of manipulation, in the form of being associated with difficult problems, actually deters incumbent officials from attempting corrective actions. The fear of being victimized by attack advertising is thus thought to contribute to irresponsible governance. Curbing the growth of entitlements may be sound public policy, but the common wisdom is that Medicare and Social Security are politically untouchable—in part because such unpopular decisions would be fuel for negative advertising: Candidate X abandons the elderly. For many incumbents, the importance of protecting one's image from attack advertisements must take precedence over the substantive merits of policy proposals. Perhaps the voters are not the only ones being manipulated by advertising.

Are these charges of distortion and manipulation deserved? Is the chorus of complaints about thirty-second advertisements and the marketing of candidates on television merited? Our research focused specifically on three problems: distortion (defined in terms of voter information or learning); manipulation (defined in terms of voter choice or autonomy); and demobilization (defined in terms of voter turnout or participation).

Our results are unexpected, in both big and small ways. They suggest that campaign advertising is not "a pack of lies." In fact, advertising on the issues informs voters about the candidates' positions and makes it more likely that voters will take their own preferences on the issues into account when choosing between the candidates. Our studies also suggest that the effects of advertisements on voters depend, among other things, upon the partisanship and gender of the sponsoring candidate, the issue being discussed, and the attentiveness of the audience. In these ways, perhaps our research might help political consultants choose the most effective tactic, but it provides no fodder for political reformers.

On the other hand, our most troubling finding is that negative or "attack" advertising actually suppresses voter turnout. Attack advertisements can be, and are, used strategically for this purpose. We would even go so far as to say that negative advertisements may pose a serious antidemocratic threat. In 1993, the Republican political consultant Ed Rollins boasted (apparently falsely) of paying black ministers in exchange for their abstaining from encouraging their congregations to vote. His claim caused an understandable firestorm of controversy. Our claim is in many ways more serious: we believe that candidates who might benefit from low turnout pay for negative advertising to discourage participation. The real concern for Twenty-First Century democracy is not manipulation of naïve voters by sophisticated "image makers," but the shrinking of the electorate by political strategists who are fully aware of the consequences of their actions.

What about the problem of distortion? Is the traditional argument valid? Clearly, the thirty-second commercial is a somewhat mindless form of communication. Candidates could surely develop their positions and arguments in greater detail were they, like Ross Perot, in a position to campaign on the basis of in-depth "infomercials." Our evidence indicates, however, that despite the typical advertisement's brevity and superficial format, voters can and do learn from advertising, even on matters of substance such as the candidates' positions on the issues. By permitting viewers to form impressions of the sponsoring candidates, advertising simplifies the task of voting. In some respects, the voters who are most likely to learn from campaign advertising are those who lack other sources of information. In terms of information, therefore, advertising works to level differences between the "haves" and "have-nots."

Our evidence also shows that political advertising is not manipulative. Instead, we find that exposure to advertising reinforces or "awakens" latent partisan predispositions. Voters who tend to prefer Democrats (such as African-Americans or blue-collar workers), for instance, are especially responsive to advertisements aired by Democratic candidates. Individuals for whom the potential for manipulation is presumably greatest—those lacking a sense of party affiliation—are, in fact, the least likely to be persuaded by campaign advertising. Overall, we find that exposure to advertising facilitates voters' "normal" or expected choice of candidates; voters exposed to campaign advertising are more likely to vote along partisan lines than those not exposed to advertising.

We found many interesting variations on the theme that advertising reinforces voters' partisanship. The persuasive effects of advertising are dependent upon several factors, including the tone of the advertising campaign, the party of the sponsoring candidate, and the particular issues under discussion. Republican candidates persuade their supporters more effectively with negative advertisements, while Democrats tend to be more persuasive with positive appeals. Moreover, whether voters react to advertising in keeping with their long-standing partisan loyalties itself depends on the issue on which the candidates advertise. Republican voters are especially drawn to "their" candidate when advertisements deal with issues on which the Republican party enjoys a favorable reputation, such as crime, illegal immigration, or national defense. Conversely, Democrats are more persuasive when they advertise on traditionally "Democratic" issues, such as unemployment or civil rights.

There's a catch to the good news findings of this book, however: advertising polarizes American elections. On the one hand, advertisements are informative and not manipulative, but they are dividing voters into more and more partisan camps. On the other hand, negative advertisements, which account for approximately half of all campaign messages, are shrinking the electorate, especially the nonpartisan electorate. As the independents in the middle stop voting, the partisans at the extremes come to dominate electoral politics. It is the voice of this increasingly small and increasingly polarized voting public that representatives hear.

Is there anything that can or should be done about the poisonous and divisive effects of advertising? Recent history offers one answer. Public concern over superficial and deceptive political campaigns reached fever pitch in the aftermath of the 1988 presidential election. Following the election, reformers took direct aim at campaign advertising. Rather than allowing the candidates and their advertising strategists the freedom to dictate the terms of campaign discourse, the press was urged to play a more interventionist and "interactive" role vis-à-vis the candidates. In particular, reporters were asked to become referees who would alert the public to inaccurate, unsubstantiated, or decontextualized claims in political advertisements. By evaluating the content of campaign advertising on a systematic basis, the goal was to deter candidates from airing misleading or superficial appeals.

These innovations had a clear impact on the 1992 campaign. The news media, both print and broadcast, devoted extensive space and resources to interpreting and scrutinizing the candidates' broadcast advertisements. These "ad-watches" were even used as the basis for rebuttal advertisements in several campaigns, including the presidential race.

The question is, were voters made more aware of the issues and capable of resisting the blandishments of broadcast advertising? Our research answers no, for two reasons. First, since voters are not mere puppets whose preferences can easily be swayed by the "sound and light" of advertising, the ad-watches aimed too low. They assumed ignorant, manipulable voters and produced copy accordingly. Second, for the audience, for whom any given advertisement tends to reinforce partisan inclinations, the ad-watches simply amplified its effects, thus playing into the hands of the candidates and their handlers. More generally, too, we argue that ad-watches miss the main threat. The use of campaign advertising to suppress turnout has escaped universal condemnation presumably because the demobilizing impact of negative advertising has been a well-kept secret, and a tacit assumption among political consultants. By demonstrating that vote suppression is indeed real, our studies suggest that the press could better serve the public by exposing the demobilizing effects of negative advertising than by refereeing the veracity and fairness of advertising content.

Normally, the competitiveness of the campaign marketplace acts as a check on the power of individual advertisers. But in the case of vote suppression, political advertisers seem to play an autonomous role. Unlike the effects of advertising on voter information and voter preference, the problem of voter withdrawal in response to negative campaigns is actually exacerbated by market forces such as competition.

In sum, advertising does pose a serious threat to democracy—but this threat is not one that is usually laid at its feet. Vote suppression is profoundly antidemocratic. It may not be the result of an explicit reaction to a particular message; voters simply grow to dislike negativity and withdraw accordingly. Nevertheless, it is a problem that cries out for consideration, if the free market approach to political speech is not to lead to a political implosion of apathy and withdrawal.

OVERVIEW

Following a chapter in which we explain our methods of research and describe the various campaigns that were studied, we present our findings in four broad thematic chapters. First, we address the debate over the effects of advertising on voter "learning"—the transmission of information about the candidates, issues, or events. As we noted at the outset, the conventional wisdom holds that advertisements are not educational and that exposure to campaign advertising impedes, rather than promotes, voter learning. Our evidence repudiates this claim overwhelmingly. We show that the messages conveyed in campaign advertisements inform voters about the candidates' positions on the issues. Exposure to advertising also allows voters to develop differentiated images of the candidates, images that play an important role in shaping voting choice.

When voters are exposed to limited amounts of campaign advertising, the information value associated with exposure to advertising is especially high for citizens who are apolitical and uninterested in campaigns. This "captive audience" is insufficiently motivated to follow other forms of campaign communication and is thus especially dependent upon advertising. For these voters, we find that exposure to a single campaign advertisement provides significant "added value" and thus narrows the information gap between more and less motivated voters.

The overall level of voter learning rises with the intensity of the advertising campaign. Voters exposed to advertising from both candidates are more informed, on average, than their counterparts exposed to one dominant advertiser. However, the educational benefits of competitive advertising are greatest for more involved and attentive voters. Competitive advertising results in a more informed and opinionated electorate, but an electorate characterized by sharp disparities between the haves and have-nots.

We also examined the effects of campaign advertising in particular races on voters' information about candidates contesting other races. In general, we found little evidence of "spillover" in voter learning; the effects of advertising on voter information are campaign-specific.

The next chapter of the book is devoted to the effects of advertising on voter choice (the issue of manipulation). All advertising, be it political or commercial, is aimed ultimately at moving the viewers' preferences. Surprising as it may seem, social scientists who study campaigns have concluded that campaign communication has little impact on voters. Our results indicate otherwise. We find that even small doses of campaign advertising are sufficient to influence voters' preferences: exposure to a single advertisement boosts the sponsoring candidate's share of the vote, on average, by nearly 5 percent. We also find that advertising influences voters indirectly—the issues on which the candidates advertise become more influential as criteria for evaluating the candidates.

Yet even though political advertising is highly persuasive, it is not necessarily manipulative. In general, unless given good reasons for doing otherwise, Americans vote along partisan lines. Our analysis of voter manipulation focuses on this benchmark role of partisanship. We find that advertisements influence voters in concert with long-standing partisan predispositions. That is, not all viewers are equally affected by advertising—the effects of advertising on voting preference are concentrated disproportionately among voters who share the partisanship of the sponsor. Advertising thus strengthens the importance of partisanship as a determinant of voting choice. Moreover, we also find that the persuasiveness of advertisements depends on the fit or match between the candidate's message and voters' stereotypic beliefs about the political parties. Republican candidates, for example, are especially able to score points with advertisements calling for "law and order," while Democrats are particularly effective when their advertisements deal with unemployment and jobs programs. Overall, we conclude that advertising is persuasive, but not manipulative.

In Chapter 5 we come to the nub: the effects of advertising on citizens' involvement in the campaign. Since the classic studies of the 1940s, political scientists have taken for granted that voter activation and mobilization are the principal objectives of campaigns. We argue, however, that the shift from party-based to media-based campaigns has meant that campaigns can be either mobilizing or demobilizing depending on the nature of the advertising campaign. Both in our experimental results and by comparing a number of 1992 Senate campaigns, we show that exposure to negative advertising, in and of itself, produces a substantial decrease in voter turnout. We also show that exposure to negative advertising increases voters' cynicism about the electoral process and their ability to exert meaningful political influence.

Unlike our findings on persuasion, the demobilizing effects of advertising are not conditioned by the direction of voters' partisan affiliation. Voters who identify with the "target" of the attack are no more likely to withdraw than voters who identify with the attacker. However, following exposure to negative advertising, voters with no sense of partisan identity are significantly more likely than partisans to lose interest in voting. To these voters, negative advertising is a signal of the dysfunctional and unresponsive nature of the political process itself.

The next chapter of the book examines the argument that campaign "markets" condition the impact of political advertisements. As anticipated by the framers of the Constitution, potentially antidemocratic effects of advertising can be countered by providing voters with the opportunity to watch advertisements from rival candidates. With respect to voter information, we find that the doctrine of "more speech" does work as intended. Voters become especially informed when they have the opportunity to watch advertisements from both the contestants. With respect to voter autonomy, our results demonstrate that competitive advertising campaigns influence voters' preferences jointly or reactively, rather than separately. Because the effects of one candidate's advertisements are conditioned or counteracted by the effects of the opponent's messages, voters become less subject to the influence of any particular candidate. In short, the presence of competition makes advertisers interdependent rather than independent actors; the effects of any one candidate's advertising depend upon the advertising strategy of the opponent(s).

Unfortunately, the interdependence of candidates only seems to strengthen the candidates' incentives to attack one another. Examined from a strategic framework, our findings in Chapter 6 support one of the most popular axioms of candidate strategy—the importance of counterattacking when attacked. Especially since Michael Dukakis's loss to George Bush in 1988, the folklore has come to include Roger Ailes's dictum—"when punched, punch back."[7] We find that candidates are driven to attack not because negative messages are more persuasive, but because that is the most prudent way to head off possible attacks by the opposition.

A further dialogue of sorts occurs between the "free" (news) and "paid" (advertising) channels of campaign communication. As described earlier, the legacy of the 1988 election was to make political advertising especially newsworthy. Most major media outlets now regularly feature ad-watch reports in which a particular political advertisement is scrutinized for its accuracy and veracity. We monitored the effects of representative ad-watch reports on voters. In Chapter 6, using examples from the 1992 campaign, we explain our finding that this new form of campaign journalism has a long way to go before it realizes its stated objective of empowering voters. It becomes almost amusing to see how exposure to ad-watch reports boosts support for the "targeted" advertiser and therefore plays into the hands of the candidates.

We conclude the book with lessons for the practice of democratic politics and for proposed reforms of the electoral process. The most important implication of our research, we argue, concerns the trade-off between the right to vote and the right to political expression. Does negative advertising embody a sufficient threat to democratic norms to warrant some form of governmental regulation, or is the time-honored doctrine of "more speech" the appropriate answer? How should we weigh the public interest in free expression against the competing public interest in widespread political participation? When, if ever, should politicians' expression be restrained or subjected to incentives to modify its form or content?

We also consider a variety of reform proposals aimed at curtailing the "antisocial" effects of advertising and conclude that, like previous efforts to reform the campaign finance laws, most would only strengthen the hostile climate of contemporary political campaigns. The evidence reported in this book suggests that the current marketplace of ideas in which candidates slug it out to woo the support of an increasingly small electorate is gradually eroding the participatory ethos of the American public and cannot be counted on to produce political campaigns that get large numbers of citizens to the polls. A more promising route to campaign reform, we argue, involves strengthening the party organizations. It is the parties, after all, and not the candidates who have the incentive to keep participation high and to bring nonpartisan voters back into the fold. Although Americans have never warmed to the idea of strong party organizations, they are our best hope for reversing the growing apathy of the American electorate.

2

THE STUDIES

Forty years after the onset of large-scale campaign advertising, there is surprisingly little agreement over the effects of broadcast advertising on voters and elections. Obviously, the candidates and their political strategists impute considerable power to the thirty-second advertisement. Academic researchers, however, have been hard-pressed to identify any effects and have concluded that campaigns in general and campaign advertising in particular are relatively unimportant determinants of electoral outcomes. In fact, political scientists routinely forecast presidential and statewide elections using models that ignore campaign-related factors altogether. Presidential elections, for instance, are thought to hinge on the state of the country's economy and the popularity of the incumbent president, with the competing campaigns having negligible effects on the outcome.[8]

For a multi-billion-dollar industry to leave no traces of influence on its targets is mysterious. And despite the claims of the academics, such an influence is hardly demonstrated. The primary impediment to a more sophisticated and thorough understanding of the effects of political advertising has been technical. Most of the "minimal effects" evidence uncovered by researchers in the political communication field rests on sample surveys or polls. Surveys are ill-equipped to detect the effects of campaign advertising. This chapter describes a more powerful alternative to surveys—the controlled experiment.

17

Survey researchers who study the effects of campaigns rely on the logic of correlation. A representative sample of voters is contacted (generally over the phone) and asked various questions about their exposure to campaign messages. How often do they watch television news, listen to talk radio, read a newspaper, or converse about politics? Which prime-time programs do they watch? Do they remember watching any campaign advertisements? Which candidate do they prefer and why? And so on.

Responses to these questions provide the basis for assessing the effects of campaign communication. In an important study of the 1972 campaign by Patterson and McClure, for instance,[9] survey respondents who reported watching television news frequently were considered under the potential influence of news reports, while those who could recall having watched a Nixon or McGovern advertisement were thought to be under the potential influence of advertising. For each medium of communication, Patterson and McClure compared users with nonusers. They discovered that people who could recall an advertisement were more informed about the candidates' positions on the issues than those who could not, whereas people who watched the news frequently were not as "advantaged" as those who watched the news less frequently. On the basis of this pattern of differences between users and nonusers, Patterson and McClure concluded that campaign advertising was more informative than television news coverage.

This inference, however, is questionable on several grounds. Individuals' memory for past events is notoriously frail, especially when the "event" in question concerns what they saw or did not see on television. Some survey respondents may have surmised that since it was election time, they must have seen a political advertisement. Among participants in our experimental studies who were exposed to *no* campaign advertisement, for example, 20 percent claimed to have seen one. Alternatively, many people who were unable to recall watching an advertisement may in fact have done so (repeatedly), only to then forget it. In our experiments, nearly half of all people who were exposed to a thirty-second advertisement could not recall that they had seen a political advertisement just one-half hour later.[10] In short, survey measures of exposure to campaign communication are likely to be riddled with errors. Since exposure to communication is basic, survey researchers are at an inherent disadvantage in the search for communication effects.

Even if we were to assume that survey researchers' indicators of exposure were "true," their ability to monitor the effects of campaign advertising would still be hindered. Consider the case of advertising recall. People who are able to remember a political advertisement differ in innumerable ways from those who cannot. In addition to having better memories, they are likely to be more interested in politics, more devoted to the candidates, more concerned about the issues, and more likely to vote. In Patterson and McClure's study, was it exposure to the candidates' advertisements that made voters who could recall watching an advertisement more aware of where McGovern and Nixon stood on the issues? Or was it their greater interest in politics that made them both more informed and more likely to attend to political advertising? Even worse, was it their superior information that allowed them to remember campaign advertisements? In general, the presence of multiple differences between voters deemed to be ad-watchers and nonwatchers makes it difficult for survey researchers to isolate the effects of advertising on any particular political response. While those who pour hundreds of millions of dollars into campaign advertising would like to know just what they get for their money, so far most survey researchers studying the effects of campaign communication have come away empty-handed.

The alternative to the sample survey is the controlled experiment. It is no accident that experimentation is the methodological paradigm of choice in all scientific disciplines. Because the researcher himself manipulates the phenomenon under investigation, he knows that the experimental participants were either exposed or not exposed to it. In the case of advertising, an "experimental" group is shown a particular advertisement, and a "control" group is not shown the advertisement. Because participants are assigned to the two conditions on a purely random basis, the researcher can be confident that the conditions will be no different from each other in composition.[11] These two basic features of the experiment—the ability to exercise physical control over the experimental stimulus and the use of comparison groups that are equivalent in all respects but the presence of the experimental stimulus—provide researchers with the all-important ability to attribute any observed difference between the experimental and control groups to the effects of the experimental stimulus. If, for example, the experimental group proves to be more informed than the control group, the researcher knows that this difference was caused by exposure to political advertising, and nothing else.

Of course, experiments are not without their own liabilities. Most experiments are administered upon "captive" populations—college students who must serve as guinea pigs to gain course credit. As the eminent experimental psychologist Carl Hovland warned many years ago, college sophomores are not comparable to "real people."[12] A further weakness of the typical experiment is the somewhat sterile, laboratory-like environment in which it is administered, an environment that bears little resemblance to the noise and confusion of election campaigns. Clearly, a considerable leap of faith is required to generalize experimental results to the real world.

Our own studies were designed to overcome the limited generalizability of the experimental method. The experimental participants represented a fair cross-section of the electorate, the experimental setting was casual and designed to emulate "real life," and our studies all took place during ongoing political campaigns characterized by extensive advertising.

GENERALIZABLE EXPERIMENTS

We enhanced the realism and generalizability of our studies in several ways. Campaigns do not occur in a vacuum, and most voters hold a variety of beliefs and expectations about the parties and candidates. We were able to capture the interplay between "old" and "new" information because each of our experiments took place during an actual campaign and featured real candidates—Democrats and Republicans, liberals and conservatives, males and females, incumbents and challengers—as the advertisers.

Second, the advertisements used in our experimental studies were highly realistic. They were either selected from advertisements being used by the candidates at the time or were produced by us to emulate typical campaign advertisements. In the case of our own productions, we spliced together footage from actual advertisements or news reports using studio-quality editing technology, making it difficult for all but the most sophisticated viewers to detect any differences between the experimental manipulations and the "real thing."

Not only did we rely on real instead of artificial presentations, our manipulations were also unobtrusive and presented in a "natural" setting. We embedded the experimental advertisements (and, in some cases, news reports) in a fifteen-minute recording of a recent local evening newscast. Candidates advertise heavily during local news programs (because the audience for news includes a large proportion of likely voters) and the appearance of the experimental campaign advertisement in the local newscast was thus inconspicuous.[13]

Significantly, the use of local news as the vehicle for the advertising manipulation permitted us to incorporate important elements of news coverage. In some cases, our studies focused on the joint effects of news and advertising. Following the 1992 Los Angeles riots, for instance, we produced advertisements that called for "law and order" and paired these advertisements with news stories about widespread looting during the riots. In other cases, we paired campaign advertisements with "ad-watch" reports that analyzed the advertisements.

We further minimized the aura of the "research laboratory" by presenting the experimental news tapes in an informal, living room–like setting. The viewing room was furnished with a couch, easy chairs, coffee table, and potted plants. Participants could snack on cookies and coffee while they watched the news, and in most cases participants came accompanied by a friend or co-worker.

We also enhanced the validity of the results by diverting participants from the true objectives of the study. Had we explained our interest in the effects of advertising at the outset, participants might have felt it necessary to pay careful attention during the commercial breaks (which would have been uncharacteristic of normal viewing patterns). We sought to eliminate the potentially biasing effects of "experimental demand" by telling participants that the research concerned "selective perception" of local news ("Do Democrats and Republicans really see the same news?"). Since the experimental stimulus consisted of a segment of a local newscast, this account of our intentions was intuitively credible. At the end of the study, of course, we fully informed the participants of the true purpose of the study.

An especially important step toward boosting the generalizability of our results was the use of a large, diverse pool of subjects (more than 3,000) who were reasonably representative of the Southern California voting-age population. Unlike the usual social science experiment, which relies heavily on conscripted college sophomores as subjects, our participants were people from many walks of life and included adults of all ages, employed and unemployed, whites, African-Americans, and Hispanics, men and women, city dwellers and suburbanites, and so forth.

Last, but not least, we administered numerous replications of each basic experimental design. These repetitions encompassed a large number of different candidates, issues, offices, campaigns, and time periods. Our studies included men and women candidates, incumbents and challengers, primary and general elections, two-candidate and multicandidate races, partisan and nonpartisan elections, and campaigns for President, U.S. Senator, Governor, and Mayor (of Los Angeles). This broad range of candidates and electoral contexts makes it most unlikely that our results are valid only for particular types of campaign or are otherwise idiosyncratic.

In summary, our studies differ from the typical laboratory experiment in several fundamental respects. We devised experimental manipulations that were relevant and realistic. The experimental setting was natural and the procedures unobtrusive. The people who participated in our studies were ordinary voters who, on election day, would have to choose between the candidates whose advertisements they had watched.

EXPERIMENTAL CONTROL

Despite our efforts to achieve a maximal degree of realism, the experiments did not compromise rigorous control over voters' exposure to campaign advertising. We devised two basic designs corresponding to the use of either one or two campaign advertisements. In the one-advertisement design, we limited the experimental manipulation to a single thirty-second commercial. In most (but not all) of the one-ad studies, we produced the experimental advertisement ourselves and aired it on behalf of several different candidates. As noted previously, our advertisements met high standards of production and, unless the viewer was a political consultant, could not be distinguished from the flurry of political advertisements confronting the typical voter every day.

The objective of the one-ad design was to assess the influence of exposure to a single advertisement and to provide a precise estimate of the effects of particular characteristics of advertisements. Because advertisements aired by different candidates differ in numerous respects, it is virtually impossible to isolate the effects of any particular attribute of actual campaign advertisements. A positive and negative advertisement for Clinton will differ not only in their tone, but in the visuals, text, voice of the announcer, and musical background as well. It can be hard to disentangle the effects of any one component of the advertisement, and the researcher cannot be sure that it is advertising tone that is responsible for any differences in the effects of the positive and negative advertisements.

The one-ad design overcomes the "confounded variables" problem and isolates the effects of a single attribute of campaign advertisements, in most cases, advertising tone or valence. The advertisements that we produced were *identical* in all respects but for their tone and the candidate sponsoring the advertisement. Figure 2.1 describes the manipulation of advertising tone in the 1992 Senate primary election study. Viewers watched a thirty-second advertisement that either promoted the sponsor or attacked the opponent(s) on the general trait of "integrity." As illustrated in Figure 2.1, the visuals featured a panoramic view of the Capitol Building and the camera then zoomed in to a closeup of an unoccupied desk inside a Senate office. In the "positive" treatments (using the example of candidate John Seymour), the text read by the announcer was as follows:

FOR OVER 200 YEARS THE UNITED STATES SENATE HAS SHAPED THE FUTURE OF AMERICA AND THE WORLD. TODAY, CALIFORNIA NEEDS HONESTY, COMPASSION, AND A VOICE FOR ALL THE PEOPLE IN THE U.S. SENATE. AS U.S. SENATOR, JOHN SEYMOUR *PROPOSED* NEW GOVERNMENT ETHICS RULES. HE *REJECTED* LARGE CAMPAIGN CONTRIBUTIONS FROM SPECIAL INTERESTS. AND JOHN SEYMOUR *SUPPORTED* TOUGHER PENALTIES ON SAVINGS AND LOAN CROOKS.

CALIFORNIA *NEEDS* JOHN SEYMOUR IN THE U.S. SENATE.

FIGURE 2.1
Manipulating Advertising Tone: Senate Primary Study

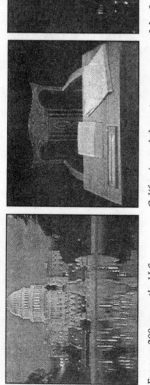

For over 200 years, the U.S. Senate has shaped the future of America and the World.

California needs honesty, compassion, and a voice for all the people in the U.S. Senate.

John Seymour proposed new government ethics rules, rejected large contributions from special interests, and supported tougher penalties on S & L crooks.

California needs John Seymour in the U.S. Senate.

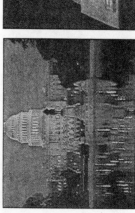

For over 200 years, the U.S. Senate has shaped the future of America and the World.

California needs honesty, compassion, and a voice for all the people in the U.S. Senate.

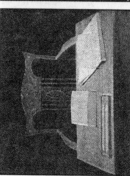

Bill Dannemeyer opposed new government ethics rules, accepted large contributions from special interests, and opposed tougher penalties on S & L crooks.

California can't afford Bill Dannemeyer in the U.S. Senate.

In the "negative" version of this Seymour spot, the text was modified as follows:

> . . . CONGRESSMAN BILL DANNEMEYER *OPPOSED* NEW GOVERNMENT ETHICS RULES. HE *ACCEPTED* LARGE CAMPAIGN CONTRIBUTIONS FROM SPECIAL INTERESTS. AND BILL DANNEMEYER *OPPOSED* TOUGHER PENALTIES ON SAVINGS AND LOAN CROOKS. CALIFORNIA *CAN'T AFFORD A POLITICIAN* LIKE BILL DANNEMEYER IN THE U.S. SENATE.

In this way, by holding the visual elements constant and by using the same announcer, we limited differences between the conditions to differences in advertising tone alone.[14] With appropriate modifications to the wording, the identical pair of advertisements was also aired on behalf of Dannemeyer, and for the various candidates contesting the other Senate primaries.

In other instances, we used the one-ad design to assess the extent to which the effects of advertising were conditioned by voters' pre-existing beliefs about the sponsoring candidate. In some studies we showed viewers the identical issue-oriented advertisement from each of the competing candidates and varied the degree to which the issue in question was stereotypically "male" or "female." As shown in Figure 2.2, the same advertisement on women's issues was presented either as an advertisement for Barbara Boxer or as a spot for Bill Clinton.

A further extension of the one-ad design assessed the extent to which the effects of advertising were conditioned by voters' partisan beliefs. In some studies we showed viewers the identical issue-oriented advertisement from each of the competing candidates but varied the degree to which the issue in question was stereotypically "Democratic" or "Republican." In one experiment, for example, the identical "law and order" advertisements were aired on behalf of Senate candidates Barbara Boxer (Democrat), Dianne Feinstein (Democrat), Bruce Herschensohn (Republican), and John Seymour (Republican). Because the advertisements were replicas of each other (with the exception of the name and party of the sponsoring candidate), any differences in the effectiveness of the advertisement can be attributed only to the attributes of the sponsor. Thus, a stronger impact for a Republican

FIGURE 2.2

Manipulating the Sponsor: Women's Issues

October 11, 1991
The Senate Judiciary Committee:
Professor Anita Hill testifies that she
was repeatedly subjected to sexual
harassment by Clarence Thomas.

The Senators reject Hill's testimony.
Some even question her sanity.

Barbara Boxer believes that sexual
harassment is a real problem and that
it is time to stand up for the rights of
women.

Elect Barbara Boxer
U.S. Senator

October 11, 1991
The Senate Judiciary Committee:
Professor Anita Hill testifies that she
was repeatedly subjected to sexual
harassment by Clarence Thomas.

The Senators reject Hill's testimony.
Some even question her sanity.

Bill Clinton believes that sexual
harassment is a real problem and that
it is time to stand up for the rights of
women.

Elect Bill Clinton
President

sponsor would suggest that Republican candidates are especially credible on the issue of crime.

The final application of the one-advertisement design concerned the effects of ad-watch news reports. In these studies, which were aimed at the 1992 presidential campaign and the Feinstein versus Seymour 1992 California Senate race, participants watched a campaign advertisement that was followed by a news report that scrutinized and evaluated the same advertisement. The ad-watch reports were taken from CNN's "Inside Politics" program.[15] In each case, the report began by replaying segments of the campaign advertisement, then raised questions about the facts and information presented, and concluded by rating the advertisement as either inaccurate or misleading. This arrangement captures the effects of exposure to ad-watch journalism as well as the extent to which the "targeted" candidate's advertising is strengthened or weakened by ad-watches.

The Two-Advertisement Design

In this design (which was used in four of our experiments), participants watched two advertisements, one from each of the candidates. Within this "paired" arrangement, we varied both the tone and content of the advertising. Thus, the spots were either negative or positive and addressed particular issues or personal attributes of the candidates. In one study, for instance, gubernatorial candidates Dianne Feinstein and Pete Wilson discussed either their competence or their integrity. In general, the content of the advertisements in the two-ad studies corresponded to the dominant theme of the respective campaigns. In one of our 1992 senatorial studies, for instance, Republican Bruce Herschensohn either attacked Barbara Boxer as a Washington "insider" who bounced checks with impunity or promoted his own "outsider" status. Democrat Boxer either promoted her legislative accomplishments on behalf of women or attacked Herschensohn as an ideological extremist. Similarly, in the 1992 presidential race, we used advertisements that varied in tone, but that focused on the state of the economy. Former President Bush either promoted his own economic record or attacked challenger Clinton's economic performance as Governor of Arkansas. For his part, Clinton either attacked Bush on the state of the economy or promoted the "Arkansas miracle."

The principal objective of the two-ad design was to pursue questions relating to advertising strategy. Voters are exposed to information from different sources, and advertising is but one element of the campaign environment. The differing elements may interact to influence voters' choices. Most important, the effects of a particular candidate's advertisements may be conditioned by the opponent's advertising. If the effects of campaign advertisements are interdependent, then what candidates can hope to accomplish depends on their ability to anticipate or outguess their opponent.

The idea that advertising is a reactive "debate" is especially important in political campaigns. Unlike product manufacturers and retailers, candidates for public office feel free to air advertisements that feature their opponents. Campaigns have increasingly turned to "attack advertising," in which candidates or their surrogates attack or discredit their opponents. Although the impact of attack messages is thought to depend on certain qualities of the sponsoring and targeted candidates (such as their popularity), practitioners generally acknowledge that it is the response of the attacked candidate that is most important. It was our two-ad studies that allowed us to test exactly which kinds of responses work best in various situations.

The question of advertising tone is but one element of the strategic equation. Candidates must also select a particular theme for their advertising campaign. A candidate whose opponent is considered especially qualified on a particular issue might prefer to organize his advertising around alternative issues or, instead, attempt to neutralize his opponent's advantage by highlighting his own credentials on the issue in question. Our two-ad studies also allowed us to explore this question in some detail.

In summary, our studies followed one of two designs. In all cases, the experimental manipulation was limited to one or two advertisements, but in no case did participants watch more than one advertisement from a particular sponsor. The scale of exposure represented by our experiments is thus quite modest. The one-ad studies either isolated the independent effects of particular attributes of campaign advertisements or the joint effects of advertising, on the one hand, and voters' partisan stereotypes, on the other. Finally, the two-ad studies addressed questions of advertising strategy by showing participants particular combinations of advertisements from each of the competing candidates.

SUBJECTS AND PROCEDURE

Our experiments all took place in the Greater Los Angeles area. We used several methods to recruit subjects, including advertising in local newspapers, distributing flyers in shopping malls and other public venues, announcing the studies in employee newsletters, soliciting the cooperation of office administrators, church pastors, restaurant managers, and others with access to large groups of people, and telephoning names from voter registration lists. Subjects were promised payment of $15 for participation in an hour-long study of "selective perception" of local news programs.

Although the "sample" was obviously nonrandom, our participants resembled the composition of Los Angeles and the surrounding area. Across all the experiments, 46 percent of the participants were male, 52 percent were white, 24 percent were black. The median age was 34. Forty-eight percent of the participants claimed affiliation with the Democratic party, 21 percent were Republicans, and 31 percent were independents. Thirty-nine percent were college graduates, with the balance being evenly divided between high-school graduates and individuals with some college.[16]

We conducted the experiments at two separate locations—West Lost Angeles and Costa Mesa (Orange County). The former is an urban neighborhood with a heavy concentration of Democratic voters. The latter, an affluent Orange County suburb, is predominantly Republican. The experimental facilities were identical in both locations— a three-room office suite consisting of two viewing rooms and a separate room for completion of questionnaires (in addition to a reception area).

When participants telephoned the facility, they were scheduled for a particular time period of their choice. Experimental sessions were available from 10 A.M. to 8 P.M., Monday through Saturday. The typical session consisted of two or three participants.

On arrival, subjects were given an instruction sheet that informed them that the research was about selective perception of local newscasts. They then completed a short pretest questionnaire, which addressed their social background, media activities, and political interest. Following completion of the pretest, participants were taken to a viewing room where, depending on the condition to which they had been assigned,[17] they watched a fifteen-minute videotape recording (complete with commercials) of a recent local newscast.[18]

In the one-advertisement studies, the experimental or "treatment" advertisement was inserted into the first commercial break midway through the tape. The political spot was always shown in the middle position in a three-advertisement break. In the two-advertisement studies, the experimental advertisements appeared during the first and second commercial breaks.

Following completion of the videotape, participants completed a lengthy posttest questionnaire, which tapped their beliefs and opinions on a wide range of campaign issues. Of course, we also ascertained participants' voting intentions and their general level of involvement in the campaign. On completion of the posttest, subjects were paid and informed in full of the true objectives of the experiment.

THE CANDIDATES AND THEIR ADVERTISING CAMPAIGNS

Our studies monitored campaigns for various public offices in California beginning with the 1990 California gubernatorial election and ending with the 1993 race for Mayor of Los Angeles. In between we studied the 1992 primary and general elections for the U.S. Senate and the 1992 presidential election. Our "sample" of campaigns thus included contests for local, state, and national office.

The 1990 California Governor's Race

This campaign featured two well-known candidates, both of whom had attained national prominence. Democrat Dianne Feinstein had previously served two terms as mayor of San Francisco and was among the "finalists" for the Democratic vice-presidential nomination in 1984. Like Feinstein, Republican Pete Wilson had also served as mayor of a major city (San Diego) before his election to the U.S. Senate in 1982.

Both candidates used extensive televised advertising throughout the gubernatorial campaign. Together, they spent approximately $15 million on broadcast time. The prevailing tone of the campaign was decidedly negative. Feinstein attacked Wilson's performance as mayor of San Diego; suggested that he was ineffective, apathetic, and manipulable as a senator; and attempted to tar him with responsibility for the streak of savings-and-loan failures in California. Wilson responded in kind through advertisements which—among other things—highlighted the large budget deficits incurred during Feinstein's tenure as mayor of San Francisco, charged that Feinstein favored racial employment quotas, and asserted that Feinstein's husband had been a major beneficiary of the federal bailout of a failed thrift institution.

The candidates began the campaign virtually even in the polls, with about 20 percent of the electorate undecided. The race remained close through September. In early October, Wilson eked out a small lead, which ultimately proved insurmountable. He was elected with 52 percent of the vote.

1992 California Senate Primaries

Due to a series of unusual circumstances, both of California's U.S. Senate seats were contested in 1992. One seat was an election in the normal course for a full six-year term. The other election was intended to fill the two remaining years of Pete Wilson's term (Wilson having just been elected Governor).

Thus, there were four contested senatorial primaries. We studied both of the Democratic primaries, but for practical reasons could examine only one of the Republican contests.[19]

The Democratic primary race for the "long" (full term) seat was contested by three candidates, each of whom had extensive political experience. These were Marin County Congresswoman Barbara Boxer, Los Angeles Congressman Mel Levine, and Lieutenant Governor Leo McCarthy. Each candidate advertised extensively, airing a mixture of positive and negative messages. The candidates emphasized their experience and problem-solving abilities. Both Levine and Mc-Carthy attempted to associate Boxer with the Congressional "bounced checks" scandal. The race remained tight until two weeks before the election, at which point Boxer established a clear lead. On election day, she won the nomination with 44 percent of the vote.

The Democratic race for the "short" seat pitted two of the state's most prominent Democrats—Dianne Feinstein and State Controller Gray Davis. Feinstein established a commanding lead over Davis in the polls. The Davis campaign attempted to narrow the gap through advertisements that emphasized Davis's support for law and order (these featured scenes from the Los Angeles riots) and impugned Feinstein's integrity. One such ad compared Feinstein with convicted tax evader Leona Helmsley. Davis's efforts made no dent in Feinstein's lead; she went on to win the nomination with 58 percent of the vote.

The Republican primary for the "short" seat featured two relatively unknown male candidates, John Seymour and William Dannemeyer. Although Seymour had served for two years on an interim basis as Pete Wilson's successor in the U.S. Senate, he had attracted little public attention. Seymour's opponent, however, was even less well known. Dannemeyer was a conservative Republican from Orange County who had served three terms in the U.S. Congress. Seymour's financial advantage in the campaign was decisive, and he won the nomination easily.

1992 California Senate General Elections

The race for the "short" seat between Dianne Feinstein and John Seymour was one-sided from the outset. Seymour attempted to capitalize on the issues of crime and immigration and aired advertisements in which he urged that illegal immigrants be returned to their country of origin.[20] Feinstein's advertising emphasized her support for employment training and other job programs, her prochoice stance, and her experience as mayor of San Francisco. Feinstein held a 20-point lead in preelection polls throughout the general election campaign. She won by 54 to 38 percent.

The race between Barbara Boxer and Bruce Herschensohn pitted a conservative southern California broadcaster against the liberal Congresswoman from Marin County. Herschensohn immediately went on the attack, pointing out that Boxer had "bounced" several checks at the House bank and that she epitomized a corrupt Washington establishment. Herschensohn also made clear his support for limited government and individualist values. Boxer's advertising concentrated on her record in Congress: she noted her exposure of Defense Department cost overruns, her leadership on environmental issues, and her constant support for women's rights. In response to the harsh tone of Herschensohn's attacks, Boxer began (toward the end of the campaign) to attack Herschensohn's ideological extremism with advertisements claiming that Herschensohn opposed Social Security and federal aid for education.

Boxer enjoyed a wide lead in the polls when the race began. Herschensohn's steady stream of attacks reduced the Boxer lead significantly, and by mid-October the race had tightened.[21] Entering the final week of the campaign, Herschensohn trailed by only five or six points. A few days before the election, the press reported damaging information about Herschensohn's frequent patronage of a risqué Hollywood nightclub. The last-minute flurry of attention to issues of character, combined with her own attacks on Herschensohn, helped Boxer and she pulled out a narrow victory of 48 to 43 percent.

1992 Presidential Campaign

Given the depth of the recession in California, President Bush faced an uphill battle to win the state. The polls indicated that Californians were profoundly dissatisfied with the incumbent, and by October the Bush campaign had virtually conceded the state to Ross Perot and the Democrats.

Bush and Clinton both relied heavily on negative advertising. Clinton's advertisements hammered away at the state of the economy, Bush's unwillingness or inability to improve Americans' standard of living, and his plans for economic recovery and "change." Realizing that the economy was not an issue on which their candidate was credible, the Bush campaign dwelled on issues of trust and character. Several advertisements reminded voters about Clinton's misrepresentations of his past actions and his record as governor of Arkansas. The

Clinton advertising campaign counterattacked by suggesting that as Vice-President, Bush had been involved in the "Iran-Contra" scandal.[22]

The Bush campaign's misgivings about California voters proved well-founded. Clinton carried the state by a wide margin, though Ross Perot also proved attractive to Californians, winning 21 percent of the vote.

1993 Los Angeles Mayoral Race

Six months after the 1992 elections, the polls in Los Angeles reopened. After twenty years in office, Mayor Tom Bradley retired from office. Following a contentious primary election, with a field of more than twenty candidates, the nonpartisan runoff to replace Bradley came down to city councilman Michael Woo and businessman Richard Riordan. Both candidates waged an intensely negative media campaign. Riordan blamed Woo for rising crime and high unemployment in the city, while Woo criticized Riordan's business deals (which he contended resulted in the loss of businesses to Mexico) and cited his support for "Reaganomics" as evidence of Riordan's ultraconservatism.

The race began tight, but Mr. Riordan eventually won by a comfortable margin.

The Sample of Advertisements

With all these races to draw on, our experiments could test many different kinds of advertising and contextual variables. Campaign advertising typically consists of two subject matter genres—image advertising and issue advertising. In the former, candidates attempt to highlight their personal strengths, particularly integrity or trustworthiness and competence or experience. In the latter, candidates attempt to position themselves advantageously (and their opponents disadvantageously) on major political issues.

Our studies featured both types of campaign advertisements. Image advertising was used in the 1992 Senate primary experiments, the 1990 gubernatorial study, the 1992 presidential campaign, and the 1993 mayoral race. In 1990, for example, some participants watched a Wilson advertisement that suggested that Feinstein's husband had improperly benefitted from the federal government's bailout of a failed savings-and-loan institution. Others saw a Feinstein advertisement that linked Wilson's opposition to stricter government regulation of S&Ls to his acceptance of campaign contributions from several thrift institutions.

Our manipulations also featured representative issue advertisements from each of the campaigns. In the 1990 gubernatorial campaign, both candidates emphasized their advocacy of the death penalty and their proenvironment stance (especially with respect to their opposition to off-shore drilling for oil). In 1992, the key issues facing the senatorial and presidential candidates included the state of the economy, crime, and women's rights. In the case of both Senate races, the presence of two women candidates and the lingering controversy over the hearings to confirm Supreme Court nominee Clarence Thomas made gender-related issues such as sexual harassment especially relevant. Not surprisingly, both women candidates made frequent reference to the Hill-Thomas hearings in their campaigns.

In conclusion, the studies span the entire gamut of political races— from local to presidential, primary to general. Our results are more generalizable than most. The "sample" of elections included races that were entirely negative in the tone of the campaign (such as the 1993 mayoral race) to races that included both positive and negative themes. Some races featured candidates who were ideologically distinct (such as Barbara Boxer and Bruce Herschensohn); others were characterized by candidates with very similar positions (such as Wilson and Feinstein in 1990). The issues central to each race were similarly varied—crime and the environment for the gubernatorial candidates, the economy and gender-related issues in the 1992 Senate and presidential races, and unemployment and crime in the 1993 mayoral campaign. All told, our studies encompass the full range of campaigns and candidates.

3

ADVERTISING AND POLITICAL DISCOURSE

Political campaigns are expected to inform voters about issues of the day, to reduce their dependence on simplistic labels, and to enable them to reach reasoned choices. Unfortunately, even as candidates have become increasingly reliant on television advertising, the information function of political campaigns has fallen into disrepute. Campaigns appear all too superficial, and the question naturally arises whether superficial campaigns breed superficial voters.

Even by the most generous of standards, the American public is poorly informed about the choices. While almost all people recognize the names of their representatives in Washington, relatively few recognize the names of the candidates challenging them. And of those who do recognize their incumbent representatives, less than half feel they know enough to state something that they like or dislike about their members of Congress. Most people's opinions of the candidates, if they have an opinion at all, take the form of generic approval or disapproval rather than agreement with or objection to the politicians' policies and ideas.[23]

Should the public's apparent lack of sophistication and expertise be attributed to uninformative or nonsubstantive advertising? As we will demonstrate throughout this chapter, the answer is quite simply no. Instead, the relatively low levels of concrete information that voters bring to political campaigns represents an enormous opportunity for candidates to educate the public.

The educational potential of campaigns, and campaign advertising in particular, was underscored by Thomas Patterson and Robert McClure's well-known study of the 1972 presidential campaign. By comparing their survey respondents who either did or did not claim to recall watching a campaign spot, they showed that "recallers" were substantially more familiar with the candidates' stances on the issues.[24]

Less well-informed voters, of course, are more likely to be "taken in" by the persuasive appeals of the candidates, but these appeals are not occurring in a vacuum. Patterson and McClure's evidence suggests that the public's lack of sophistication and expertise concerning political issues should not necessarily be attributed to uninformative or nonsubstantive advertising. Voter ignorance may be attributed to several alternative factors. Large segments of the public may pay selective attention to campaign-related issues and may find nonpolicy issues (such as the candidates' personal traits or electoral prospects) more relevant or compelling. In addition, the public may "tune out" information concerning policy positions if the positions are seen as insincere, impossible to implement, or unimportant. When these factors are at work, the candidates could debate the issues at length with only negligible impact on voter information.

It could also be argued (and it is) that voters' limited awareness of the issues is due to the failings of the news media. The dominance of market-oriented television news and the increasing "tabloidization" of the print media have meant that the candidates' issue positions receive only minimal coverage. Indeed, the candidates' television advertisements are often more substantive and serious than news reports on the campaign. It is only too well-documented that media outlets of all stripes devote far more attention to the details, however sordid, of the candidates' personal lives and to the horse-race and conflictual aspects of the campaign than to matters of public policy. It is hardly surprising, then, that voters learn rapidly about the personal attributes of the candidates, and that the level of voter opinionation on questions of character invariably exceeds opinionation about the candidates' positions on issues.[25]

The evidence presented in this chapter suggests that the nonsubstantive appearance of campaigns may be more illusory than real: we find that exposure to campaign advertising is, in fact, a significant learning experience. When advertisements reveal candidates' positions on the issues, voters become significantly more informed about these positions.

We will examine the contributions of campaign advertising to informed voting using two different indicators of learning. First, we consider the effects of advertising on voters' awareness of the candidates' positions on major issues. While it is obvious that candidates cannot provide detailed programmatic information within the framework of a thirty-second advertisement, they can and do convey meaningful information about their own (and their opponents') positions or records on well-known issues and policies.

From the beginning, political issues have been at the forefront of campaign advertising, though we often bridle at the manner in which issues are raised. Consider an infamous commercial run by North Carolina Senator Jesse Helms in 1990. Helms, who found himself locked in a tight race against Harvey Gantt (a black state senator), used the "white hands" advertisement to arouse white voters' opposition to affirmative action. Against the backdrop of a white applicant crumpling a rejection letter into a wastebasket, the text reads, "You needed that job. And you were the most qualified. But they had to give it to a minority because of racial quotas. Is that really fair?" This ad was widely criticized—both in North Carolina and nationally—for hitting below the belt. But for all of the controversy, the advertisement squarely confronted issues of affirmative action and fairness in the workplace on which there were clear, demonstrable differences in the candidates' positions.[26]

Helms's "white hands" commercial is typical: ominous, negative, but definitely issue-oriented. In fact, a recent survey of the content of political advertising in major campaigns found that approximately half of the broadcast advertisements provided "clear statements" about the candidates' positions on issues. This same study also showed that the prominence of issues in political advertising campaigns has increased since 1980.[27]

Our studies dealt with the main issues in the 1990 gubernatorial election (between Democrat Dianne Feinstein and Republican Pete Wilson), both of the 1992 U.S. Senate races (featuring the "women's team" of Barbara Boxer and Dianne Feinstein versus Republicans Bruce Herschensohn and John Seymour), and the presidential race

TABLE 3.1

Candidates' Issue Orientation

	1990 Gubernatorial Election	1992 Senate Election	1992 Presidential Election
Crime	Both candidates favor mandatory sentencing and the death penalty; both claim to have reduced crime rates while mayor.	All four candidates pledge to support tougher sentencing and increased police forces in order to eradicate "gangs and lawlessness."	
Environment	Both candidates oppose off-shore drilling for oil and favor tougher auto emission standards.		
Economy	Both candidates take credit for balanced budgets and economic growth while mayor.		
Unemployment		All four candidates pledge to support government-supported job training programs and tax incentives to encourage companies to stay in California.	Clinton points to increased unemployment and pledges to initiate government-supported retraining programs. Bush argues that his administration's trade policies will open foreign markets and boost employment opportunities.
Abortion		Both Democratic candidates pledge to support a woman's right to choice and to address the problem of sexual harassment of women.	Clinton pledges to appoint prochoice federal judges and attacks Bush for opposing the rights of women.

between George Bush and Bill Clinton. The issues on which the candidates advertised heavily included crime, the environment, unemployment, and abortion. Table 3.1 summarizes the positions taken by the candidates in the advertisements used in our studies.

Our own advertisements picked up those same themes. During the 1992 Senate campaigns, for instance, we produced an advertisement that described the economic devastation of California.

AUDIO

SINCE 1990, CALIFORNIA HAS LOST TWO AND A HALF MILLION JOBS. THE STATE NOW HAS THE HIGHEST UNEMPLOYMENT RATE IN THE NATION.

CALIFORNIA NEEDS ELECTED OFFICIALS WHO WILL FIGHT TO END THE RECESSION. ————WILL WORK TO BRING JOBS BACK TO OUR STATE. AS A U.S. SENATOR, HE/SHE WILL INTRODUCE LEGISLATION TO INCREASE FEDERAL SPENDING FOR JOB TRAINING PROGRAMS AND GIVE CALIFORNIA COMPANIES INCENTIVES TO MODERNIZE THEIR FACTORIES AND PLANTS.

CALIFORNIA NEEDS————IN THE U.S. SENATE.

VIDEO

EMPTY FACTORIES AND BOARDED-UP STOREFRONTS; A GRAPH OF THE STATE'S UNEMPLOYMENT RATE; CLOSE-UP PICTURE OF THE CANDIDATE; WORKERS AT A MCDONNELL-DOUGLAS PLANT AND A CONSTRUCTION SITE.

After the participants had watched the local newscast into which this advertisement had been inserted, they were asked to place both the sponsoring candidate and the opponent on a "government jobs programs" scale.[28] The results showed that advertisements are powerful sources of substantive information, especially in nonpresidential campaigns. Exposure to a single campaign advertisement such as this one significantly boosts voters' information about the candidates' positions on political issues. (Appendix B provides information about the specific questions used to measure information about the candidates' positions on the issues.)

Our second approach to voter learning during campaigns considers an alternative and more subjective form of political information. Even though most voters are unaware of the specific details of candidates' positions on particular issues, they can and do utilize more inexpensive substitutes for factual knowledge. While the majority of Americans remain unfamiliar with the funding mechanisms and coverage provisions included in the Clinton administration's ill-fated health care proposal, they do know that President Clinton stands for expanded access to health care. More generally, researchers have established that the public can differentiate between the political parties on major issues.[29] Democrats, for instance, are considered proponents of social welfare and other public assistance programs, while Republicans are seen as protectors of business interests and supporters of a strong military. These stereotypes and expectations, however crude, enable voters to form beliefs about particular candidates' positions on issues.

We ascertained our participants' impressions of the various candidates' positions and credentials on the issues by asking them to list what they particularly liked or disliked about each candidate. Their responses covered the entire gamut of candidate attributes, from physical appearance, group connections, personal traits, and chances of victory to their positions on campaign issues. Candidate by candidate, we tallied the number of likes and dislikes that referred to specific issues and examined whether their frequency was affected by exposure to campaign advertisements. The results could not have been more clear-cut: exposure to advertising makes voters much more likely to refer to issues as reasons for supporting or opposing a candidate.

We pursued several specific questions of interest. We examined differences in voter learning in relation to different types of campaign advertising, paying particular attention to the question of advertising valence or tone. Here, contrary to conventional wisdom, our findings suggested that negative and positive advertisements were equally informative. Second, we considered whether the effects of advertisements used by candidates in one race could have an effect on how much voters know about candidates contesting other races. Such simultaneous or "spillover" learning effects turned out to be minimal; the effects of advertising on information were generally campaign-specific. Third, we identified groups of voters who were more or less likely to learn from advertising. We found that exposure to just one advertisement tended to level chronic differences in political information stemming from differences in education and various indicators of political interest. As the level of advertising increased, however, the information gap between the "haves" and "have-nots" returned and even widened.

Finally, we considered the issue of information parity among the candidates—how much do voters know about each of the contestants? Parity is important for both candidates and voters. The ability to convey information is vitally important to candidates because the more voters come to know about a candidate, the more inclined they are to vote for the candidate. Indeed, even minimal information about a candidate (such as mere name recognition) is strongly associated with voter preference for the candidate, at least in situations where the voter has even less information about the opposing candidate. Moreover, as advertisers, candidates are able to reach a large segment of the public with selectively favorable information designed specifically to influence voting decisions.

From the perspective of voters, encountering information from both (as opposed to only one) of the candidates is useful because reasoned choice requires a comparative assessment of the competing candidates. We further monitored voters' ability to engage in comparative judgments by monitoring their relative familiarity with both candidates. There was nothing surprising here: we found that each candidate's share of voter information depended on the level of advertising. When voters were exposed to only one candidate's advertising, that candidate became more familiar vis-à-vis his opponent. Exposure to both candidates' advertising, however, made voters more likely to be equally informed about both the candidates.

THE EVIDENCE

The remainder of this chapter will identify more precisely the relationships revealed by our experiments. We begin with voters' ability to correctly place candidates on the issues. The top panel of Figure 3.1 graphs the level of voter awareness of the candidates' positions in the various campaigns under consideration. With the exception of the presidential election, exposure to campaign advertising significantly boosted the level of issue information. In the dual Senate races, a single campaign advertisement provided a significant impetus to voter learning. Voters became even more informed when provided the opportunity to see an advertisement from each of the Senate candidates. In the Feinstein-Wilson gubernatorial race, exposure to advertising from both candidates was necessary to raise the level of issue information.

The distinctiveness of the presidential results is understandable. It is well-established that presidential candidates generate vast amounts of news coverage. Voters (and candidates) are thus less dependent on advertising. It is also clear that voters attain a much higher level of familiarity with the presidential candidates; some two-thirds of our experimental participants could correctly place Bush and Clinton on the issues of abortion and unemployment. In contrast, less than one-third of the sample could identify where Senate hopefuls Feinstein and Seymour stood on the issues of crime, abortion, and unemployment.

The underlying pattern is clear. Exposure to even small doses of campaign advertising is a significant educational experience. Aggregated across all four campaigns, the percentage of informed voters increased by 5 percent as a result of exposure to a single advertisement, and by 9 percent when both candidates advertised. Campaign advertising makes voters more aware of the issues.

The bottom panel of Figure 3.1 tracks the effects of advertising on our measure of subjective information—the number of spontaneous references to both candidates' positions on issues (any issues) in voters' lists of likes and dislikes of the various candidates. Here, the impact of advertising was even more pronounced. With the exception of the 1990 gubernatorial campaign (where issue-based likes and dislikes were unusually frequent irrespective of exposure to campaign advertising), voters became significantly more likely to refer to issues as a result of exposure to one or two campaign advertisements. Even the highly visible presidential candidates elicited a greater outpouring of issue-oriented comments when they advertised. Averaging across the four campaigns, the prominence of issues in voters' lists of likes and dislikes was nearly *doubled* when participants watched an advertisement from each of the competing candidates.

By either measure of issue information, therefore, exposure to campaign advertising is a significant learning experience. Advertisements

FIGURE 3.1
Learning about Issues

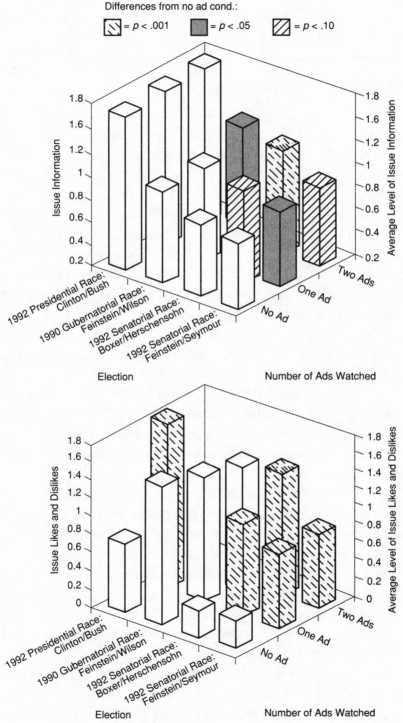

impart information about their sponsors' positions on policy issues and leave voters with impressions that are more strongly tinged with issue considerations.

The Question of "Spillover" Learning

We turn next to the question of whether the effects of advertising can spread or piggyback to other candidates and campaigns. In a presidential election year, the voter typically encounters television advertising from a multiplicity of candidates vying for various positions (from Insurance Commissioner to U.S. Representative to President). Can voters distinguish between the candidates on the roster in any given year, or do they instead simplify their task by assimilating or linking the positions of candidates from the same party? If information about candidates is sorted by party affiliation, advertising on behalf of a particular Democrat should be applied to other Democratic candidates. We would then expect a cascading form of information "coattails" by which candidates who advertise more extensively provide voters with cues about the positions of lesser known candidates. Alternatively, it may be that voters are inclined to treat candidates and races as distinct entities. In this case, advertisements that promote Bill Clinton's support for health care reform would not reflect on Barbara Boxer's or Dianne Feinstein's positions on this issue, and voters' information about the Senate races would be unaffected by Clinton's advertising campaign.

As we noted earlier, California voters were exposed to a spate of advertising during the 1992 campaign from presidential candidates Bush and Clinton, as well as the four senatorial contenders. Given the fact that voters knew considerably more about the positions held by Bush and Clinton, we naturally expected that exposure to advertising from the presidential campaign would boost information about the Senate candidates. We also considered the possibility that advertising from candidates in one of the simultaneous Senate races would affect learning about the candidates in the other race.

As revealed in Figures 3.2a–3.2b, the only traces of spillover between the presidential and senatorial campaigns concerned voters' likes and dislikes of the candidates. Exposure to an advertisement from the presidential campaign, for instance, boosted (by a significant margin) the likelihood that voters would cite issues when asked about their impressions of the candidates in either Senate race. In reciprocal fashion, exposure to advertising from either of the Senate races more than doubled the frequency of issue-oriented comments aimed at Bush and Clinton.

Unlike the frequency with which voters invoked issues in their comments about the candidates, concrete information about the candidates' positions on the issues did not spread across campaigns. A Clinton advertisement on unemployment, for example, did not make voters any more able to identify the positions held by Boxer or Herschensohn (even though the Senate and presidential candidates held the same positions on jobs programs). Similarly, neither of the Senate races' advertising had any impact on information about the presidential candidates. In fact, the only instance of information spillover occurred within the Senate elections. Voters who watched two issue advertisements from the Boxer-Herschensohn race (one from each candidate) not only learned about the sponsors' positions, they also became significantly more informed about the positions taken by Feinstein and Seymour. This particular spillover effect, however, was not reciprocal—issue advertisements aired by Feinstein and Seymour did nothing for voters' information about Boxer and Herschensohn.

FIGURE 3.2A

Spillover Effects on Issue Likes and Dislikes

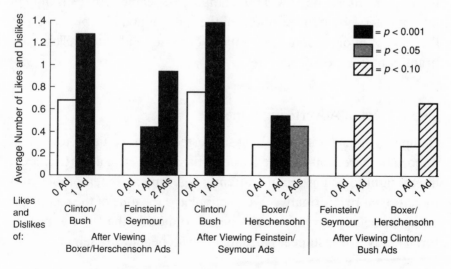

FIGURE 3.2B

Spillover Effects on Issue Information

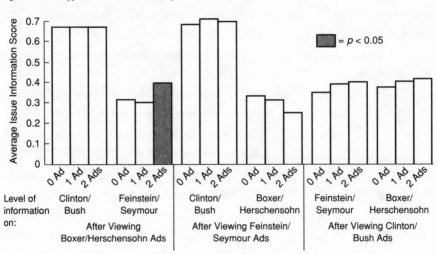

The evidence thus suggests that the scope of what voters learn from advertising varies with the indicator of information. Exposure to advertising from *any* candidate served to raise the frequency of issue-based likes and dislikes of *all* candidates. Voters who watched an advertisement describing one candidate's position on some issue became sensitized to issues when they were asked to comment about that candidate and various others. However, the effect of advertising on voters' ability to correctly identify the candidates' positions on the issues was more narrow and campaign-specific. Advertisements inform voters about the positions of the sponsor and his opponent, but they do not inform about the positions of these candidates' fellow partisans contesting other races.[30]

The Effects of Advertising Tone

Campaign consultants have long suggested that advertising tone is an important ingredient of effective advertising. Negative advertisements are thought to be particularly attention-getting and memorable, and therefore more informative. We manipulated the tone of the campaign advertisement in several of our one-ad studies. In the 1990 gubernatorial study, for instance, participants watched advertisements from

Dianne Feinstein and Pete Wilson on the issues of crime and the environment. In the positive versions of these advertisements, the sponsor was depicted as "tough" on crime and a friend of the environment. In the negative versions, the opponent was depicted as "soft" on crime and a foe of environmental protection. In all other respects (visuals, the announcer, etc.), the positive and negative versions of the advertisements were identical. Any differences in the effects of the positive and negative advertisements, therefore, can be attributed only to advertising tone. Table 3.2 provides a capsule summary of our tone manipulations.

In our two-advertisement studies, we varied advertising tone so that participants watched either one or two positive (or negative) advertisements. Our ability to assess the effects of advertising tone in these studies was necessarily less precise because the advertisements we used were selected from those that were actually aired by the various candidates. The positive and negative advertisements thus differed in many attributes other than their tone (such as the voice of the announcer, the musical backdrop, visuals, thematic focus, etc.). Our definition of negative tone in these studies corresponds to the conditions that featured two negative advertisements; conversely, positive tone encompasses conditions in which participants were exposed to a positive advertisement from each candidate.

The differences in voter information attributable to the tone of campaign advertising are displayed in Figures 3.3a–3.3b. In general, we find that advertising tone counts for little; voters come away from positive and negative advertisements with about the same level of issue information. In addition, they are no more nor less likely to talk about issues after watching positive or negative advertisements. In the few scattered instances where tone produced a difference, no consistent pattern could be detected. In the Boxer-Herschensohn Senate race (which, in reality, was entirely negative in advertising tone), negative advertisements proved more informative and more evocative of issue-based likes and dislikes of the candidates. In the presidential campaign, however, the difference was in the opposite direction—positive advertising resulted in significantly higher information and more frequent references to issues in voters' lists of likes and dislikes of the candidates.[31]

TABLE 3.2

Experimental Manipulations of Advertising Tone

1990 Gubernatorial Campaign—Environment

Positive Ad	Negative Ad
When federal bureaucrats asked for permission to drill for oil off the coast of California, ——— said no. When the automobile industry wanted to weaken pollution controls, ——— said no. The Russian river, the giant Sequoias, Yosemite Valley, Mono Lake; these are the treasures that make our state great. ——— will protect these wonders. California needs a Governor like ———.	When federal bureaucrats asked for permission to drill for oil off the coast of California, ——— said yes. When the automobile industry wanted to weaken pollution controls, ——— said yes. The Russian river, the giant Sequoias, Yosemite Valley, Mono Lake; these are the treasures that make our state great. ——— will destroy these wonders. California can't afford a Governor like ———.

1990 Gubernatorial Campaign—Crime

Positive Ad	Negative Ad
It's happening right now, in your neighborhood. A generation of youths slowly dying. ——— intends to stop this tragedy and preserve California's future. As Mayor of ———, ——— added police officers, built new jails, and fought hard against drugs. The result? Major crime rates fell by 12 percent. This record won the endorsement of the California Association of Police Chiefs. California needs a Governor like ———.	It's happening right now, in your neighborhood. A generation of youths slowly dying. ——— is not the candidate who intends to stop this tragedy and preserve California's future. As Mayor of ——— cut the police force, blocked new jails, and opposed drug education programs. The result? Major crime rates increased by 12 percent. This record was condemned by the California Association of Police Chiefs. California can't afford a Governor like ———.

1992 Senate and Presidential Campaign—Women's Issues

Positive Ad	Negative Ad
The Senate Judiciary Committee. Professor Anita Hill testifies that she was repeatedly subjected to sexual harassment by Clarence Thomas. The Senators reject Hill's testimony; some even question her sanity. Barbara Boxer (Dianne Feinstein, Bill Clinton) believes that sexual harassment is a real problem and it is time to stand up for the rights of women. <Candidate's sound bite.> Elect Barbara Boxer (Dianne Feinstein) U.S. Senator (Bill Clinton President).	The Senate Judiciary Committee. Professor Anita Hill testifies that she was repeatedly subjected to sexual harassment by Clarence Thomas. The Senators reject Hill's testimony; some even question her sanity. Bruce Herschensohn (John Seymour, George Bush) does not believe that sexual harassment is a real problem and has opposed laws that stand up for the rights of women. Not Barbara Boxer (Dianne Feinstein, Bill Clinton). <Candidate's sound bite.> Elect Barbara Boxer (Dianne Feinstein) U.S. Senator (Bill Clinton President).

Table 3.2, continued

1992 Senate Campaign—Unemployment

Positive Ad	Negative Ad
Since 1990, California has lost 2.5 million jobs. The state now has the highest unemployment rate in the nation. California needs elected officials who will end the recession. ———— will work to bring jobs back to our state. ———— will introduce legislation to increase government funding for job training programs and to provide California companies with incentives to modernize and expand their factories and plants.	Since 1990, California has lost 2.5 million jobs. The state now has the highest unemployment rate in the nation. California needs elected officials who will end the recession. _____ has done nothing to bring jobs back to our state. _____ opposes legislation to increase government funding for job training programs and to provide California companies with incentives to modernize and expand their factories and plants.
California needs ———— in the U.S. Senate.	California can't afford ———— in the U.S. Senate.

Based on the results shown in Figures 3.3a and 3.3b, we conclude that negativity does not bolster the information value of political advertising. How much voters learn about the candidates' positions and the extent to which they think about political issues when evaluating the candidates does not depend on the tone of the advertising campaign.

Who Learns?

To this point we have assumed that all voters learn uniformly from advertising. Of course, this is implausible. Academic researchers have devoted considerable effort to identifying the factors that discriminate between people who comprehend and learn from campaign messages and those who do not.[32] These studies have demonstrated that the reach of campaign messages is limited by built-in differences in recipients' political attentiveness and information. We know that the more attentive and informed are drawn disproportionately from the ranks of the affluent, educated, and politically engaged strata of society. Of course, attentive and informed voters are more likely to monitor campaigns and messages about the candidates' positions on the issues. In this sense, the effect of campaigns is to exacerbate existing information inequalities—the smart get smarter, the uninformed stay uninformed.

FIGURE 3.3A

Effects of Advertising Valence on Issue Information

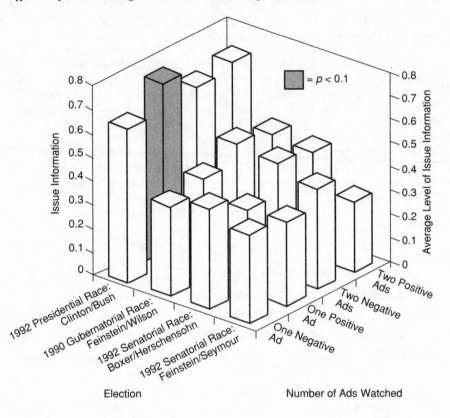

Political advertising may not fit the general pattern described above. Unlike most channels of campaign communication, advertising allows candidates to reach uninterested and unmotivated citizens—those who ordinarily pay little attention to news reports, debates, and other campaign events. After all, the "audience" for political advertising is primarily inadvertent—people who happen to be watching their preferred television programs. Of course, viewers can choose to tune out or channel-surf during advertising breaks, but the fact remains that the reach of advertising extends beyond relatively attentive and engaged voters.

We distinguished between more and less attentive voters using a variety of measures. These included years of formal education (high school versus college), prior knowledge about current events, interest in public affairs, prior voting history, and attentiveness to the print

FIGURE 3.3B

Effects of Advertising Valence on Issue Likes and Dislikes

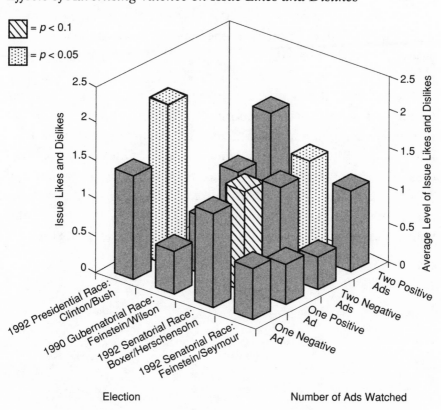

media.[33] In addition to these indicators, we also examined differences in learning associated with party affiliation and gender. Party affiliation is especially important, for it enables us to assess whether learning is politically motivated or "selective." Perhaps voters find advertisements from one of their "own" more interesting, credible, or relevant than advertisements from the opposition. Gender is also relevant because three of the candidates contesting the races under consideration were women (Dianne Feinstein in 1990, Feinstein and Barbara Boxer in 1992). The presence of two women Senate candidates in 1992 attracted considerable publicity and discussion concerning a potential "year of the woman." Research suggests that men tend to be more attentive to the political world, but analysts have wondered whether the presence of strong female candidates might close this gender gap.

For the purpose of assessing group differences in learning, we pooled across all four campaigns. In the case of participants who watched advertising from the 1990 gubernatorial candidates, learning was defined as information about the gubernatorial candidates; in the case of the presidential study, it was learning about Bush and Clinton, and so on.

The results of this pooled analysis (shown in Figure 3.4) were intriguing. As we expected, the information boost produced by exposure to a single campaign advertisement was much greater among less-advantaged groups. However, when the level of advertising was increased to two advertisements, the learning effects became more pronounced among the more attentive and engaged. The more educated and informed, frequent users of the print media, and regular voters all registered no increase in information after exposure to a

FIGURE 3.4

Individual Differences: Issue Information

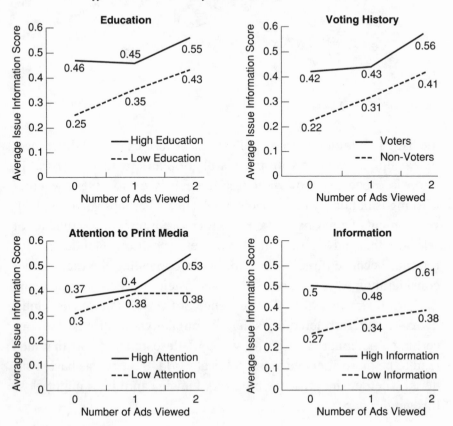

single advertisement, but showed substantial increases after watching two advertisements. Among their less-advantaged counterparts, however, exposure to two advertisements induced only modest gains in information. As a result, the information gap between the more and less attentive was narrowest when participants encountered advertising from only one of the candidates, and widest when participants encountered either none or two political advertisements.[34]

The case of voters' prior political information is illustrative. Among our participants who watched no campaign advertisements, the high-information group enjoyed a lead of 23 percent in awareness of the candidates' positions. Among participants who saw a single campaign advertisement, the lead dropped to 14 percent. And when the newscast included two advertisements, the lead was back to 23 percent.

Extrapolating from these results, we may surmise that as campaigns generate more extensive amounts of advertising, the less attentive and informed either tune out or fall victim to information overload. Either way, they fail to learn. The more attentive voters, on the other hand, only begin to acquire new information as the level of advertising surpasses some threshold. Given the vast amounts allocated to broadcast advertising in most major races, our results lead to the conclusion that advertising is not as egalitarian a form of campaign communication as expected—the more the candidates advertise, the more their message reaches only the better-informed segments of the electorate.

We turn next to the effects of party identification and gender. As noted above, the importance of party labels in American politics leads us to expect that advertising is particularly informative when the sponsor and viewer hold the same party affiliation. As Figure 3.5 indicates, this expectation was amply confirmed: partisan agreement enhances learning about the candidates' positions.[35] When the candidate who advertised was Republican, Republicans were more informed than Democrats by a margin of 14 percent. But when the sponsor was a Democrat, Democrats were more informed than Republicans by a margin of 13 percent.[36] Aggregating across both parties, viewers who affiliated with the sponsoring candidates were more informed than those affiliating with the opponent as well as those with no sense of party identity.[37]

FIGURE 3.5

Partisan and Gender Differences in Learning: One-Ad Studies

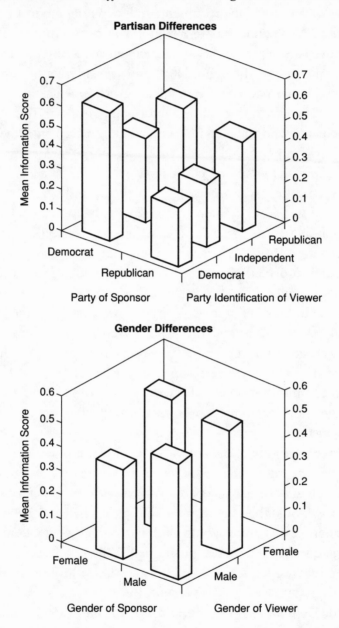

Did women learn more from women candidates than men? Clearly they did. As shown in the bottom panel of Figure 3.5, men were more informed than women when the sponsoring candidate was a man. The tables were turned, however, when the candidate was a woman. Now women were more informed than men.[38]

Information Parity among the Candidates

Finally, we return to the question of differences between individual candidates in their "share" of what the public learns and the extent to which the distribution of information about the candidates is affected by campaign advertising.

From the candidates' perspective, the ideal world would be one in which voters learn a great deal about them and little about their opponent(s). Since voters tend to shy away from relatively unknown candidates, familiarity is tantamount to preference. A one-sided distribution of information, though beneficial to the dominant candidate, impedes voters' ability to choose on the basis of issues. Voters need to know about both candidates' positions so that they may determine which of them is closer to their own positions.

We examine individual candidates' level of familiarity vis-à-vis their opponent in Figure 3.6. Our measure expresses voters' information about particular candidates as a fraction of their total information about both candidates.[39] A score of 1.0 for Barbara Boxer, for example, would mean that voters knew something about her and nothing about her opponent, Bruce Herschensohn. A score of zero would show the opposite, and .5 would be the point of equality under which voters possessed the same amount of information about both candidates.

As Figure 3.6 indicates, the presidential election was clearly the most closely contested campaign in terms of voter information. Despite Bush's incumbent status, our participants were just as familiar with Clinton's positions on issues as they were with Bush's. Each candidate's share of voter information remained even regardless of the level of campaign advertising. Our results thus confirm the argument (noted earlier) that presidential candidates' access to alternative sources of communication makes political advertising relatively unimportant in the battle for public visibility.

FIGURE 3.6

Candidates' Share of Voter Information

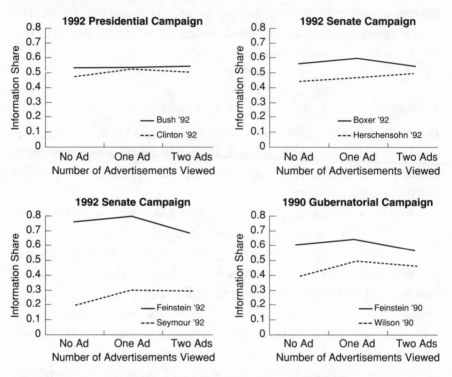

The nonpresidential races fluctuated considerably with regard to the individual candidates' relative familiarity. Among participants exposed to no advertising at all, the Democratic candidates enjoyed a substantial edge in familiarity over the Republicans. In all three races, the candidates were able to increase their share of voter information when they advertised and their opponent did not. As might be expected, the gain in relative familiarity was especially prominent for the candidates who were initially less visible (the Republicans). In the cases of Pete Wilson and Bruce Herschensohn, "solo" advertising enabled them to achieve parity with their Democratic opponents. Averaging across the sponsoring candidates, the increase in relative familiarity was 5 percent. Advertising by one candidate makes the advertiser more familiar with voters at the expense of the opponent.

As expected, the distribution of voter information was most equitable when voters were equally exposed to both candidates. The information edge enjoyed by gubernatorial candidate Feinstein and Senate candidate Boxer was substantially eroded when both candidates had access to voters. In the Feinstein-Seymour Senate race, although Seymour's share of information increased slightly when both candidates advertised, Feinstein's dominant familiarity was generally unaffected by the level of advertising.

In summary, exposure to competitive advertising campaigns increases voters' familiarity with both candidates. In the process, by evening the candidates' level of visibility, advertising benefits less well-known and less well-established candidates. Competitive advertising also benefits voters by enabling them to compare the candidates on the issues.

CONCLUSION

Though political advertisements are generally ridiculed as a serious form of campaign communication, our results demonstrate that they enlighten voters and enable them to take account of issues and policies when choosing between the candidates. Just why are campaign advertisements informative?

In the first place, as campaign consultants are quick to point out, the inherent brevity of the campaign advertisement does not necessarily preclude the transmission of substantive information. Even the slowest-speaking of candidates can articulate a portion of their positions and records within the span of thirty seconds. In the 1992 Senate race between Barbara Boxer and Bruce Herschensohn, a Boxer advertisement noted Herschensohn's position on *six* different issues—his support for increased defense spending, his opposition to Social Security and the home mortgage tax deduction, his proposals to abolish the Department of Education and terminate federal funding for AIDS research, and his prolife stance on abortion.

When a political advertisement is aimed at a single issue (as is often the case), candidates can describe their position in considerable detail. Consider the following statement on abortion with a running time of twenty-four seconds.[40]

I BELIEVE THAT THE QUESTION OF ABORTION OUGHT TO BE RESERVED EX- CLUSIVELY TO A WOMAN AND HER DOCTOR. I FAVOR GIVING WOMEN THE

UNFETTERED RIGHT TO ABORTION. I ALSO FAVOR THE FEDERAL FUNDING OF
ABORTIONS THROUGH MEDICAID FOR POOR WOMEN AS AN EXTENSION OF
THE RIGHT TO ABORTION, AND I OPPOSE ANY STATUTORY OR CONSTI-
TUTIONAL LIMITATIONS ON THEIR RIGHT.

The brevity of the advertising message may actually strengthen its
information value. The typical person's attention span for political
information is notoriously short-lived; few of us are sufficiently motivated to send away for the candidates' position papers, tune in to the
ten-minute excerpts from campaign speeches on the "MacNeil-Lehrer
Newshour," or watch the entire speech on C-SPAN. Those who do so
are political aficionados and experts. The great majority of voters
bypass or ignore information that entails more than minimal acquisi-
tion costs, preferring to use messages that are simple to digest and
easily obtained. Of course, campaign advertising meets the demand
for both simplicity and access.

In addition to the convenience benefits of advertising, political advertisements may be informative because of their reliance on widely
shared cultural symbols and scripts—the Social Security card, construction workers in their hard hats, Soviet troops marching through
Red Square, and so on. The imagery of campaign advertising serves
to remind voters about what they already "know" about the candidates' positions on issues. Most Americans are socialized to believe,
for example, that Democrats favor jobs programs and that Republicans favor balanced budgets. Advertising on the issues evokes these
stereotypic beliefs about the candidates. In effect, political advertising
informs voters both by providing new information and by refreshing
their existing store of knowledge. This characteristic of political advertising also explains why people are more able to recall information
from political advertisements than from product advertisements.
Unlike their beliefs about political parties and candidates, most Americans are not brought up to believe that Anacin and Aspirin have particular strengths and weaknesses. Product advertising, being less likely
to evoke prior knowledge, is thus more difficult to retain. In one national study conducted during the 1972 presidential campaign, for
instance, over 50 percent of people were able to recall information

from political advertisements. Few, if any, product advertising campaigns can hope to achieve this level of recall.[41] In short, the continuous interplay between advertising and voters' prior beliefs provides an important impetus to learning. As we will show in Chapter 4, the intermingling of new and old information is also crucial to understanding the effects of advertising on voter preference.

4

STRIKING A RESPONSIVE CHORD

Campaigns ought to empower voters to choose candidates who will best represent their interests. The popular belief, though, is that the sound and light of advertising manipulate and deceive voters, especially those ignorant about the candidates to begin with. This is not a trivial concern, especially when we consider how little people know about their representatives in the U.S. House and Senate.[42] In this view, the gullible masses can be easily swayed by a carefully crafted marketing campaign. Electoral victory, then, belongs not to the men and women who have the voters' interests at heart, but to those who hire the best advertising agencies.

Voters, however, are not fools, nor are they fooled by political advertising. Although people command few facts about the candidates, they do hold strong beliefs about politics in general. They desire that the government address particular concerns, such as unemployment and crime, and they harbor definite opinions about the political parties and political leaders who are responsible for addressing the problems high on the public's agenda. These attitudes temper the electorate's receptiveness to political commercials.

The potential for manipulation is real enough. Campaign messages can influence how people vote, and they can influence what people think the election is about when they vote. As we show below, exposure to even a single advertisement can raise support for its sponsor by a significant amount. What is more, a single advertisement can re-direct the issues on which the race hinges.

Advertising, however, affects the electorate unevenly and in ways that leave very little room for electoral manipulation. Among our find-ings:

- Exposure to a single advertisement solidifies the support of parti-sans, especially those who are poorly informed or wavering in their loyalty.
- Advertisements induce few Republicans to vote Democratic and few Democrats to vote Republican. Exposure to an opposition candi-date's advertisements, in fact, can sometimes strengthen a voter's loyalty to his or her party.
- Candidates do best on those issues on which their party is generally perceived to be better. Republicans do better than Democrats when crime is the issue; Democrats do better than Republicans when un-employment is the issue.
- So-called "women's issues" reach Democrats more than they reach women.
- Republican viewers find negative advertisements to be significantly more persuasive than positive messages. Democratic viewers find positive commercials to be more compelling.
- Independents are generally unresponsive to political advertising, with the important exception of negative commercials.

While these results reflect several complicated and interconnected phe-nomena, they underscore a basic axiom of political advertising: Advertising works—or fails—to the extent that it speaks to the voters' political interests and beliefs, to the extent that it resonates with voters' partisan predispositions.

Consider the case of Willie Horton. Perhaps the most infamous po-litical commercial of recent times, "Willie Horton" and its cousin "The Revolving Door" are widely credited with reviving George Bush's 1988 presidential bid and sealing Michael Dukakis's fate as an also-ran. Whatever else can be said about these ads, they were certainly effective. Not all viewers, however, judged the messages and the mes-sengers equally. The anticrime stance shored up Bush's support among the Republican-leaning suburban voters. But among African-

Americans the Bush campaign message stank of racism, driving these voters—who did not support Dukakis wholeheartedly at the outset of the general election campaign—firmly into the Democratic camp.[43]

The many commentaries about the 1988 election pointed with disgust at the divisions and prejudices in the public that the campaign commercials tapped. The story of Willie Horton, though, suggests that advertising might not be the darkly manipulating force of American politics after all. Manipulation involves leading voters to select politicians who ultimately do not represent the individual's interests and preferences.[44] Extensive crossover voting in response to campaign commercials would be clear evidence of electoral manipulation. Conceivably a sophisticated advertising campaign could sway large numbers of Republicans to vote Democratic or large numbers of Democrats to vote Republican or win the growing segment of the electorate that considers itself to have no party attachments or leanings. The case with Willie Horton, and with advertising more generally, is the opposite. As we will demonstrate throughout this chapter, advertising reinforces and invigorates existing partisan preferences and beliefs.

This argument was largely overlooked in the postmortems on the Bush-Dukakis race, but it is hardly new. It has been recognized as a basic fact of voting behavior since the first wave of academic survey researchers in the 1940s descended on Elmira, New York, to find out how people make up their minds over the course of the campaigns.[45] It squares with subsequent survey research on the dynamics of campaigns, which finds that people learn a lot over the course of the campaigns but usually vote in-line with their partisan predisposition.[46] But more important, it is a basic precept of practitioners in the worlds of product advertising and political advertising.[47] One consultant put the matter quite bluntly: "You can only give the voters what they want."[48]

The resonance principle comes to life in our experiments. While advertising may speak to voters' many different ideas and interests, we find that reactions to political advertising are structured primarily by the political parties. Party affiliation produced striking and consistent patterns of reinforcement. Democratic partisans who saw commercials of Democratic candidates and Republican partisans who saw commercials of Republican candidates registered significant increases in support for their parties' nominees. Comparatively few voters, however, crossed party lines in reaction to the commercials of opposition candidates. These effects are especially pronounced among partisans who pay little attention to public affairs and know little about the candidates. In the end, political advertising does not produce wholesale manipulation and deception of the electorate. Rather, it leads partisans to cast "informed" votes. Exposure to advertising induces less-informed Democrats and Republicans to vote like their fellow partisans who are more knowledgeable about the candidates and public affairs.

The powerful reinforcing effects of campaign advertising do not stem just from the labels Democrat and Republican, but are based on the issues that distinguish the parties and give those labels meaning. Voters align themselves with a particular party because they believe that party best represents their interests and concerns. Those who care about crime tend to be Republicans; those who fear racial discrimination tend to be Democrats. Our studies reveal that partisan voters are especially responsive to those issues that their party is seen to be best at, and partisans consider their own candidates to be more credible messengers on those issues. Of course, not all issues fit neatly into partisan categories; some candidates can capitalize on an issue because of other stereotypes. Being an incumbent or a man may give candidates a special edge in their commercial appeals. Or, those features may be liabilities, as, for example, when a scandal in Congress lowers public regard for all incumbents or when media hype about the Year of the Woman gives a female candidate an edge. Most issues, however, are highly politicized and divide along party lines, allowing one party's candidates to appeal strongly to voters who care most intensely about those issues.

What of the Independents—the supposed swing-voters in American elections? They are the exceptions that prove the rule. People who claim no partisan attachments are extremely unreceptive to campaign advertising. This is true regardless of the Independent voter's interest in public affairs or knowledge about the candidates. This is true regardless of the issue discussed in the advertisements or the candidate promoted in the commercials. Rather than a readily manipulable mass of swing voters, politicians face a highly unresponsive group at the center of the electorate.

Negative advertising also fits with our resonance theory of political advertising. Recent elections have seen the proliferation of campaign commercials that attack the political beliefs and personal characters of opponents. Campaign consultants justify the use of such messages as simply being more persuasive than positive messages. As a matter of grand strategy, consultants may be right: attack advertising may be the most reliable route to victory. Not all viewers, though, are receptive to negative advertising. Our experiments demonstrate that how one reacts to negative and positive advertisements depends on one's views of government. Democratic viewers actually prefer positive messages about the candidates to negative ones. Democrats have a proactive view of government, and positive commercials reinforce their belief in a positive role for government and the competence of politicians.

Republicans and Independents, on the other hand, possess negative views of government, and negative advertising speaks directly to those beliefs. Central to the GOP's ideology is the image that government fails at most things; free markets produce the public good much more efficiently and effectively. Advertisements pointing up the failures of particular programs, the corruption of government, and the incompetence of politicians speak directly to the Republican voters' beliefs that less government is better. Independents are largely distrustful of, and alienated from, politics. If they vote at all, it is to throw out one bum or the other. Any message attacking Washington, politics, or particular politicians speaks more strongly to the nonpartisan voters' cynicism than do messages detailing what a candidate will do once elected.

ADVERTISING AND VOTE CHOICE

Before addressing the more complex questions of who is affected by advertising and why, it is useful to put advertising in context. People vote for candidates for a host of reasons—party identification, evaluations of the economy and the president, issue stances, personalities, gender, race, and so on. Given the importance of these factors, how much change in voting preferences can campaign commercials produce? How much bang is there in the advertising buck?

Our single-advertisement experiments were designed expressly to measure the effect of advertising exposure on voting preferences. In these experiments we first determined who saw an advertisement for a particular candidate and who did not. After a participant in our experiments watched one of the videotapes, we then ascertained what that viewer thought of the candidates and how he or she intended to vote. Contrasting the opinions of those who saw an experimental advertisement with the opinions of those who did not provides a ready measure of the ability of advertising to persuade viewers.[49]

Our immediate concern is whether advertising affects how people vote. We asked the participants whom they intended to vote for in the coming election. Respondents could choose one of the candidates, none of the candidates ("not sure yet"), or not to vote in this election. Since an advertisement may increase support for the sponsor or decrease support for the opponent, we examined the *lead* of the sponsoring candidate, the percent voting for the sponsor minus the percent voting for the opponent(s).

Party identification, past voting behavior, and other factors that tap voters' political predispositions account for most of the variability in voting intentions across individuals. Party identification alone goes a long way to explaining why people vote the way they do. Among those people who saw no experimental advertisements (the control groups), 62 percent of the Democrats intended to vote Democratic and 10 percent intended to vote for the Republicans, with the remaining 28 percent being undecided. Forty-one percent of the Republicans intended to vote Republican, 22 percent preferred the Democrats, and 37 percent remained uncommitted. Independents leaned to the Democrats (26 percent Democratic versus 12 percent Republican), as was to be expected in races where the Democrats were heavily favored, but the bulk of the Independents, 62 percent, were undecided or intended not to vote. Appendix B contains a detailed statistical analysis of the factors that affect voting preferences.

Even in the face of such strong determinants of the vote, campaign advertising significantly changed viewers' electoral preferences. In our experiments, exposure to a single campaign advertisement increased support for the sponsoring candidate by nearly eight percentage points. Table 4.1 displays the effects of advertising exposure on the sponsors' leads in each of the six one-ad experiments as well as the average (or overall) effect of advertising on voters' preferences. Each entry in the table is the change in the vote margin (or lead) of the sponsoring candidate attributable to exposure to an advertisement, holding party, gender, race, and past voting behavior constant. That is, each entry is the difference between the voting intentions of those who saw an ad and similar people who did not.

In each of the six experiments, exposure to a campaign commercial produced a strong increase in the sponsor's lead. On average, support for the sponsoring candidates rose 7.7 points (with a margin of error of 3.8 points).[50] The persuasive effects of the ads ranged from a low of 5.4 points, when the Senate candidates focused on government jobs programs, to a high of 11.5 points, when Barbara Boxer and Dianne Feinstein discussed abortion rights, the Thomas-Hill hearings, and other concerns high on the agendas of women voters.[51] Each experiment produced statistically significant movement in voting preferences.[52]

A seven- to eight-point shift in voting intentions may seem small, especially compared to the importance of partisanship, but it is hardly trivial. In the 1988, 1990, and 1992 elections, the victors in one in three U.S. Senate races, one in three gubernatorial contests, and one

TABLE 4.1

Effect of Exposure to a Single Advertisement on Voting Preferences

Experiment	Estimated Effect	Standard Error	Number of Cases
1990 Governor	.074	.042	240
1992 Senate: primary	.076	.032	747
1992 Senate: riots	.058	.036	329
1992 Senate: women's issues	.115	.034	400
1992 Senate: unemployment	.054	.040	225
1993 Mayor	.068	.043	233

Average effect   .077
Margin of error ± .040

Note: Estimates are controlling for party identification, past vote, and gender, race. In Appendix B we present the full analyses.

in nine U.S. House races won by seven percentage points or less.[53] Very few incumbents lost their seats in these elections, but more intensive advertising by the losers might well have reversed many of these outcomes.

Elections, of course, are about more than winning and losing. The vote itself is a coarse expression of public sentiment, and any politician worth his or her salt has a more nuanced view of public opinion. Politicians understand, or at least try to understand, what their strengths are among the voters and what the voters think is important and want from government. After the ballots are counted, the winners must divine the mandates behind their elections. What problems do voters want their new presidents, governors, and legislators to address? What will the electorate hold them accountable for come the next election? Voters' reasons for choosing a candidate, as much as the number of votes that a candidate receives, give meaning to election victories.

Campaign advertising influences the meaning of the vote in two ways. First, advertising can change the viewers' evaluations of the candidates on specific issues and personality traits. For example, an advertisement expounding a candidate's accomplishments on crime may make people think that politician is able to reduce crime rates. Second, advertising can influence how much weight voters give to various factors. An advertisement about crime may make viewers think that crime is an important problem, regardless of what they think of the candidates. Also, advertisements that emphasize personality traits of the candidates may make elections depend on charisma more than on the issues.

To examine the effects of advertising on how people think about the choices, we asked subjects to evaluate the candidates on various personality traits and issues. Participants rated how well the traits "honest," "hard-working," "strong," and "inexperienced" described each candidate. The total number of favorable ratings offers a measure of the overall image of a candidate, and the margin by which the sponsor's traits exceeded the opponent's, the "net trait rating," captures the relative strength of a candidate's personality.[54]

We also asked people to rate the candidates on various issues. Participants identified their own positions on an issue and the positions of the candidates on that same issue. We have already seen in Chapter

3 that advertising exposure increases the ability of people to rate the candidates on the issues. Here we examine the extent to which those ratings were favorable. In addition, we can examine how voters reacted to the specific content of the advertisements or whether the advertisements had any effects. For example, did the crime advertisements lead viewers to develop more favorable evaluations of the sponsoring candidate on that issue?[55]

Advertising strongly influences evaluations of the candidates on the traits or issues addressed in the commercials. The Senate primary election study dealt with personal images of the candidates—integrity, competence, and experience. Exposure to the experimental advertisement changed voters' assessments of the candidates' personality traits by a significant margin. With the solitary exception of Gray Davis, all of the candidates enjoyed positive personal images relative to their opponent(s) when they advertised. Even in Davis's case, though he was viewed less positively than his opponent, Dianne Feinstein, his advertisements significantly raised voters' relative evaluations of him. Averaging over all of the candidates, the trait ratings of the candidates (which ranged from +1 for entirely positive to −1 for entirely negative) were .17 when the candidates advertised and −.13 when they did not—a significant difference.[56] This .30 increase in the assessments of the candidates' personalities translates into a 4.4 percentage point increase in intentions to vote for that candidate.[57]

The general election studies focused on issues rather than personalities. Here too, advertising exposure produced significant improvements in the relevant evaluations of the sponsors of the ads. Exposure to advertising led people to rate the sponsoring candidate more favorably on the death penalty when the ad addressed crime, on job creation when the ad addressed unemployment, on abortion when the ad addressed women's issues, and on environmental protection when the ad addressed pollution. Overall, the approval rating of the sponsoring candidates' position on the relevant issue rose by 4.8 percentage points in response to a campaign advertisement, a highly significant change statistically speaking, which translates into a direct increase in the sponsor's lead of roughly two points.[58]

In addition to producing more favorable evaluations of the sponsoring candidates, advertising also changes the criteria by which voters make up their minds. Psychologists refer to this as "priming." Like decision makers in other walks of life, voters are notorious simplifiers. They look for ways to economize on deliberative effort by finding a single reason to vote for or against a candidate. Rather than ransack their memories for every fact that they have ever learned about the candidates and the election, voters rely primarily on information that happens to be momentarily salient. Simply by focusing on one issue to the exclusion of others, candidates can alter the criteria on which voting choices are based and, indirectly, change voting intentions. For example, when campaign advertisements emphasize economic issues, voters' beliefs about the economy and the candidates' abilities to deal with economic problems become especially important determinants of voting preferences. When candidates focus on women's issues, opinions on sexual harassment or reproductive rights or gender equality take on added importance as criteria for judging candidates.

Both our primary and our general election studies produced strong priming effects. In the senatorial primaries, the ads focused on the candidates' competence and integrity. In all three primaries, the candidates' personalities proved powerful ingredients in the vote, as noted earlier. Exposure to an advertisement made evaluations of candidates' traits even more prominent, producing an indirect increase in the sponsor's share of the vote of roughly one and a half percentage points. This indirect effect is smaller than the direct effect of the advertisement, but it is still quite significant.[59]

In our general election studies, the experimental advertisements dealt with issues of crime, unemployment, and gender. Participants indicated their positions on the death penalty, the right of a woman to have an abortion, and government-sponsored jobs programs. Advertising on crime and unemployment doubled the effects of the participants' issue opinions on voting intentions.[60] The consequence was to boost the vote margin of the sponsoring candidate by an additional two points. The women's issues advertisements, on the other hand, produced no significant evidence of priming.

The difference between women's issues and crime and unemployment is likely due to the nature of the issue. Crime and unemployment are valence issues: everyone would like less crime and less unemployment, all other things being equal. Many women's issues, on the other hand, are divisive. Public opinion is deeply split on abortion rights, on pay equity for men and women, and on the appointment of Clarence Thomas to the Supreme Court, which was the opening hook for the experimental advertisement. Divisive or "position" issues can still produce priming, but the response to them is likely to be more complex than with valence issues. As we discuss below, the women's issues study reminded Democratic men of the Thomas-Hill hearings and the issues it raised. Democratic women needed no reminding, and Republicans, regardless of gender, reacted against the themes stressed in the ads.

The strength of the priming effect for unemployment and crime suggests a subtle way that campaign advertising may manipulate elections. By hammering away at particular issues, candidates may distract voters from other important concerns. People may care most about crime or unemployment, but by calling their attention to health care, campaign commercials may lead people to vote according to their preferences on that issue, rather than on problems of greater concern to them over the long run.

While advertising certainly affects how people vote and what people think the election is about, our findings should not be taken as evidence that campaign commercials manipulate public opinion. None of the results to this point show whether people are actually led to vote against their underlying interests or partisan preferences. Do large numbers of people defect from their party allegiances simply because they saw a political appeal from the opposition party's candidate? Are people who care about a particular issue led to abandon that issue in their voting decisions? To determine whether political advertising manipulates voters requires that we examine how different people react to particular messages.

THE IMPORTANCE OF PARTISANSHIP

Americans' political preferences fall into three broad categories: Democrat, Republican, and Independent. To some extent, this division has been forced on the electorate by the two-party system, which is itself largely a product of the first-past-the-post voting rule.[61] Nonetheless, partisan preferences and labels in the United States do have real meaning for people. Party allegiances reflect the degree to which the parties and the candidates who run under their banners represent, and have represented, the voters' interests. They are shorthand for what people want and expect from government and what the parties, as governing organizations, can claim credit for or should receive blame for.

While much has been written about the rise of the Independent voter and the decline of party organizations, the simple labels Democrat and Republican continue to command high degrees of loyalty from most voters. Today, two-thirds of the electorate claims an affiliation with one of the two major parties, and most of these people stick by their party allegiances when they vote.[62] In the last five presidential elections, for example, only 14 percent of the party identifiers who voted chose the candidate of the opposite party.[63] Although a growing number of people vote one way for president and another for Senator or Representative, the frequency of such split-ticket voting is an order of magnitude lower among partisans than it is among Independents.[64]

Loyalty at the polls, however, is not an immutable habit, but an outcome of political campaigns and the electoral context. Candidates work to strengthen the support of their own parties' voters and coax Independents and members of the opposite party to abandon their previous attachments. Political parties occasionally suffer serious lapses of discipline among their adherents. More than a quarter of all Democratic voters crossed party lines to vote for Ronald Reagan in 1980; one in five crossed over to vote for Reagan again in 1984.[65] Even during a single campaign, partisan loyalties can vary considerably. Media polls during the 1992 election, for example, showed that 19 percent of Republicans intended to abandon their party and vote for Bill Clinton. On election day, however, only 7 percent of Republicans voted Democratic.[66]

Appealing to one's own partisans and attracting Independents and opposition party members are actually quite different tasks. Advertising persuades viewers who are of the same party as the candidate by *reinforcing* their prior beliefs, and it persuades viewers of the opposite party by *converting* them. When a candidate's advertisement reaches a voter with the same party identification, the message will generally agree with and strengthen the favorable predispositions of the voter toward that candidate. When that same commercial reaches a citizen who identifies with the opposite party, the message will impart new information that cuts against the unfavorable stereotype that the viewer holds of that candidate. Reinforcing voters' predispositions is relatively easy since a party's message speaks to the preconceptions of that party's adherents. Converting voters is typically a much harder task, since conversion requires that voters abandon beliefs that have accumulated over many years and for some people date back to childhood.[67]

Voters reactions to our experimental advertisements show the overwhelming strength of party reinforcement.[68] Figure 4.1 displays the persuasive effects of the experimental advertisements in our general election studies among three different groups of party identifiers—viewers of the same party as a candidate, viewers of the opposite party, and independents.[69] Since the candidates in each primary are of the same party as the viewers, the primary election experiment is omitted from this analysis. The figure shows the effects of advertising exposure and partisanship on voting preferences. Each bar represents the change in the sponsoring candidate's vote margin attributable to advertising exposure for each of these three partisan groups.

Our general election studies reveal that, while advertising both reinforces partisans and converts the opposition, reinforcement is much stronger. Among viewers of the same party as the sponsor, the experimental advertisements produced a 14-percentage-point increase in the sponsoring candidate's lead. Among viewers of the opposite party, the ads led to only a 5-percentage-point increase in the sponsor's lead. Statistically, this 9-point difference in the persuasive effects of the advertisements is highly significant.[70]

Party identification is, of course, a crude measure of voter's political predispositions. Even though some people may stick with their habitual attachments in name, they may not abide by that identification in the voting booth. In the 1980s, for example, large numbers of Democrats crossed party lines and voted Republican. The disloyalty of the "Reagan Democrats" at the polls reflected their growing disenchantment with the policies and performance of the Democratic party. Liberal Republicans also abandoned their own party's ranks over issues such as abortion rights and school prayer.

Although weak partisans are less committed to candidates of their party, they respond very favorably to advertisements from their own

FIGURE 4.1

*Effects of Advertising on Vote Preferences by Party
(General Elections Only)*

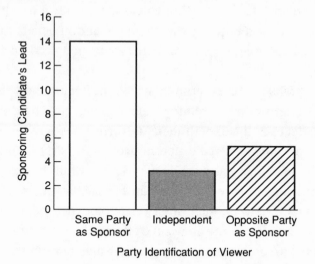

Party Identification of Viewer

parties' candidates and seem resistant to the appeals of the opposition party. We identified weak partisans as those who reported that they had abandoned their party in the last presidential election—i.e., Democrats who reported that they voted for George Bush and Republicans who reported that they voted for Michael Dukakis. Only 23 Republicans in our sample admitted that they voted for Dukakis, too few to permit a separate statistical analysis of their response to the political advertisements. Reagan/Bush Democrats were sufficiently numerous, and they responded quite favorably to the Democratic candidates' appeals. Among weak Democrats who saw no experimental commercial, the Democratic candidate's lead, holding other factors constant, was twelve percentage points; among weak Democrats who saw a Republican advertisement, the Democratic candidate's lead was, astonishingly, even higher, at 15 points; and among weak Democrats who saw a Democratic advertisement, the Democratic candidate's lead was 31 percentage points. Not only is this 19-point increase distinct from the negligible effect of Republican advertisements among weak Democrats, but it is *higher than the reinforcing effects among strong Democrats*, whose support rose 10 percentage points in response to a Democratic advertisement.[71] In other words, weak partisans are easily made into strong partisans. They are difficult to convert to the opposite party's camp. Rather than manipulation, political advertising appears to produce *stronger divisions* among voters.

The most surprising feature of Figure 4.1 is the behavior of the Independents. Recent elections have often been portrayed as battles for the support of the nonpartisan voters. This segment of the electorate, however, appears to be the least receptive to political advertising. Nonpartisans' voting preferences moved only 3 percentage points in the direction of the sponsor, a statistically insignificant shift and the smallest among all of the partisan groups. The predominance of partisan reinforcement and the unresponsiveness of nonpartisans suggest that advertising cannot produce widespread electoral manipulation. Rather, the cumulative effect of advertising is to bring partisans home to roost, while leaving the preferences of nonpartisans largely unchanged.

It may still be the case that advertising misleads important groups within the electorate to vote against their preferences. In particular, less knowledgeable and less attentive individuals may be very susceptible to campaign appeals. Well-informed voters are unlikely to be persuaded by a campaign commercial since that message is just one scrap of information out of many. Campaign advertising offers low-information voters a costless way of learning about the electoral choices. As we saw in Chapter 3, low-interest viewers do register significant gains in information from political commercials. These voters may, in turn, be easily swayed to vote against their underlying interests. If so, then campaign advertising may actually hurt those whom it has the greatest potential of helping.

To gauge the receptiveness of low-information voters to political appeals, our pretest questionnaire contained a battery of factual questions about current affairs and political personalities as well as an item in which viewers described their general attentiveness to politics. These questions allowed us to determine the viewers' levels of interest in and information about politics. We distinguish three groups: low-, moderate-, and high-interest voters. The low-interest voters report that they follow public affairs "never" or "hardly at all," and they could identify only one or two important names in politics, including the President of the United States and the Speaker of the House. The

moderate-interest voters follow public affairs "now and then" and recognize a handful of prominent politicians. High-interest voters follow
politics "most of the time" or "always" and could identify all or almost
all of the public personalities.

The reactions of low-interest partisans to our experimental advertisements confirm our general story of partisan reinforcement.
Advertising exposure strongly *reinforces* the party loyalty of lower-
information voters who have the same partisan identification as the
sponsor. This reinforcement effect makes lower-interest partisans
almost as loyal as their high-interest brethren. By contrast, advertising
exposure converts only a trivial fraction of Independents and members
of the opposite party, regardless of their level of information. Our evidence for these conclusions comes from comparing the degrees of
party loyalty exhibited by those who saw no experimental advertisements with those exposed to our advertisements.

First, consider how people vote in the absence of an advertisement.
Figure 4.2 displays Democratic candidates' vote margins for different
types of party identifiers and different levels of interest in public affairs,
among the participants in our experiments who were *not* exposed to a
political commercial (the control groups).[72] The vertical axis is the
Democratic candidate's lead (i.e., the vote share of the Democrat
minus the vote share of the Republican). The horizontal axis corresponds to the level of interest of the voters. On the far left are
those expressing low levels of interest in politics; on the far right are
those with high levels of interest. Within each level of interest we display the vote preferences of Republicans, Independents, and Democrats. In each panel Republicans are on the left, Democrats are on the
right, and Independents are in the middle. A large spread in the
Democrat's lead between Democratic and Republican identifiers indicates a high degree of party voting and loyalty.

Independents show no particular political leanings across the three
levels of political interest. Among nonpartisans, the Democrat's vote
margin hovers near 15 percentage points across levels of information.[73]
In contrast to the Independents, the degree of loyalty among partisans
grows with the level of interest in politics. Among low-interest partisans, the vote margin of Democratic candidates is only 6 percentage
points higher for Democratic identifiers than it is for Republican iden-

FIGURE 4.2

Differences in Party Voting in the Absence of Advertising

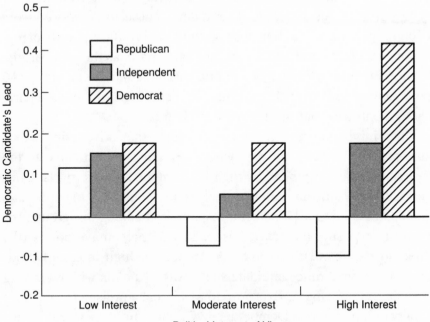

tifiers. Among moderate-interest partisans, the vote margin of Democratic candidates is 20 points higher for Democratic voters than for Republican voters. And among high-interest partisans, the spread between Democratic and Republican voters is 50 points: the margin of the Democratic candidate's lead is 41 percentage points among high-interest Democrats and −10 points among high-interest Republicans.

Now consider the effects of advertising exposure on different partisan groups and different levels of interest in politics, displayed in Figure 4.3. The vertical axis is the change in the sponsoring candidate's lead attributable to advertising exposure, or the persuasive effect of the advertisement. The horizontal axis shows the three types of partisans: those whose identifications are the same as the sponsor, Independents, and those whose identifications are the opposite of the sponsor. We have further divided each partisan group according to the respondents' interest in politics. Within each panel, low-interest voters are on the left, high-interest voters are on the right, and moderate-interest voters are in the middle.

Low-interest voters who have the same party identification as the sponsor stand out. Exposure to an advertisement from their own party's candidates produced a 24-percentage-point shift in their voting preferences toward that candidate. These voters moved from being largely undecided or not voting back into their party's camp. Among medium-interest voters of the same party as the sponsor, the reinforcing effects were again significant, but somewhat smaller (16 percentage points). Finally, the high-interest voters of the same party showed only a 7-point shift to their candidate.

Combining Figures 4.2 and 4.3 reveals that advertising exposure produces loyalty among low-interest partisans on par with the degree of loyalty exhibited by their high-interest counterparts. Consider the low-information Democrats in Figure 4.2. Democratic candidates enjoyed a 17-percentage-point lead among this group. Advertising exposure increased this lead by 23 percentage points (the effect in Figure 4.3), to 40 points. Among the high-interest Democrats, the Democratic candidate's lead was 41 points without having seen an advertisement. Exposure to a political ad raised the partisan loyalty of high interest Democrats by 7 points. In other words, expo-

FIGURE 4.3

Effects of Advertising on Vote Preference by Party and Interest in Politics

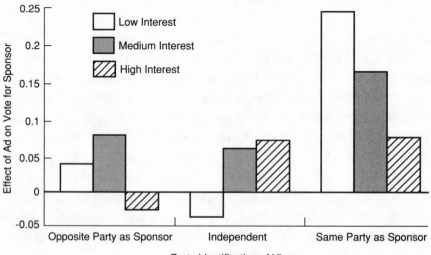

sure to a campaign commercial equalized the party loyalty of the low- and high-interest groups.

Opposition partisans showed little conversion, regardless of their level of interest. Among people whose party identification was the opposite of the sponsor, exposure to an advertisement produced no consistent pattern of conversion. Low-interest voters of the opposite party moved 4 percentage points in the direction of the sponsor. Medium-interest members of the opposition moved 8 percentage points.[74] High-interest opposition voters shifted 3 points *away* from the sponsor.

Independents also ran contrary to fears of manipulation. The lower the level of interest, the more nonpartisans resisted the appeals of campaign advertising. High-interest nonpartisans moved 7 percentage points toward the sponsor of the advertisement. Medium-interest nonpartisans moved 3 percentage points toward the sponsor. And low-interest nonpartisans shifted 2 points *away* from the sponsor.

This small, but troubling, shift goes to the heart of America's current problems of apathy and nonparticipation and disillusionment with political campaigns. Being an Independent in the United States has two different meanings. Some people are nonpartisans because they are truly indifferent between the parties. They like certain policies of one party and certain policies of the other, but they do not prefer the overall ideals of one party to the other. High-interest Independents are of this type and find campaign advertising to be mildly persuasive. Other people claim no party affiliation out of apathy. They simply have no interest in politics and even look with disgust on the governmental process. In our experiments, the low-interest Independents are further turned off by exposure to a campaign commercial. Unfortunately, most Independents are largely of the second type. Nationwide survey data show that a majority of independents follow politics "hardly at all"; a majority of them cannot name which party controls Congress; a majority of them do not vote.[75] Ultimately, the bulk of the Independent voters simply tune out the political advertising and even, at the extreme, take advertisements as further cause to dislike the process and the candidates.

On the whole, then, campaign advertising does not manipulate people to vote against their political preferences. Partisans respond with renewed vigor for their parties' nominees. Over the course of the campaign, advertising will tend to strengthen the partisan bonds between candidates and the electorate. Low-interest and weak partisans benefit the most. These voters, who seem to be at greatest risk of manipulation, exhibit the highest degrees of partisan reinforcement in response to advertising exposure. The other group at risk of manipulation are the Independents. Nonpartisans, however, respond little, if at all, to advertisements from the parties' candidates.

THE ISSUE OF ISSUES

Campaign advertising may do more than awaken and reinforce partisan loyalties. It may shape the agenda of the political campaign and determine what people think the election is about. John Cooper, a political consultant in Tennessee, put the matter this way:

> Every election asks and answers a question. And everybody who's running tries to make it his or her question, an election about the question that could be answered in no other way but that it would be favorable to yourself. Any manager wants to control the idea and the question.[76]

This is no easy task. Short-term fluctuations in the economy, momentary foreign policy crises, and domestic issues of the day can command public attention, leaving campaigns little room to maneuver. A candidate's ability to define **the** question is further constrained by the reputations of the parties. The issues that distinguish the parties give substance to the labels Democrat and Republican and determine what candidates can credibly claim in their advertising. Candidates often bog down when they campaign on issues that break with the overall image of their party. The more successful candidates play to their strengths; they advertise on those issues that their party is perceived to be best at.

To explore the role of issues in advertising, we designed three experiments around the themes of the economy and crime. The economy was chosen because it was far and away the most important issue on the minds of California voters and because Democrats "own" the issue of jobs. Crime was chosen because Republicans have traditionally held an edge on this issue and because George Bush's 1988 crime ads were widely touted as the most effective commercials of recent campaigns. As described in Chapter 2, the advertisements devised for our experiments had identical videos, but the soundtracks were varied to accommodate changes in the sponsoring candidate's name and in the main message of the commercial. One set of participants, for example, saw a commercial from Dianne Feinstein discussing rising unemployment and the need for job training programs and economic development money. Another set of people saw John Seymour making the same pitch. Still others watched a Seymour (or Feinstein) advertisement that stressed crime as the blight of the cities and the need for tough anticrime measures.[77] By comparing the reactions to these advertisements, we could see which candidate had higher credibility with which message.

Our findings about issues underscore the basic philosophy of advertising espoused throughout this chapter: Candidates can only tell the voters what they want to hear. Here we present three basic variations on this theme.

1. Effective advertising speaks directly to the voters' concerns

In 1992, public enemy number one was the recession. Nationwide polls found a public pessimistic about the short-term and the long-term health of the American economy. Southern California, the locus of our experiments, limped through the year with double-digit unemployment, something previously unheard of in the "recession-proof" Golden State. Californians wanted the government to ease the state's economic woes, and no candidate could skirt the issue. Eighty-three percent of the participants in our study listed the economy, unemployment, or the recession as the most important problem facing the state. Accordingly, all candidates did better with an economic appeal in our experiments than they did with an advertisement geared toward crime. On average, the sponsoring candidate's vote margin was 9 percentage points higher when the experimental advertisements focused on unemployment rather than on crime.

However, promises of economic renewal did not resonate with all voters. Some people voted, instead, on the basis of crime, personal character, or other considerations. The division between voters who emphasized unemployment and those who gave higher priority to crime followed party lines. Democrats cared about job creation and unemployment; Republicans were more concerned with crime when choosing between candidates.[78]

Voters responded most strongly to the issues to which they were predisposed. Republicans found crime advertisements significantly more persuasive than advertisements that called for jobs programs, while Democrats and Independents were significantly more receptive to messages about the economy. What is more, the direction of the responses followed party lines. The vote margin of Republican candidates was 14 percentage points higher among Republican voters who watched an advertisement about crime than it was among Republicans who saw an advertisement about the economy (regardless of the source). The vote margin of Democratic candidates was 7 points higher among Democratic voters who watched an advertisement about unemployment instead of an advertisement about crime. In effect, the mere mention of crime to Republicans and unemployment to Democrats strengthened each partisan group's support for their own party's candidates.

2. Effective advertising capitalizes on the policies, performance, and reputations of the parties

The Democratic and Republican parties "own" certain issues. Regardless of their party affiliation, voters perceive the parties to have specific strengths and weaknesses. The Democratic party has the reputation for keeping unemployment low even at the risk of higher inflation; the Republicans are willing to tolerate higher unemployment for lower inflation.[79] A majority thinks that the Democratic party pursues more sensible policies for environmental protection and poverty. Republicans are widely thought to be better in the areas of crime and foreign affairs. These reputations carry over to the parties' nominees. For voters, the party labels serve as handy informational shortcuts, signaling the overall ideological leanings and issue positions of the candidates. Although people know little about the candidates themselves, even the least attentive voters know roughly where the parties stand and whether a Democratic politician or a Republican would better represent their interests.[80]

Likewise, voters give little credence to promises by candidates that do not fit with their partisan reputations. There are, of course, exceptions. As the coauthor (with Edward Kennedy) of the Job Training Partnership Act, Senator Dan Quayle rescued federal jobs training programs, and Indiana papers and politicians widely praised their freshman Senator's efforts in his 1986 reelection campaign.[81] Usually, however, politicians are constrained to campaign on those issues on which their party is widely perceived to be more capable. In 1988, Michael Dukakis could not have stolen the Republicans' thunder by attacking George Bush for the rising rates of violent crime under the Reagan administration. Four years later, George Bush's promises of economic renewal rang hollow. High unemployment had destroyed the reputation established during the Reagan administration that the Republicans were better at producing economic growth. In 1992, for the first time in twelve years, the Democrats were seen as the party better for prosperity.[82]

Attempts to coopt the opposition's issues can be ineffective, or even dangerous. In 1988, Bush tried to reach parity with the Democrats on education and the environment with his proclamations of being the "Education President" and the "Environmental President." Both messages got lost in the furor over crime and national defense. In 1994, Democrats tried to steal crime from the Republicans with gun control (which was favored by three-fourths of the American public). The emphasis on gun control backfired. The three-fourths who supported it were weak supporters or cared more about other issues. Instead, the issue served only to activate the one-fourth who had intense preferences on that issue, who were disproportionately conservative, and who were opposed to the regulations passed by the Democratic Congress. The Clinton administration's main legislative successes—the Crime Bill, the North American Free Trade Agreement, and the 1993 Budget Act—also emphasized traditional Republican issues of crime, free trade, and budget reduction. Come the midterm election, Democratic House incumbents found themselves sounding like Republicans whenever they campaigned on the major legislative initiatives of the last term.

As events push particular issues onto the public's agenda, the party judged to be better at those issues or problems benefits. A candidate whose party "owns" the most important problem can ride the wave of favorable news, while a politician of the opposite party must swim against the tide of events.

California's economic ills were particularly damaging for Republican candidates in 1992. Not only was the economy bad, but people were hurting in such a way that their party had little hope of being judged as part of the solution. The California electorate rated George Bush's economic performance so low that the Republican presidential campaign chose not to purchase any spot advertising time in the state. John Seymour and Bruce Herschensohn had no choice. As the Republican senatorial candidates, if they hoped to take a seat in the Senate, they had to win Southern California, and they had to do so with an economic appeal.

The economic theme of the 1992 election translated into a considerable Democratic advantage. The participants in our experiments were at once more responsive to unemployment than crime and more receptive to a Democrat's than to a Republican's commercial about unemployment. Among viewers who saw a Republican advertisement about the economy, the Republican candidate's vote margin was 5 percentage points higher than it was among those who saw the same candidate discussing crime. Yet, among viewers who saw a Democratic advertisement about the economy, the Democratic candidate's vote margin was thirteen percentage points higher than it was among those who saw the same candidate discussing crime. Thus, Republicans in California in 1992 faced a Catch-22: it paid to push the issue of the economy, but it also played into the hands of their Democratic opponents.

While voters were not as acutely attuned to crime in 1992 as they were in 1988, our crime advertisements showed evidence of continued Republican ownership of law and order. Although the effects of the crime advertisements are too small to reach statistical significance, the overall pattern squares with the conventional wisdom about issues in elections. When crime was the message, Republican candidates did somewhat better than Democrats (by roughly 5 percentage points in the vote margin).

The issue of gender politics is similarly ensnared in partisanship. 1992 was widely touted as the Year of the Woman. To see how men and women reacted to the hype about the year of the woman, we created advertisements that featured questions high on the political agendas of women—sexual harassment in the workplace, breast cancer research, representation of women in Congress, and reproductive rights. On these issues a majority of the American public agreed with the positions of the Democratic party.

The reactions of our participants suggest that women's issues evoked responses along partisan rather than gender lines. The reactions of male Democrats and female Republicans and Independents provide the sharpest test of issue ownership. Female Republicans and Independents showed an increase in support, albeit modest, for Boxer and Feinstein in response to the experimental advertisements. Among female Republicans and Independents who did not see a campaign commercial, Boxer and Feinstein held a 22-point lead. Exposure to a women's issues ad increased that lead to 28 points. This 6-percentage-point increase in support for Boxer and Feinstein is marginally significant statistically, and it is only slightly higher than the 4-percentage-point increase in support for the sponsoring candidates that the advertisements produced among male Republicans and Independents.[83] Male Democrats, by contrast, moved from tepid to enthusiastic support for Boxer and Feinstein in response to a women's issues advertisement. Among male Democrats who did not see an advertisement, the Democratic candidates led by 50 percentage points. Among male Democrats who saw the women's issue advertisement, the Democratic candidates led by 83 percentage points. This 33-point increase in Boxer's and Feinstein's vote margins is highly significant. It also dwarfs the effect among Democratic women, who registered no significant increase in support for the Democratic candidates, because among these voters Boxer and Feinstein held 80 point leads over their male Republican opponents.[84]

This is not to deny the obvious edge that Boxer and Feinstein enjoyed among women voters, especially those who were also Democrats, or the boost that Boxer and Feinstein received from favorable press. Rather, our advertising experiments reveal that even issues whose appeal seems narrowly targeted to one group are, in fact, broadly construed by voters and produce partisan reactions. Events such as the Clarence Thomas hearings, the prolonged California recession, and sensational murders can push issues like gender politics, unemployment, and crime onto the public's agenda. When an issue is thrust into the limelight, the party judged better on that issue will have a significant electoral edge.

3. Effective advertising directs the voter's attention to issues that the voter already believes to be priorities

We have shown that campaign commercials about a particular issue increase the extent to which people rely on that issue in making their electoral decisions. This priming effect suggests that candidates might be able to change the public's agenda. By addressing only "Republican" issues, Republican candidates might lead all people to think that those issues are the most important. Priming, however, turns out to be a highly partisan phenomenon. Candidates can direct the voters' attention to an issue only if the voters are predisposed to care about that issue to begin with and only if the candidates are themselves credible messengers. Republican candidates can direct Republican voters' attention away from the economy and onto crime, but Republican advertising cannot distract Democrats from their basic concerns about unemployment and other "Democratic" issues.

Consider, once again, the crime and unemployment experiments. The simple priming effect was that exposure to an advertisement raises the weight that voters ascribe to the issue mentioned in the advertisement. The priming effect turns out to be concentrated within just two subgroups: Republicans who saw Republican crime ads and Democrats who saw Democratic unemployment ads. Among Republicans exposed to a Republican crime advertisement, the weight assigned to crime in the vote decision was double that of other voters. Among Democrats exposed to a Democratic unemployment advertisement, the weight given to job creation was three times the weight that other voters gave to that issue.[85] No other subgroups in our experiments (e.g., Democrats who saw Republican ads about unemployment) exhibited significant priming effects.

The power of partisan priming suggests that the meaning of partisanship in political campaigns runs much deeper than mere labels. The Democratic and Republican parties champion specific causes and embody different ideas about the proper role of government. Ordinary voters separate along these lines. People who fear crime gravitate to the Republicans and listen to the Republicans when they speak out on crime. People who care intensely about lessening unemployment identify with Democratic candidates and respond readily to Democratic messages on the economy.

The effect of issues in advertising carries a simple lesson about political advertising. Candidates succeed not by distracting voters, but by addressing the problems that individuals believe to be important. This, of course, means that campaign advertising and campaigns in general play a much more limited role in the electorate's voting decisions. Through their advertising, candidates can exploit favorable electoral circumstances and they can solidify the support of their own partisans, but they cannot convert nonpartisans and members of the opposite party, and they cannot redirect the interests of most voters and change the substance of the election.

ATTACK ADVERTISING: ADVANTAGE, REPUBLICAN

To this point, we have ignored what is perhaps the most important development in recent political campaigns: attack advertising. Over the last two decades, negativity, as much as any issue or idea, has become the hallmark of political campaigns. Today, candidates assail their opponents' track records or their lack of experience or the mere fact that they are members of Congress—the institution that voters love to hate. Candidates malign each other's integrity, character, and competence. And, without a hint of irony, candidates criticize their opponents for having used attack advertising.

Political attacks are nothing new to election politics. Indeed, the punches packed in thirty-second spots seem mild compared to the invectives directed against candidates in the 19th century. Abraham Lincoln was called

Ape, Buffoon, Coward, Drunkard, Execrable, Fiend, Ghoul, Hopeless, Ignoramus, Jokester (in the face of war tragedies), Knave, Lunatic, Murderer, Negro, Outlaw, Perjurer, Robber, Savage, Traitor, Usurper, Vulgar, Weakling.[86]

And that was Abraham Lincoln.

Television makes negativity more pervasive and pernicious. Television spreads political messages much more quickly and much more widely than was ever possible with pamphlets, newspapers, or speeches. The breadth of television's reach makes it difficult to dispel rumors or counteract the effects of negative information.

Even within the television age, the tone of political campaigns has become increasingly bitter and hostile. A decade ago, attack advertisements were just a small fraction of the messages aired by candidates. Now, politicians come out swinging.[87] By the most comprehensive accountings, fully half of all political commercials emphasize the weaknesses of the opposing candidates rather than the strengths of the sponsors.[88] Some candidates even rely solely on negative advertising in what has come to be known as the "Cranston strategy," named for Senator Alan Cranston's unrelenting attacks on his 1986 challenger, House Member Ed Zschau.

In a disquieting exhibition of art imitating politics, product advertising has witnessed a similar transformation. A 1971 Federal Trade Commission found that only one in ten product advertisements openly compared competing brands. A similar study in 1990 found that just over 50 percent of the product advertisements sampled were "comparative," the product advertisers' euphemism for negative.[89]

There is a wide sense that negative or comparative commercials are more potent than positive ones. A recent survey found that most advertising executives believe that negative ads are very persuasive, provide consumers with useful product information, and allow small, relatively unknown firms to successfully compete with much larger firms.[90] Campaign consultants, pundits, and political scientists offer similar justifications for the power of political attacks. Like consumers, voters tend to be risk-averse and prefer candidates who are perceived to have fewer negative attributes. As pollster Mark Mellman surmised, "if you're going to fill empty heads, it's a lot easier to do it with negatives."[91] Individuals also accord negative information greater weight when forming judgments of the candidates. Indeed, one of the oldest axioms of politics is that people never vote for, only against.

Despite their vogue, negative advertisements are not without risks. Candidates who use attack ads increase the opponents' "negatives"; they can also appear in a more negative light themselves, creating a backlash against their candidacy. In the 1993 Los Angeles mayoral race, the voters echoed that very sentiment. An exit poll by the *Los Angeles Times* asked people how they voted, what they liked about the candidate they chose, and what they most disliked about the candidate they did not choose. The single most common complaint against the candidate not chosen was "his negative advertisements."[92]

Our experiments manifest both the power and the dangers of attacking. In the general election experiments, the negative advertisements proved on the whole to be more persuasive than the positive ads. But in the primary experiment, the opposite held true.

Table 4.2 presents the effects of advertising tone on voting preferences in our primary and general election studies. The first column in the table presents the results for the primary election study, and the second column, the results in the general election studies, which we have pooled for the sake of improving the statistical precision of the estimates.[93] The rows of the table correspond to the sponsor's lead in the positive and in the negative conditions.

The general election experiments confirmed the received wisdom that negative ads carry a more powerful punch than positive ads. Among subjects who saw the positive version of an advertisement, the candidate who sponsored the ad led by 9.5 percentage points. Among subjects who saw the negative version of the ad, the sponsor led by nineteen points.[94] In other words, negative advertising in the general elections gave the sponsor an electoral boost that was nearly ten points higher than positive advertising.

The primary election experiments, on the other hand, showed a strong backlash against negative advertising. When candidates promoted, they commanded healthy leads. Among subjects who saw positive versions of the advertisements the sponsor lead by 7.4 percentage points. When candidates attacked, they fell behind the rest of the primary field. Among those who saw negative versions, the sponsor actually trailed by two points, a statistically significant drop in support.[95]

The difference between the general and primary elections suggests that negative advertising is volatile material indeed. The discrepancy, however, is not all that difficult to explain. Closer examination of our data show that it is due, again, to party. In the primary election study,

TABLE 4.2

Effect of Advertising Tone on Voting Preferences: Primary versus General Elections

Tone of advertisement	Primary Election Experiment		General Election Experiment	
	Sponsor's lead (*N*)		Sponsor's lead (*N*)	
Positive	.074	(229)	.095	(692)
Negative	−.020	(345)	.190	(384)

Note: Regression analyses controlling for effect of other variables are presented in Appendix B.

attack advertising backfired in the Democratic races, but it actually worked in the Republican races. The primary election experiments involved three separate races, as described in Chapter 2. On the Democratic side there was a two-way contest between Dianne Feinstein and State Controller Gray Davis and a three-way race among U.S. Representative Barbara Boxer, U.S. Representative Mel Levine, and Lieutenant Governor Leo McCarthy. On the Republican side, we examined the two-way race between appointed U.S. Senator John Seymour and U.S. Representative William Dannemeyer. In both Democratic races, each candidate had significantly lower vote margins when he or she attacked. In the Republican race, the candidates did somewhat better by attacking.

Examination of the general election studies shows, further, that the nexus between attack advertising and party is driven by the partisanship of the voters, rather than the candidates. Independents and Republicans are very receptive to attacks, while Democrats tend to prefer positive messages. There appears to be a gradient of "Republicanness": the more Republican and conservative the electorate, the less they like governments and its politicians, and so the more effective negative advertisements are.[96]

The evidence for this conclusion is summarized in Figure 4.4, which shows how the effect of advertising tone varies across party of the candidate and partisanship of the viewers. The effect here is the difference in voting preferences between the group that saw the positive version of an advertisement and the group that saw the negative version. Positive numbers reveal the extent to which viewers responded more strongly to the positive than to the negative versions of the advertisements. Along the horizontal axis are the three groups of party identifiers—Republicans, Independents, and Democrats. The broken line connects the groups that saw the Democratic ads; the solid line, connects the groups that saw the Republican ads:

Three features of Figure 4.4 stand out. First, the more Republican or conservative a viewer is, the more receptive he or she is to attacks. Democrats are the least receptive to negative campaign commercials and even show a slight preference for positive messages; Independents tend to favor attacks over promotions; and Republicans are extremely receptive to negative campaign commercials.

Second, it is the viewers' partisan predispositions rather than the party of the sponsor that determines the reaction to advertising tone. Republican viewers were largely unmoved when they saw a positive advertisement from either candidate. However, a negative advertisement from a Democratic candidate increased the Democrat's vote margin by 9 points among the Republican viewers. Republican voters

FIGURE 4.4

Effect of Advertising Tone on Vote Preferences by Party

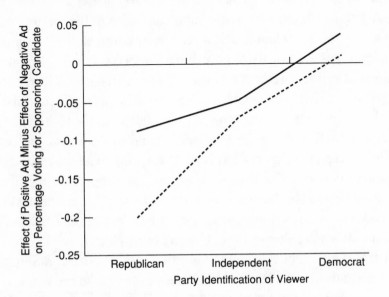

registered an even greater increase in the support for the source (20 points) when the negative commercial came from a Republican candidate. Democratic voters, on the other hand, moved more strongly toward the source when a positive ad was shown. This was true regardless of whether the candidate was a Democrat or Republican.[97]

Third, to the extent that Independents are responsive to any form of advertising, it is negative advertising. When nonpartisans saw a positive campaign commercial, they registered no response at all. When they saw a negative commercial, from either a Democrat or a Republican, they showed a 6 percent shift in preferences toward the sponsor.

This may not exactly qualify as manipulation, since advertising in general does not lead Independents to vote against their predispositions. But it is worrisome, to say the least, that Republicans and Independents find negative advertising from candidates of both parties to be quite persuasive.

The source of this pattern is ideological. Identification as either an Independent or a Republican generally carries with it a strong belief in the fallibility of government. Republicans and to some extent Independents tend to oppose new or expanded government programs; they tend to believe in private, rather than public, solutions to social problems. Promises of new government actions and spending, whether on jobs programs or jails, will resonate less well with these voters than messages that implicate an opposing candidate in the failures of existing policies. The Democratic ideology, by contrast, has developed a firm faith in the necessity of government interventions to alleviate the failures of private markets and the inequities in society. Democratic voters want to hear not what has failed, but what a candidate will do to fix what ails us. Democrats generally have faith that the federal government will do the right thing; Republicans and Independents do not.[98]

One alternative explanation is that attacking resonates with being the minority party. The Republicans were the out party at the time of our studies, and had been for forty years. They may have been skeptical about government not because they believed it to be fallible, but because they weren't part of it. The test of this alternative is upon us, now that the Republicans hold majorities in the House and Senate. If this alternative holds, Democratic voters will begin to see politics in a negative light and Republican voters will look for positive messages about government. It may, however, take some time for politicians to break old habits.

Whatever the ultimate reason behind the interaction between party identification and advertising tone, the pattern in Figure 4.4 carries a very powerful explanation for why candidates of either party feel pressured to attack. Independents are increasingly numerous in American politics. In fact, in only a handful of states do the identifiers of one of the parties constitute an outright majority, and neither party enjoys the support of a majority nationally. In every state and in every national election, candidates must capture both their base and the support of Independents to win. Candidates can solidify their base with all sorts of advertising, but they must also sway the Independent vote, and doing so *requires* negative advertising. As Independents become more numerous in the American electorate, attack advertising will become more common in American campaigns.

The responsiveness of Independent voters to attacks puts Democratic candidates in a dilemma. Candidates must accomplish two ends in their campaigns: they must reinforce their own supporters, and they must appeal to nonpartisans. To appeal to Independents, Democratic candidates must go on the attack. Negative campaign commercials, however, are much less effective than positive advertisements at reinforcing the preferences of the Democrats' own partisans. Consequently, the Democratic candidate must choose between two fairly risky alternatives. Attack the Republican and be less effective among some voters of your own party, or promote yourself and risk losing the Independent vote.

Republicans, by contrast, have a strong incentive to attack. Like Independents, Republican viewers find negative commercials much more persuasive than positive ones. By going on the attack, Republican candidates can strongly reinforce support among their political base, and they can persuade nonpartisans to vote Republican.

Of course, Democratic candidates often go on the attack, and they do so with as much vigor as any Republican. The logic of when to attack is driven by many other considerations, such as the response of journalists and the appropriate reaction to the opposition's advertising. The principal implication of the findings here is that, whatever the ultimate reason, negative advertising gives Republicans a considerable electoral advantage.

CONCLUSIONS

Our experiments manifest one basic theory of advertising: campaign commercials work to the extent that they resonate with the viewers' concerns and political beliefs. Voters cull out of political advertisements information that squares with their predispositions; this, in turn, leads voters to choose politicians with whom they fundamentally agree. In many respects, this means that advertising is a much healthier form of political communication than is often thought: partisan reinforcement provides a hedge against political manipulation. Republicans and Democrats are strengthened in their convictions; nonpartisans are largely unmoved.

There's a kicker hidden here. Though manipulation is not a concern, divisiveness is. Advertisements do not induce widespread crossover voting, but they do send each side scurrying back to its respective corner. On election day, the electorate speaks with a highly partisan voice, for that is the mindset reinforced by the candidates' campaign messages.

These findings also reveal that advertising is not what ails the political parties. As we explained in the introductory chapter, television advertising is often thought to have undermined the political parties by allowing candidates to establish personal followings independent from their parties. This conclusion has been bolstered by survey research that has found negative correlations between the voters' ratings of the parties and the amount of money spent by individual candidates. Consider the following conclusion offered by Martin Wattenberg in *The Decline of American Political Parties 1952–1980*:

> If partisanship were stressed in campaigns, one might expect both sets of correlations [between spending and ratings of the candidates and ratings of the parties] to be positive. But apparently the effect of candidates' media advertising is solely the projection of candidate images, and not that of the parties. Although the negative correlations between media expenses and partisanship are not of great magnitude, the cumulative effect

of such a pattern over time could possibly account for a significant portion of the long-term trend [in the decline of partisanship].[99]

Our experiments point to a very different conclusion. Successful candidates run with, rather than away from, their parties. Since the proper functioning of campaign advertising is to reinforce partisans, voter loyalty is an outcome of the campaign process. Vigorous advertising by competing partisan candidates allows people to hear and see what their own party's nominees have to offer. It reassures voters that their party's nominee indeed represents the policies and ideals that attracted them to the party to begin with. It energizes their otherwise weak partisan attachments. The cumulative effect of free and open campaigning over the airwaves is to produce high degrees of loyalty and to provide candidates with powerful incentives to tailor their messages to their political base, the issues and stances that appeal to their own partisans. Thus even on issues that appear to cut across party lines, like gender politics, the images that candidates project in their advertisements necessarily come off as "projections of their parties."

The negative correlations between candidates' campaign expenditures and voter support for the parties are not inconsistent with our own data. Our finding that advertising reinforces partisans but persuades relatively few independents suggests that the conventional interpretations of these correlations impute the wrong causal connections. It is not the case that candidates' advertising necessarily weakens the parties. Instead, it is the weakness of the parties that forces candidates to rely heavily on advertising. Because Independents are less responsive to political appeals, candidates who face increasingly nonpartisan constituencies must spend ever larger amounts of money simply to persuade the voters.[100]

The inability of campaign commercials to persuade Independent voters of a candidate's strengths provides protection against electoral manipulation. This may ultimately be the silver lining to a more ominous cloud. Today, one person in three considers him or herself to be an Independent; a generation ago, less than one in four did. Whatever the causes of the decline of partisanship in the United States—and they are legion—the growing mass of Independent voters means that American political campaigns have become dysfunctional for an increasingly large segment of the electorate. Advertising is the main form of campaign communication in the United States, and an increasingly large part of the electorate takes only negative information away from the process.

Negative advertisements appeal to the nonpartisan voter because they resonate with the already negative view that Independents have of American politicians, government, and the political parties. To stir nonpartisans to vote, American politicians must attack, even though doing so fuels the already low opinion that voters hold of political institutions and politicians. The problem is that campaign advertising is not bringing the Independent voter back to the parties, and as we will see in the next chapter, it is actually driving people away from the electoral process.

5

THE WITHDRAWAL
OF THE VOTER

There has been no shortage of hand wringing and outrage over the depths to which campaigns have sunk. The rhetoric of political advertising is often vicious, strident, and shallow; the candidates and their consultants are unaccountable for the kind of campaigns they have chosen to run.[101] The toll on the electorate has been considerable. The cost of political advertising, however, is not that people cast uninformed votes or that they are tricked into voting for someone with whom they generally disagree. Rather, political advertising—at least as it is currently practiced—is slowly eroding the participatory ethos in America. In election after election, citizens have registered their disgust with the negativity of contemporary political campaigns by tuning out and staying home.

California, 1986. The day after the Republican primary, Democratic Senator Alan Cranston began pounding away with ads that attacked his opponent, Representative Ed Zschau, for flip-flopping. One of the Cranston ads featured two photos of Zschau, one on the left half of the screen, the other on the right. "Compare two candidates. . . . One says clean up toxic waste. The other voted against it. Funny thing is, both candidates are named Ed Zschau." The assault never let up: four months of continual attack advertisements. Zschau also got into the act, labeling Cranston a liberal and calling attention to the Senator's opposition to both the death penalty and tough drug laws. The electorate, though, never really learned who Ed Zschau was, and in the end, they lost sight of Alan Cranston as well. Turnout was low, fully eight percentage points below the 1982 turnout, and though Cranston won by a narrow margin, neither candidate could attract a majority of votes.

New Jersey, 1988. The Senate contest between Republican House member Peter Dawkins and Democratic Senator Frank Lautenberg started harmlessly, with Dawkins spending nearly $2 million on a feel-good ad in which Dawkins proclaimed his admiration and devotion to New Jersey. After Labor Day, the defoliants hit the Garden State. Lautenberg's first advertisement replayed the audio part of Dawkin's feel-good commercial. "I've lived in a lot of places. But . . . I never found a single place that had as good people or as much promise as I've found right here in our Garden State." Meanwhile, the video displays, in bold letters, "Be real, Pete." Dawkins quickly went into the dirt as well, alleging that Lautenberg "personally pocketed tens of thousands of dollars trading stocks of companies that do business with the government. . . . He'll deny anything to get elected. As long as he can make some money on the side." Then from Lautenberg the voters heard that Dawkins "misled us about when he moved here. His campaign lied about his being wounded in Vietnam. He's a hypocrite because he's financed by polluters. . . . He'll move anywhere, say anything to get elected." And so went the months of September and October in New Jersey. On election day, the voters told the candidates what they thought. Lautenberg won, but turnout was down sharply. In fact, 120,000 New Jersey voters—6 percent of those who went to the polls—cast ballots for president, but chose to leave the Senate column blank.

New York, 1992. Senator Alfonse D'Amato defended his turf with a barrage of attacks on his challenger, Robert Abrams. "Abrams never met a tax he didn't like—except his own." "Abrams demanded a $6 million a year luxury office suite." During the final month of the campaign, D'Amato aired 18 separate advertisements in the state; 12 of them attacked Abrams. Abrams perished by the sword, but also lived by it. He had beaten Geraldine Ferraro and Liz Holtzman in a nasty three-way race for the Democratic nomination, and Abrams relentlessly slammed D'Amato as "Senator Sleaze" and for allowing "his office to be systematically misused for personal gain." In the end, it was the New York electorate who paid the price. Only 43 percent of the voting-age population (fully 8 percent less than the national average) decided to vote in the 1992 New York Senate election. Of those who did go to the polls, 430,000 voters cast a ballot for one of the presidential candidates, but couldn't stomach voting for D'Amato or Abrams.

Alabama to Wyoming, New York to California—across the country candidates have taken the "attack dog" tenor, and their bark has kept many voters away from the polls.

Campaigning doesn't have to be like that. In an earlier era, when parties relied heavily on grass-roots organizing, campaigns were won and lost according to who was better at mobilizing the electorate. Political campaigns weren't clean and debate wasn't high-minded, but politicians had every incentive to get the voters to the polls, and they ran their campaigns accordingly. In the days before broadcasting, it wasn't cost-effective to reach the supporters of one's opponents; even partisan newspapers were bought only by partisans. In the age of television, can campaigns still energize voters?

Yes and no. Our experiments, and corroborating evidence from actual Senate election results, reveal that high-tech advertising campaigns can stimulate people to vote and instill a sense of confidence in government, but only through *positive* campaign messages. In the 1992 Idaho Senate race, for example, the lines between the candidates were sharply drawn over water rights and land use, but the candidates focused on their own positions on those issues. The race was a drawing card: turnout was up in Idaho, and more Idahoans voted in that Senate race than even voted for President!

Unfortunately, Idaho is not the norm. As we will demonstrate throughout this chapter, the practice of attack advertising, which has become the dominant message of modern political campaigns, alienates people, especially nonpartisans, from politics and actually depresses intentions to participate in the electoral process. It is through political participation that negative advertising can truly distort the representative process.

ADVERTISING TONE AND POLITICAL PARTICIPATION

Attack politics are widely thought to turn people off. Editorial writers disparage the practice. Consultants brag about using negative advertising to depress turnout, when higher turnout may hurt their candidate. Pollsters increasingly find a public that is angry about the tenor of political campaigns and at the enmity within government.[102]

Quite part from the hostility of campaigns, many observers fear that campaigning on television destroys the participatory spirit of the public.[103] Television is an inherently passive medium, and it may breed a passive electorate. One recent psychophysical study found that watching television takes less concentration than eating a bowl of cereal, and at the same time, it increases the stress felt by the viewers. Others have concluded that television stifles thought, and if people do learn from television, it is learning without involvement.[104] This is hardly the civics book vision of democracy, nor is it entirely accurate.

Our one-advertisement studies reveal that whether political advertising depresses or stimulates voting depends on the tenor of the message. The essence of these experiments was that we could manipulate the tone of the experimental advertisement while *keeping all other features identical*. Consider, for instance, the positive and negative versions of the advertisements created for Dianne Feinstein in the 1992 Senate primary election experiment. The video track was the same for both advertisements. The positive version of the text read:

FOR OVER 200 YEARS THE UNITED STATES SENATE HAS SHAPED THE FUTURE OF AMERICA AND THE WORLD. TODAY, CALIFORNIA NEEDS HONESTY, COMPASSION, AND A VOICE FOR ALL THE PEOPLE IN THE U.S. SENATE. AS MAYOR OF SAN FRANCISCO, DIANNE FEINSTEIN *PROPOSED* NEW GOVERNMENT ETHICS RULES. SHE *REJECTED* LARGE CAMPAIGN CONTRIBUTIONS FROM SPECIAL INTERESTS. AND DIANNE FEINSTEIN *SUPPORTED* TOUGHER PENALTIES ON SAVINGS AND LOAN CROOKS.

CALIFORNIA *NEEDS* DIANNE FEINSTEIN IN THE U.S. SENATE.

In the negative version of this Feinstein spot, the text was modified as follows:

FOR OVER 200 YEARS THE UNITED STATES SENATE HAS SHAPED THE FUTURE OF AMERICA AND THE WORLD. TODAY, CALIFORNIA NEEDS HONESTY, COMPASSION, AND A VOICE FOR ALL THE PEOPLE IN THE U.S. SENATE. AS STATE CONTROLLER, GRAY DAVIS *OPPOSED* NEW GOVERNMENT ETHICS RULES. HE *ACCEPTED* LARGE CAMPAIGN CONTRIBUTIONS FROM SPECIAL INTERESTS. AND GRAY DAVIS *OPPOSED* TOUGHER PENALTIES ON SAVINGS AND LOAN CROOKS.

CALIFORNIA *CAN'T AFFORD A POLITICIAN LIKE* GRAY DAVIS IN THE U.S. SENATE.

Since everything else about the videotapes was identical, any differences between the reactions of the participants who were exposed to the positive and negative versions of the experimental advertisement can be attributed to the tone of the message—*and to no other factor.* The results of the one-advertisement studies, in short, are unequivocal about the role of negative campaigning as a determinant of citizen involvement.[105]

Citizen involvement in politics, of course, has many elements, and no single measure can capture the nuances of public preferences. We examined three measures of participatory attitudes. First, and most basic, we asked our participants whether they intended to vote in the upcoming election. Second, we asked them to evaluate the electoral process. Do elections make government more responsive to the views of the people; are elected officials willing to tackle the problems facing the country; do candidates keep in touch with voters once they get elected; is the political process more attuned to "special interests" than to the public good? The average of these four responses provided an index of the viewers' confidence in the electoral process.[106] Finally, we asked our participants to assess their own influence over the political process. Do ordinary people like them have any say about what the government does, and is politics too complicated and confusing for them to understand?[107]

On all three measures we found substantial differences between positive and negative campaign commercials. People exposed to the negative versions of the advertisements registered lower intentions to vote, expressed less confidence in the political process, and placed less value on their own participation. These results appeared in simple statistical analyses and held up after we had controlled for a host of factors that social scientists have found to predict participation—such as age, income, partisanship, and past participation. Appendix B presents the statistical analysis that led to this conclusion. Here we discuss the basic findings.

Table 5.1 shows the difference between the positive and negative versions of the experimental advertisements for each of our measures of citizen involvement, pooling all of the experiments into one analysis.[108] The first row presents the effect of advertising tone on intentions to vote; the second row the effect on confidence in the process; the third row the effect on political self-confidence. The first column is the effect, the difference between the average response of those who saw the positive message and the average response of those who saw the negative message. The second column is the margin of error, which is commonly presented with public opinion data and can be used to gauge the statistical significance of the effects.[109]

The negative versions of our advertisements clearly lowered the participatory spirit among our audiences. Intentions to vote were 4.6 percentage points lower among those who saw a negative advertisement than among those who saw the positive version of the same spot. The percent expressing confidence in government was 2.8 points lower among those who saw the negative versions of the ads. And the fraction who felt that their own vote counted were 5.2 points lower among those who saw the negative versions of the ads. The relatively small margins of error for each effect indicate that the difference be-

TABLE 5.1

Effect of Advertising Tone on Participatory Attitudes

Measure of Citizen Involvement	Effect	Margin of Error
Intentions to vote	4.6	± 1.8
Confidence in the process	2.8	± 1.2
Political self-confidence	5.2	± 1.3

tween positive and negative advertising for all three measures is highly significant in statistical terms.[110]

The magnitude of these effects is cause for considerable concern. Since 1960, voter turnout in presidential elections has dropped 10 percentage points, from 62 percent of the voting-age population to 52 percent in 1992. The public's sense of its own effectiveness has taken an even more dramatic dive. In 1960, nearly 75 percent of the American public felt confident in the capabilities of government and their own efficacy; today only 40 percent do.[111] Our experimental data suggest that the tone of political campaigning contributes mightily to the public's dwindling participation and growing cynicism.

Our experiments show that advertising has an upside, as well. Just as negative advertising turns people away from the electoral process, positive advertising can bring them back. The data in Table 5.1 reflect the difference between positive and negative television advertising. To isolate the effects of positive and negative advertising on citizen involvement, we compared the reactions to those positive and negative versions of the advertisements by those people who saw no political advertisement—the control group.

We found the effects of positive and negative advertising to be symmetric. On average, positive advertising increased each of the participatory attitudes by approximately the same amount that negative advertising depressed them.[112] Specifically, exposure to a positive advertisement raised intentions to vote by 2.3 percentage points over the baseline group who saw no advertisement, and exposure to a negative advertisement dropped intentions to vote by roughly the same amount. Exposure to a positive advertisement raised the percentage of people who expressed confidence in the political process by 1.4 points, while negative advertisements dropped them by a similar amount. And exposure to a positive advertisement raised the percentage of people who stated political self-confidence by 2.6 points, while negative advertisements dropped people's sense of efficacy by that amount.

Television advertising, then, can strengthen citizen involvement, but to do so, the messages must be positive. They must stress the sponsoring candidate's own accomplishments and abilities. Unfortunately, the trend in political advertising is in the opposite direction.

1992: THE BIG TURNOFF

Given the strength and magnitude of the experimental findings, one would expect to see sizable differences in participation across actual political campaigns. The anecdotes recounted at the outset of this chapter are suggestive and certainly not isolated cases, but is the relationship between negative campaigning and turnout as strong as these examples imply? Might other factors, like education, income, and the civic culture of the state, explain the exceedingly low turnout in highly negative elections? And is there evidence that positive campaigns actually stimulate participation, as our experiments suggest?

To answer these questions, we monitored each of the 34 U.S. Senate campaigns in 1992. Senate elections provide an especially good test of our claims, since Senate candidates rely heavily on advertising and since many of our experiments dealt with the two California Senate campaigns during the 1992 elections.

We recorded whether the tone of the overall campaign in the state was negative, mixed, or positive. Our assessment of campaign tone was based on a systematic analysis of news coverage of the various Senate races and on the opinions of two campaign consultants, who were actually involved in several of the races. A race was negative if both candidates in the general election relied heavily on attack advertisements. A race was positive if both candidates largely avoided personal or issue-based attacks and, instead, focused on reasons to vote for the candidates. A handful of campaigns were at neither extreme. A race had mixed tone if one candidate relied on positive and the other on negative messages or if both candidates used a fairly even mix of positive and negative messages. Figure 5.1 shows the tone of the 1992 Senate elections. States with negative campaigns are black; mixed campaigns are gray; and positive campaigns are white.

Although 1992 was "the year of hope and change," the tenor of the 1992 Senate campaigns was overwhelmingly negative. Positive campaigns occurred in twelve states: Alaska, Hawaii, Idaho, Iowa, Kansas, Maryland, Nevada, North Dakota, South Dakota, Utah, Vermont, and Wisconsin. While these states accounted for a third of the Senate races, they contained only 13 percent of the nation's voting-age population. The rest of the electorate feasted on negative advertising. Six

FIGURE 5.1
Tone of the 1992 U.S. Senate Campaigns

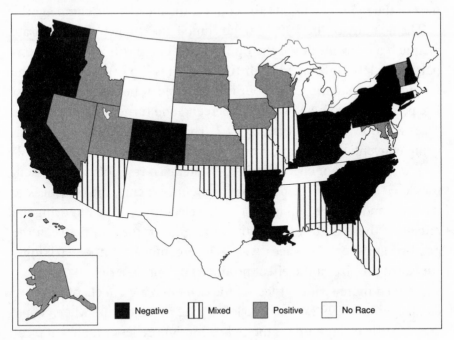

states, containing a quarter of the electorate, had mixed campaigns: Alabama, Arizona, Florida, Illinois, Missouri, and Oklahoma. Fifteen states, with 62 percent of the voting-age population, had full-blown negative campaigns: Arkansas, California (two Senate seats), Colorado, Connecticut, Georgia, Indiana, Kentucky, New Hampshire, New York, North Carolina, Ohio, Oregon, Pennsylvania, South Carolina, and Washington.

Aside from the fact that the negative campaigns tended to occur in the more heavily populated states, attack politics have scattered widely and evenly across the United States. Negative campaigning was not limited to the Republican side of the ticket. Nor did it seem to be a uniquely male activity. Two women (Barbara Mikulski in Maryland and Charlene Haar in South Dakota) were engaged in positive campaigns, and the tone of the contest between Carol Mosely-Braun and Richard Williamson was mixed. But Barbara Boxer and Dianne Feinstein were both involved in highly negative campaigns in California, as were Lynn Yaekel in Pennsylvania and Patty Murray in Washington. The best single predictor of campaign tone, it turns out, is the closeness of the race. The tighter the contest, the meaner the campaign.[113]

The hostility of the 1992 Senate campaigns drained the electorate as much as it wore down the opposition. The positive Senate campaigns in 1992 averaged high turnout rates—57.0 percent of the voting-age population. Turnout in the mixed-tone races was almost five percentage points lower, 52.4 percent, and turnout in the negative races was down even further, to 49.7. These differences are significant using conventional statistical tests,[114] and they hold up after controlling for the sense of civic duty in the state, past rates of participation, the dollar volume of the campaign (amounts spent), the closeness of the race, and the age and income of the electorate. After removing the effects of these other factors, the difference in turnout between the positive and negative races was 4.5 percentage points—strikingly similar to the size of the effect produced by our experiments.[115]

An even more stringent test of the demobilizing effects of negative campaigning in 1992 is ballot rolloff. Ballot rolloff occurs when people vote for offices high up on the ticket, but ignore less important elections. This happens, naturally, in almost every election. The top of the ticket—every four years the presidency, otherwise often a Senate or governor's seat—typically involves the best-known politicians in the election, and some voters turn out simply to vote for one of those people. More obscure offices, like city auditor, are often sought by people who are unknown to even well-informed voters. Negative campaigning affected not only how many people went to the polls, but how many voters cast a vote for one of the Senate candidates once they were in the voting booth. In the positive Senate races in 1992, 3.3 percent of those who voted for President did not vote for Senator. In the negative Senate races, the rate of ballot rolloff was 6.0 percent. As with the simple turnout rate, the effect of negative campaigns on rolloff was statistically significant and remained so after controlling for other things that affect participation.[116]

A couple of percentage points in turnout or rolloff may seem trivial, but they correspond to millions of votes. Holding all other factors (such as the intensity of the campaign) constant, we estimate that if all of the Senate campaigns in 1992 had been positive 6.4 million more people would have gone to the polls. Rolloff would have also been cut substantially, leading 1.2 million people who voted for President to make their voices heard in the Senate as well.[117]

THE MEANING OF THE PUBLIC'S DISCONTENT

The act of not voting often sends as potent a signal to politicians as the preferences expressed by those who do go to the polls. A candidate who wins a narrow majority in a low-turnout election is vulnerable in two ways at the next election. The opposition may be able to persuade enough of the *voters* to switch. Alternatively, the opposition may be able to convert some nonvoters to voters, mobilizing enough people to win, and when turnout is low, a little mobilization goes a long way.[118] What is the message of nonvoting engendered by attack advertising, and how might more positive campaigns change the contours of the active electorate?

Negative campaigning may keep people away from the polls for three different reasons. First, negative advertising may discourage supporters of the candidate who is attacked. Campaign consultants often state that their objective in using negative campaign commercials is to "drive up the opponent's negatives." Attack advertising might defuse partisan support for the opposition, just as advertising in general reinforces partisan preferences. For a supporter reacting to negative information, dropping out may be easier than switching to the attacker. Candidates might air negative advertisements with the objective of systematically reducing turnout among those intending to vote for the opposition. Accordingly, the demobilizing effects of negative campaigns should be concentrated among the ranks of the target candidate's partisans.

An alternative explanation is that negative advertising makes the public disenchanted with both candidates. The electorate may curse a "plague on both houses."[119] The fact that a candidate has stooped to negative campaigning may make people disparage the attacker, and the content of an attack ad may lead people to dislike the candidate who has been attacked. By this account, candidates unintentionally depress turnout among their own supporters by using negative advertising. If this were true, the effects of negative advertising would set in equally among the ranks of both the candidates' supporters and non-partisans.

Finally, negative campaigning may diminish the power of civic duty and may undermine the legitimacy of the entire electoral process. Viewers may learn from the mudslinging and name-calling that politicians in general are cynical, uncivil, corrupt, incompetent, and untrustworthy. Campaigns that generate more negative than positive messages may leave voters embittered toward the candidates *and* the rules of the game. By this account, negative advertising is likely to engender the greatest disenchantment among those whose ties to the electoral process are weakest—the nonpartisans and the poorly informed. Partisans, on the other hand, are generally immune to the opposition's messages and are reinforced by their own candidates.

This third form of voter alienation was borne out in our experiments.

The first two arguments depend on whether voters penalize the attacker and whether partisan groups exhibit different rates of demobilization. The evidence cuts both ways. On the one hand, while voters do learn the negative messages about the candidates, they do not seem to penalize the attackers. To test this idea we examined participants' ratings of the personal traits of both the sponsors and the targets of attack advertisements. In addition, we tallied the number of negative comments about the sponsors and the targets offered by viewers in response to an open-ended question asking them to list what they like and disliked about each of the candidates. Using either approach, our results indicate that the targets generally suffered as a result of negative advertising. The targeted candidates had considerably lower trait ratings and were more intensely disliked when the commercials attacked them than when the commercials promoted the opposition.[120] The exception was Dianne Feinstein in the 1992 Senate race, in which John Seymour's attacks consistently failed to raise Feinstein's negatives. Viewers, however, ascribed no additional negative traits to the attackers. The difference in the sponsor's trait ratings between the positive and negative versions of the advertisements was almost exactly zero.

On the other hand, negative advertising did not produce significantly different rates of demobilization between the partisan groups.

If the first argument discussed above—that advertising discourages partisans—is true, then Democrats should exhibit disproportionately lower intentions to vote and lower levels of efficacy when they see Republicans attack, and vice versa. No such asymmetry resulted among our respondents. Partisans exhibited the same degree of demobilization regardless of the sponsor. Democrats and Republicans do not drop out differentially depending on whether their candidate is the "victim."

However, this is not evidence that the second argument—a plague on both houses—is correct either. In our experiments, negative campaign messages produced an overall decline in participatory attitudes. All partisan groups showed lower levels of confidence in government, lower levels of confidence in their own activity, and lower intentions to vote. These effects were largest among nonpartisans. Intentions to vote showed the clearest evidence that Independents are particularly sensitive to attacks. Among partisans (Republicans and Democrats alike), the drop in turnout produced by negative advertising was 3 percentage points. Among nonpartisans, the decline was an astounding 11 points.[121] This pattern is most consistent with the third account of how negative advertising depresses voting. People infer from negative advertisements that the entire process, not just the targeted candidate, is deeply flawed.

The strikingly different reaction of partisans and nonpartisans to attack advertising highlights the fundamental difference between the processes of reinforcement and mobilization. Reinforcement is often a matter of moving people from being undecided to decided. Mobilization typically means moving people from nonvoting to voting, or at least increasing the likelihood that they will vote.

Advertising is primarily a matter of loyalty for partisans. They're likely to vote regardless of the tone of the message; the question is for whom. While partisans generally abide by their affiliations, many still require reinforcement. The sponsor and the tone of the advertisement strongly affect how partisans vote, but these features of the advertisement have little effect on whether partisans vote.

By contrast, advertising tone pulls nonpartisans in two very different directions. Nonpartisans find negative advertising somewhat persuasive; it resonates with their pessimistic view of politics. But unlike Republican viewers, Independents do not take attack advertisements as a call to take back their government. Instead, negative messages tend to alienate nonpartisans from politics further and to discourage their participation in a tainted process.

Thus, if candidates conducted more positive campaigns, they would not change the partisan balance of the electorate. They would, however, bring large numbers of nonpartisan voters back. How this might change electoral competition between the parties and the representativeness of government is a matter of speculation. We suspect that it would be an improvement. Nonpartisans tend to be more centrist than die-hard loyalists. A more Independent electorate is likely to pressure party leaders in government to seek common ground and compromise. That strikes us as a more sensible way of governing.

Beyond these partisan differences, our findings show that negative advertising demoralizes the electorate. It eats away at the individual's sense of civic duty, especially in those people whose connection to the political process is marginal. In the long-run, negative campaigns contribute to the general antipathy toward politicians and parties and the high rates of disapproval and distrust of political institutions.

CONCLUSION

Our findings are likely to dishearten even the most optimistic observers of American politics. Negative campaigning has long been suspected to be antithetical to fundamental democratic values, but no one has suspected how much so. Negative advertising drives people away from the polls in large numbers. In our experiments the effect of seeing a negative as opposed to a positive advertisement is to drop intentions to vote by nearly 5 percentage points. The disillusionment engendered by attack politics goes much deeper than dissatisfaction with the candidates. Negative advertising breeds distrust of the electoral process and pessimism about the value of an individual's own voice. The 1992 Senate elections manifested the enormity of the public's discontent with attack advertising. The negative campaigns run by most Senate candidates in 1992 led over 6 million people to stay home and another 1 million *voters* to skip the Senate election.

Negative advertising is also fueling the polarization of American politics. Attack politics heightens the partisan flavor of political discourse by driving the Independent voter from the active electorate. Though the numbers of nonpartisans have grown in public opinion polls, Independents have not emerged as a great force in American politics because they do not vote in proportion to their numbers.[122] As we have demonstrated, the hostile tenor of political campaigns contributes in no small part to the disaffection of the Independent voter. In response to our negative advertisements, nonpartisans registered significantly lower intentions to vote and lower levels of political efficacy than did partisans. Advertising not only fails to resonate with nonpartisans, as we showed in Chapter 4, but the practice of negative advertising actually turns them off.

Polarization of electoral politics translates directly into greater polarization of Congress. Members of the House and Senate work very hard to represent their constituents—especially those who vote for them.[123] Legislators assiduously avoid casting votes that will alienate key interests in their electoral coalitions. As their bases of support become more partisan (or at least less Independent and centrist), members of Congress will work harder to represent those partisan interests. As campaigns become increasingly negative, Independents increasingly drop out and politicians will increasingly come to represent either one of the political opposites embodied by the parties.

There is a silver lining to this cloud. Positive campaigns, in which the candidates promote their own ideas, successes, and abilities, can rejuvenate the electorate, especially the nonpartisan voters. Exposure to positive television advertising, surprisingly, acts much the way old-fashioned forms of campaigning did. People become more public-spirited and politically energized by watching advertisements that promote the virtues of the candidates. In addition to boosting turnout, positive advertising strengthens the public's confidence in elections and in representative government. It is not the pervasiveness of broadcast advertising that spawns public cynicism; it is, instead, the tone of the advertising campaign. If campaigns were to become more positive, people would be less embittered about politics as usual and more willing to vote.

Unfortunately, the trajectory is downward. By all accounts, campaigns will only continue to become more negative and nasty. Many political consultants have come to believe that all Americans are cynical about their government and that the electorate responds only to negatives and, thus, that they must go negative.[124] We believe that this attitude is folly; it is dangerous, and it is very hard to reverse.

6

THE SPECTACLE

The electorate has grown weary of the nastiness and negativity of campaigns. They are mad at the candidates, mad at the parties, mad at the media, and mad at anyone else who steps into the electoral arena. Many people now choose to stay home on election day; others openly express their dissatisfaction with the candidates and the parties among which they must choose. People no longer feel that they vote *for*, only against. If venom isn't really what the public is after, why do candidates insist on going negative?

Politicians and campaign consultants are, by and large, not mean-spirited people who conspire to scare voters away from the polls. The reality is more complex. The negative tenor of campaigns can be traced to the competitive nature of political advertising, to the activities of organized interests, and, last but not least, to the ways in which reporters cover the campaign. Politicians, interest groups, and journalists all act in ways that serve their own best interests. Few of these players really want to produce highly negative campaigns, but the interplay among them produces the kind of campaigns that voters have come to loathe.

"Politics," Lloyd Bentsen reflected after the 1988 election, "is a contact sport."[125] The main event is the head-to-head competition between the candidates. This, above all else, drives candidates to assail one another with thirty-second spot ads. Put bluntly, candidates attack out of fear: fear that the opposition will throw the first punch, fear that they will appear weak if they don't respond in kind. In politics, the best defense is a strong offense, and negative advertising is the most expedient way to fend off the opposition's attacks.

In addition, candidates attack to expand the scope of the political conflict, to drag organized interests and the media into the fray. Political campaigns have about them the same excitement as a prize fight. The more intense the conflict, the more people are drawn to it. Political campaigns, however, are not nearly as orderly as professional boxing matches. No ropes keep the audience from joining in. The more a candidate attacks, the more she makes news; the more conflict there is, and stories about the conflict, the more likely the candidate's proponents are to join the fray. Corporations, professional associations, unions, and other organizations have large stakes in the outcomes of elections, and they don't remain on the sidelines long. These organizations put up millions of dollars to underwrite the candidate's campaign activities; they also aggressively publicize their support of and opposition to politicians independent of the candidate's own campaigning. Through unrestrained independent advertising, interest groups can and do influence the tone, the issues, and even the outcome of elections.

The media are less partisan, but have an equally important effect on the tenor of campaigns. Journalists report the campaign with the verve of sportswriters covering a title fight. Their job, after all, is to sell papers and attract viewers, and elections are full of great material— the mistakes and weaknesses of the candidates, the twists and turns of public opinion, and the jabs and hooks of political debate. Campaign commercials, especially the negative ones, are ideally suited to the dictates of a good news story. They pack a sensational story with good visuals and good sound into thirty brief seconds. Nothing grabs the public's attention like the smell of a scandal or the prospect of a political upset. Such stories make for entertaining reading, but they don't instill confidence in the political system.[126]

COMPETING FOR VOTES

The 1988 presidential election made the adversarial nature of political advertising painfully clear. George Bush's commercials assailed Michael Dukakis for releasing dangerous criminals on furlough, for polluting Boston Harbor, for being ignorant about foreign affairs, for vetoing a bill requiring Massachusetts schoolchildren to salute the American flag, and for being a card-carrying member of the American Civil Liberties Union. The Dukakis camp was slow to react to these criticisms. Dukakis himself felt that the attacks were either unfounded or so ludicrous as to be unworthy of a response.

Worthy or not, the attacks sank Dukakis's presidential ambitions. Bush successfully portrayed Dukakis as ideologically extreme, unpatriotic, and incapable of handling important problems. By not fighting back, Dukakis created the image that he was ineffectual and indecisive. Ed McCabe, a New York marketing director who worked on Dukakis's advertising for a time, wrote after the election: "I don't think he ever realized that there's one thing the American people dislike more than someone who fights. That's someone who climbs into the ring and won't fight. That's what really happened here. He threw the fight."[127]

Four years later, Republican strategists reran the same themes. Bush impugned Bill Clinton's integrity, questioned his patriotism, and demonized him as a tax-and-spend liberal. Even though Clinton carried considerably more personal baggage than Dukakis, Bush's attacks did not work in 1992. They failed because Bill Clinton did something that Dukakis didn't do: he fought back. GOP advertisements were quickly countered with Democratic advertisements. Speeches by Bush or Quayle met prompt responses by Clinton or another prominent Democrat. Criticisms of the Republicans' daily messages zipped to newspapers and radio and television stations around the country via fax and satellite.[128]

The 1992 Democratic campaign team won the battle of the airwaves because they had anticipated the Republican strategy and responded appropriately. Here lies the true art of campaigning. Candidates must decide when to take the initiative and when to follow, when to take the high road and when to take the low, when to seize an issue and when to change the subject. There are few hard-and-fast rules, except when it comes to negative advertising.

As we noted in Chapter 1, most consultants subscribe to Roger Ailes's first dictum of politics: "If you get punched, punch back." The best way to defuse an attack is typically to counterattack. Here are examples of three common tactics.

1. Defend against the charges

Attack by Representative Wayne Dowdy against Senator Trent Lott, Mississippi U.S. Senate race, 1988.

> SCENE: A STRETCH LIMOUSINE BARRELS THROUGH A SMALL TOWN.
>
> ANNOUNCER: TRENT LOTT SAYS HE NEEDS TO KEEP HIS TAXPAYER-PAID, $50,000-A-YEAR CHAUFFEUR IN WASHINGTON. YOU CAN VOTE FOR A PARTY POLITICIAN WHO LOOKS AT LIFE THROUGH TINTED WINDOWS. OR YOU CAN VOTE FOR A SENATOR WHO SEES MISSISSIPPI THROUGH THE EYES OF ITS PEOPLE.

Response by Trent Lott.

> GEORGE AWKWARD [LOTT'S AFRICAN-AMERICAN BODYGUARD, SPEAKING DIRECTLY INTO THE CAMERA, WITH THE AMERICAN FLAG IN THE BACKGROUND]: I'VE BEEN A DETECTIVE IN A SECURITY POLICE FORCE IN WASHINGTON, D.C., FOR 27 YEARS. WAYNE DOWDY CALLS ME A CHAUFFEUR. HE OFFENDS EVERY LAW ENFORCEMENT OFFICER WHO PUTS HIS LIFE ON THE LINE EVERY DAY. MR. DOWDY, I'M NOBODY'S CHAUFFEUR. [PAUSE] GOT IT?

2. Counterattack on the same question or on issues that are of greater concern to voters.

Attack by Bruce Herschensohn on Barbara Boxer, California Senate race, 1992.

> HERSCHENSOHN [SPEAKING DIRECTLY INTO THE CAMERA]: YA KNOW. A HUNDRED AND FORTY-THREE BOUNCED CHECKS. WOW, THAT'S . . . THAT'S . . . A LOT. THAT'S REALLY A LOT. THAT'S WHAT MY OPPONENT DID. IT ADDED UP TO MORE THAN WHAT MOST CALIFORNIANS MAKE IN WELL OVER A YEAR. FORTY-ONE THOUSAND DOLLARS IN BOUNCED CHECKS. BOY. I MEAN, DO YOU WANT HER TRYING TO BALANCE YOUR BUDGET? OUR GOVERNMENT'S BUDGET? GEE.
>
> ANNOUNCER: FIGHT BACK WITH HERSCHENSOHN.

Boxer's response.

> HERSCHENSOHN [NEWSCLIPS]: "WHAT I WANT IS THE REPEAL OF ROE V.
> WADE" . . . "WE NEED MORE OFFSHORE OIL DRILLING AND NUCLEAR POWER
> PLANTS" . . . "DEMOLISH THE DEPARTMENT OF ENERGY AND EDUCA-
> TION" . . . "I OPPOSE ANY CUTS IN DEFENSE."

> ANNOUNCER: THAT'S WHAT BRUCE HERSCHENSOHN WANTS. IS THAT WHAT
> YOU WANT?

3. *Assail the opposition's credibility*

Attack by Russell Feingold on Senator Robert Kasten, Wisconsin U.S.
Senate race, 1992.

> FEINGOLD [HOLDING NEWSPAPER WITH HEADLINE ABOUT SENATOR ROBERT
> KASTEN'S NEGATIVE CAMPAIGN TACTICS]: IF THINGS ARE GOING TO CHANGE
> AROUND HERE, THIS MAN MUST BE DEFEATED IN NOVEMBER. NOT MUCH
> HAS BEEN WRITTEN ABOUT RUSS FEINGOLD TO ATTACK. SO THE ONLY
> OPTION IS TO MAKE SOMETHING UP.

> FEINGOLD [HOLDING UP MOCK TABLOID ENDORSEMENT BY ELVIS PRESLEY]:
> YOU VOTERS KNOW BETTER THAN TO BELIEVE EVERYTHING YOU READ.

Senator Robert Kasten's counterattack.

> ELVIS IMPERSONATOR [SITTING IN PINK CADILLAC WITH 1950S MUSIC BLAR-
> ING, LOOKING AT CARDBOARD CUTOUT OF FEINGOLD HOLDING MOCK
> TABLOID]: I DON'T MAKE MANY APPEARANCES. BUT WHEN I HEARD THAT HE
> WAS TELLING TALES HOW I ENDORSED HIM, I HAD TO COME FORWARD. YOU
> KNOW THAT RUSS HAS BEEN IN POLITICS FOR MORE THAN A DECADE. FEIN-
> GOLD PLANS TO RAISE OUR TAXES OVER $300 BILLION. WELL, THE KING
> WOULD NEVER SUPPORT THAT. TAKE IT FROM THE KING, THIS RUSS FEIN-
> GOLD RECORD HAS GOT ME ALL SHOOK UP.

Feingold's parting shot:

> FEINGOLD [CLOSE UP]: A WHILE AGO, I WARNED YOU ABOUT MY OPPO-
> NENT'S HISTORY OF MAKING THINGS UP. I FIGURED WHEN HE STARTED

DISTORTING THE TRUTH ABOUT ME, YOU'D TAKE IT WITH A GRAIN OF
SALT.

[FEINGOLD PICKS UP A JAR OF SALT AND STARTS POURING IT ON THE
GROUND. THE CAMERA ZOOMS IN ON THE GROWING PILE.]

FEINGOLD: WELL, GET READY, BECAUSE NOW HE'S TELLING YOU I HAVE A
PLAN TO RAISE THOUSANDS OF DOLLARS OF TAXES ON THE MIDDLE CLASS.
NOT TRUE. SENATOR KASTEN KNOWS I HAVEN'T PROPOSED ANY SUCH TAX
INCREASES. PERIOD. THE TRUTH IS THE SENATOR HAS MADE UP SOMETHING
SO BIG THAT A FEW GRAINS OF SALT WON'T BE ENOUGH. A SHOVELFUL
WOULD BE MORE LIKE IT.

[CAMERA PULLS BACK TO SHOW FEINGOLD HOLDING A SHOVEL.]

Tit-for-tat. And so it goes with many campaigns today. A negative
advertisement triggers a negative response and, in turn, a negative
reply. Increasingly, even positive commercials provoke attacks. Candidates who promote a particular ideology or program seem especially
susceptible to criticism. Stick your neck out and get your head
chopped off. Consider the race between Ohio Senator John Glenn and
his 1992 challenger Mike DeWine. In one commercial John Glenn
tried to pick up on the issue of health care reform.

GLENN: ONE OF THE WORST THINGS ABOUT WASHINGTON IS THAT FOR ALL
THE MONEY THAT'S WASTED ON PROGRAMS THAT DON'T WORK AND THAT WE
DON'T NEED, WE DON'T EVEN HAVE NATIONAL HEALTH INSURANCE. NO ONE
IN AMERICA SHOULD HAVE TO GO WITHOUT A DOCTOR, AND NO FAMILY
SHOULD BE FORCED INTO POVERTY BY OUTRAGEOUS HEALTH INSURANCE
PREMIUMS.

DeWine countered:

ANNOUNCER: THIS IS WHAT'S WRONG WITH POLITICS IN WASHINGTON. FOR
18 YEARS, JOHN GLENN NEVER SUPPORTED NATIONAL HEALTH INSURANCE.
HE NEVER VOTED FOR IT. . . . NOW, IN THE TOUGHEST CAMPAIGN OF HIS
LIFE, JOHN GLENN IS SUDDENLY PROMISING HEALTH INSURANCE. WHERE
HAS HE BEEN FOR 18 YEARS?

DeWine narrowly lost, but in his actions lie a corollary to Ailes's Law: attack early and often. The reasoning is simple enough. If political campaigns are likely to turn negative, it is best to get in the first blow. It does not matter if the candidate is a liberal or conservative, incumbent or challenger, Republican or Democrat. Anticipation of attacks from the opposition has led to preemptive strikes by candidates as different as Mitch McConnell (a conservative Republican challenger in Kentucky in 1984) and Alan Cranston (a liberal Democratic incumbent in California in 1986). McConnell's ads wore down the incumbency advantages of Senator Walter Huddleston; Cranston's attacks crushed Congressman Ed Zschau, a little-known, but well-financed Republican challenger.

The need to punch back and the temptation to get in the first blow are driven by the same electoral forces. Voters are often most receptive to attack advertisements when the candidate who is attacked responds with self-promotional advertisements rather than a counterattack. The victim of the attack can appear flawed and unwilling to defend himself. As we find below, partisanship further accentuates this effect. Republicans and Democrats want to see their own candidate score points. Partisans get an extra charge when the man or woman they support blindsides the opposition with a negative ad. By the same token, partisans are averse to seeing their own candidates on the receiving end of such a blow. This sort of judgment by voters drives candidates to run negative commercials. Even candidates who would in principle like to run wholly positive campaigns are led to attack to protect themselves from the airborne assault of the opposition.[129]

Two simple experiments demonstrate these principles. Like the experiments presented in earlier chapters, participants in our two-advertisement experiments viewed a local newscast into which we inserted political commercials. In these studies, however, we inserted two advertisements, one from each of the competing candidates, into the video. The advertisement of one candidate went into the first commercial break, and the advertisement of the other candidate went into the second.[130] Unlike the one-ad studies discussed in Chapters 4 and 5, the political advertisements were actual spots used during ongoing campaigns in California, and each commercial was either positive or negative. Viewers saw either two positive commercials (one from each candidate), two negative commercials (one from each candidate), a negative Democratic ad paired with a positive Republican ad, or a negative Republican ad paired with a positive Democratic ad.[131]

The smaller of the two experiments was conducted during the 1992 California Senate race between Barbara Boxer and Bruce Herschensohn. This experiment highlights the vulnerability of candidates to negative messages when they air positive commercials. Table 6.1 shows the reactions of people to the competing messages. The entries in the table are Boxer's lead in the sample (i.e., the percent intending to vote for her minus the percent intending to vote for Herschensohn). The columns correspond to the Boxer advertisements, and the rows correspond to the Herschensohn advertisements. The entry in the first row and column, then, shows Boxer's lead among those people who saw a positive commercial from both candidates.

Voters' reactions to competing campaign messages square with our findings in Chapter 4. The Republican candidates generally benefit from negative messages; the Democrats, from positive ones. But this simple experiment also reveals the problem faced by candidates who, while being attacked, try to promote their own ideas. Bruce Herschensohn's margin was higher among viewers who saw his negative messages, regardless of the tone of the Barbara Boxer advertisements. For instance, when Herschensohn's positive message was paired with a Boxer attack, he trailed by 27 points (his second-worst outcome). Herschensohn's support was slightly higher when he countered a Boxer attack with an attack. Barbara Boxer, by contrast, did best when

TABLE 6.1
Voting Preferences in Two-Ad Studies: Boxer-Herschensohn (Cell entries Are the Democratic candidate's lead)

		Tone of Barbara Boxer Ad	
		Positive	Negative
Tone of Bruce Herschensohn Ad	Positive	.33	.27
	Negative	.00	.24

viewers saw positive messages from both candidates. In that case, she enjoyed a 33 point lead. Positive advertising, however, would not guarantee Boxer an easy victory. The positive ad strategy made Boxer at once appealing and vulnerable to attack. While Boxer's best outcome occurred when both candidates aired positive messages, her worst outcome arose when viewers saw a positive Boxer advertisement paired with a negative Herschensohn commercial. In this situation, the candidates ran even.

What should Boxer do? Should she promote herself and gamble that Herschensohn will also take the high road? Or, should she go on the attack, which would guarantee her a smaller electoral margin than the case where he promotes and she attacks? The theory of games developed by economists offers a useful way to think about this choice. The central insight of this theory is that candidates develop campaign strategies based on their own objectives and their beliefs about how the opponent will behave. Appendix C contains a brief discussion of the game theoretic ideas used here.

Looking at Table 6.1 from a game theoretic perspective counsels the more cautious approach. The key to Boxer's strategy depends on what Herschensohn is likely to do. Since Herschensohn always does better with negative advertisements, Boxer can expect him to attack. Boxer's best response to a negative campaign by Herschensohn is to go negative herself. If she airs a positive commercial, he can easily counter with a negative. That would be the best possible outcome for Herschensohn and would allow him to pull even. If Boxer attacks, her margin is somewhat lower than her best outcome (positive-positive), but it avoids the potential disaster of her being attacked while running positive commercials.

The actual course of the Boxer-Herschensohn campaign mirrored these laboratory findings. Boxer came out of the primary election with a comfortable 16-point lead over Herschensohn. In August and September, Herschensohn attacked Boxer for abusing congressional perks and for bouncing 143 checks at the House bank. Boxer, meanwhile, promoted herself on women's issues and the economy. By October, Boxer's once considerable lead had vanished, and with three weeks left in the campaign the polls showed that she held only a 3 point edge, a statistical dead heat. Boxer finally fought back. The last Democratic

commercials of the campaign painted Herschensohn as an ideological extremist, who would dismantle the Department of Education,
who supported nuclear power, and who opposed a woman's right
to choose. Boxer's counterattack apparently stemmed Herschensohn's momentum, and on election day, she eked out a 5-point victory.

The larger of our two-advertisement experiments was designed to
see how competitive advertising played out among different partisan
groups. This experiment was conducted during the 1990 California gubernatorial race between Dianne Feinstein and Pete Wilson.[132] As noted
earlier, the partisan attachments of the voters actually strengthen the
pressures on the candidates to attack. Like our 1992 Senate study,
viewers saw two advertisements, one from each candidate, and each ad
either promoted the sponsoring candidate or attacked the opponent.
The commercials were actual advertisements run by the candidates
during the campaign. Though the 1990 and 1992 two-ad experiments
involved very different candidates and electoral circumstances, voters'
reactions to competing messages and the resulting campaign dynamics were strikingly similar.

Table 6.2 shows the responses of Democrats, Independents, and
Republicans to competing advertisements by Pete Wilson and Dianne
Feinstein. Each panel of the table represents a particular group; the
rows of each panel correspond to the Wilson advertisements, and
the columns of each panel correspond to the Feinstein advertisements.
For example, the first row and the first column of the first panel shows
Feinstein's lead among Democratic voters who saw a positive Fein-
stein advertisement paired with a positive Wilson advertisement.

The results again reflected the general finding of Chapter 4: Democrats usually do better with positive messages and Republicans usually
do better with negatives. Wilson's negative advertisements were more
effective than his positive advertisements among all partisan groups.
In contrast, Feinstein's best outcome among Republicans and Independents and second-best outcome among Democrats occurred when
her positive advertisement was paired with Wilson's positive advertisement. But like Boxer, Feinstein's positive advertisements carried
considerable risks. When viewers saw a positive Feinstein ad paired
with a negative Wilson ad (the lower left cell in each panel), she

TABLE 6.2

Voting Preferences and Partisanship in Two-Ad Studies: Feinstein-Wilson (Cell entries Are the Democratic candidate's lead)

Democratic identifiers		Tone of Dianne Feinstein Ad	
		Positive	Negative
Tone of Pete Wilson Ad	Positive	.55	.66
	Negative	.50	.51

Independents		Tone of Dianne Feinstein Ad	
		Positive	Negative
Tone of Pete Wilson Ad	Positive	.33	.19
	Negative	.17	.18

Republican identifiers		Tone of Dianne Feinstein Ad	
		Positive	Negative
Tone of Pete Wilson Ad	Positive	−.32	−.40
	Negative	−.73	−.54

scored her lowest levels of support across all three partisan groups, trailing by as much as 75 points among Republicans.

The 1990 gubernatorial study also makes it clear that partisans are highly responsive to the antagonism of negative campaigning. Feinstein and Wilson did best among their own partisans when their negative ads were paired with the opponents' positive ads. Among Democrats, Feinstein's lead reached 66 points when Wilson promoted and she went on the attack. Among Republicans, Wilson led by 73 points when Feinstein promoted herself and he attacked. When the tables were turned, partisans felt far less supportive of their own candidates. Among Democrats, Feinstein led by just 50 points, her lowest level of support in this group, when she promoted and Wilson attacked. Among Republicans, Wilson's lead fell to 40 points when he promoted and Feinstein attacked.

Thus, again, although positive advertising holds great potential for Democrats, negative advertising offered the most prudent strategy. For Republicans, the choice is clear: negative advertisements work best. Among Democratic and Independent voters, the difference between Feinstein countering an attack with a positive or a negative ad was minimal. However, among Republican voters, Feinstein invited disaster by running a positive campaign when Wilson went negative. In that case, she ran 73 points behind Wilson among Republicans, compared with a 54 point deficit when she counterattacked.

The California gubernatorial campaign was touted as one of the most negative races of 1990, but the election started out positively enough. In the primaries Feinstein established herself and her credentials in February 1990 with the "Forged from Tragedy" ad that we described in Chapter 1. The commercial (among other things) produced an 18-point swing in voting preferences in the primary election polls, giving Feinstein a ten point lead over her opponent John Van deKamp, a lead that she never relinquished.

The general election campaign, however, began on a sour note. Pete Wilson opened with an advertisement that claimed that Feinstein and her husband had received a sweetheart deal from a failed Oregon savings-and-loan bank. Feinstein quickly countered with a commercial listing "Five S&L Facts," including the fact that, while in the U.S. Senate, Wilson himself had received $250,000 in campaign contributions from savings institutions and had voted for the bailout of the savings-and-loan industry. The issue was dropped, and Wilson turned to Feinstein's record in San Francisco. One Wilson ad portrayed Feinstein as a tax-and-spend liberal; another showed clippings from the *San Francisco Chronicle* and claimed that Feinstein "broke the bank and left the city holding the bag." Feinstein did not sit idly by. She assailed Wilson's record in San Diego, claiming that as mayor he had turned San Diego Bay into a toxic waste dump, which cost taxpayers millions of dollars to clean up.

As the attacks continued, Feinstein slowly cut into Wilson's double-digit lead. Looking for a final push, the Feinstein team decided to resurrect the "Forged from Tragedy" ad. This time there was little movement in the polls, and if anything, Feinstein lost the momentum that she had built at the end of September and the beginning of October. The "Forged from Tragedy" advertisement was a bust in the general election because the context differed. When Feinstein aired the ad in February, it was the only political message on television. The ad established her credentials without the countervailing effects of other candidates' advertisements. By October, the airwaves were saturated with attacks from Feinstein, Wilson, and candidates for other offices. When pitted against Wilson's negative advertisements, "Forged from Tragedy" was fated to fail.

The 1990 and 1992 campaigns carry a more general lesson about the tone of political advertising. Against the backdrop of a negative campaign, promotional advertising appears particularly weak. This is true of both Republican and Democratic candidates. A candidate is demeaned in the voters' eyes when he or she promotes while the opposition attacks. Clearly, this places enormous pressure on candidates to go negative, even when voters are fed up with the nasty tone of campaigns.

ORGANIZED INTERESTS

Many observers trace the negative climate of current political campaigns to the activities of interest groups. In 1980, the National Conservative Political Action Committee (NCPAC) attacked six prominent Democratic Senators—George McGovern in South Dakota, Frank Church in Idaho, Birch Bayh in Indiana, John Culver in Iowa, Warren Magnuson in Washington, and Herman Talmadge in Georgia—as being too liberal and out of touch with their constituents. All six were defeated, giving NCPAC instant notoriety and the Republican party control of the U.S. Senate for the first time since 1954.

The NCPAC legend carries two morals. First, interest groups are as belligerent as any candidate and operate primarily to destroy their opponents in Congress. Second, conservative and Republican groups are especially negative. However, a closer look at interest group campaign activity reveals that only the second of these conventional wisdoms has any merit, and even the groups that campaign on behalf of Republicans tend to promote their friends much more than they attack their foes.

Interest groups are drawn into the fight by the prospect of being able to knock their foes out of Congress. Unlike direct contributions to candidates, which are subject to strict limits, independent expenditures remain unregulated. Interest groups are allowed to contribute no more than $5,000 a year to a candidate. That limit was set in 1974 and inflation has greatly eroded its value: a $5,000 contribution today is equivalent to an $1,800 contribution in 1974.[133] Independent expenditures, on the other hand, enjoy the First Amendment protection of free speech, so groups can spend as much as they like for or against candidates.[134] "Considering that," says Dr. Joseph Hatch, who chairs the American Medical Association's political action committee, "we're additionally enthused about making independent expenditures. We see that as the way of the future to express our political influence."[135]

Elected officials are far less excited. Politicians fear ambush from hundreds of extremist and single-issue groups that can readily spend large sums to push their particular agendas. A congressional vote for gun control or for restrictions on abortion funding or for reform of social security may trigger a barrage of negative advertisements from groups with heavy stakes in those issues. Organized interests seem to have a unique edge in going negative. Attack advertisements from interest groups convey all of the negatives about the candidate who is attacked without the risk of a political backlash against the candidate the group supports.[136]

Many single-issue and ideological organizations have aped NCPAC's strategy of independent attacks. In 1992 alone, interest groups spent a total of $1.6 million in opposition to House and Senate candidates, with much of that money coming from a few groups and concentrated in a few key races. The National Rifle Association, for example, spent $136,000 in opposition to Mike Synar, a Democratic Congressman from Oklahoma. The National Abortion Rights Action League spent $144,000 against Massachusetts Republican Steven Pierce, a House challenger. Together, Public Citizen, Inc., and the Clean Up Congress Committee of the Willamette Citizens PAC poured $100,000 into a campaign to defeat House Minority Whip Newt Gingrich.

Organized interests have been no less innocent in presidential campaigns. The infamous Willie Horton commercial was actually the handiwork of the National Security PAC. Seeing that the interest group's anticrime message had scored points with the electorate, the Bush campaign picked up the attack in an advertisement called the "Revolving Door," which discussed Massachusetts' prison furlough program and showed a stream of men dressed in blue prison uniforms walking into and then out of a revolving door. All told, conservative groups pumped $3.4 million dollars into the independent campaign against Michael Dukakis.[137]

Examples such as these have stirred no end of furor about the negativity of interest groups' independent expenditures.[138] These, however, are the exceptions. When groups jump into the political arena, it is usually to praise their friends, rather than to assail their foes. Elected officials dread making decisions on controversial issues that may bring independent money into campaigns. Even still, independent money isn't bad for elections, since it goes overwhelmingly to produce positive messages.

The Federal Election Commission (FEC) records independent expenditures for and against candidates for President, House, and Senate. The classification is done by the interest groups themselves. Organizations that make independent expenditures in House, Senate, and presidential campaigns must file detailed reports with the FEC, specifying the candidate about whom the expenditure was made, the amount of the expenditure, and whether the funds were spent "for" or "against" the candidate. These data reveal that interest groups promote candidates much more frequently than they attack.[139]

Figure 6.1 shows the independent expenditures for and against House and Senate candidates from 1980 to 1992.[140] The decade began with a flurry of negative campaigning by interest groups. In the 1980 election, organizations used their independent expenditures primarily to attack candidates. The volume of independent negative campaigns trebled in the next election, and 1982 saw the most intense negative campaigning by organized interests. In that year groups like NCPAC and the NRA spent $3.7 million in opposition to Democratic Senatorial candidates and another $930,000 against Democratic candidates running for the House. However, the tone of interest group campaigns changed abruptly in the middle of the 1980s. Since 1984, interest groups have spent approximately three dollars in support of candidates for every dollar they have spent in opposition. At the same time that candidates began to step up their attacks on one another, groups began to actively promote their own ideas and candidates.

The reasons for the reversal can, again, be traced to NCPAC, but this time to its failures. In 1982, NCPAC tried to repeat its earlier success, targeting six prominent liberal Senators. The group spent three million dollars, only to lose in all six races. Defeat spelled declining contributions and, eventually, the death of the organization. The fall of NCPAC exploded the myth among consultants and interest group strategists that attack advertising is a group's best means of defeating opponents, shaping the campaign agenda, or securing the organization's long-range interests.

Since 1984, organizations have tended to run positive advertising campaigns. The National Rifle Association (NRA), the National Abortion Rights Action League (NARAL), and a handful of NCPAC knock-offs (such as the Midwest Conservative PAC and the East Coast Conservative PAC) still run negative campaigns. Even these groups,

FIGURE 6.1

Independent Expenditures For and Against U.S. House and Senate Elections (in thousands)

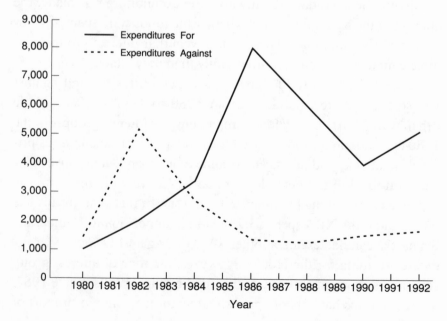

however, balance their attacks with expenditures in favor of candidates to their liking. In 1992, for instance, the NRA spent $139,000 in support of Democrat Gene Green of Texas, and NARAL supported the Senate candidacies of Ben Campbell in Colorado and Russ Feingold in Wisconsin to the tune of $140,000 each.

The predominance of positive campaigning by interest groups stems from the fact that the biggest independent spenders in national politics are not ideological and single-issue groups, but trade associations, which invariably run positive campaigns. Two organizations, in particular, stand out: the Realtors and the American Medical Association (AMA). In 1992 the Realtors spent $170,000 in support of Rod Chandler, a Republican House member in Washington running for the Senate; $125,000 for the reelection of Gene Shaw, a Republican House member of Florida; and $330,000 in support of Democrat Les AuCoin's Senate bid in Oregon. Lined up behind incumbent Senator Robert Packwood, AuCoin's opponent, were the AMA and the Automobile Dealers, who spent $228,000 and $66,000, respectively, to push their candidate. The AMA also spent $258,000 in favor of Vic Fazio, a Democratic House member from California; $119,000 for Michael Andrews, a Democrat from Texas; and $185,000 for Scott McInnis, a Republican from Colorado. The list goes on, with one important theme running throughout. Trade associations use independent expenditures to promote Representatives and Senators who have proven their support for the groups in the past. They are careful not to attack any opponents of these lawmakers, because, after all, they might win—and it's a lot easier to throw positive money at successful incumbents than to overcome the ill will engendered by an attack.

While legislators generally have less to fear from interest group attacks than is commonly thought, interest group expenditures do have a serious partisan slant. Groups campaign much more intensely on behalf of Republican candidates. Organizations independently spent $42 million on House and Senate campaigns during the 1980s and 1990s. Of that, 62 percent went either in favor of Republicans or against Democrats. Presidential elections showed an even steeper Republican advantage among independent expenditures. Of the $78 million in independent expenditures spent during the 1980s and 1990s, 92 percent were "for" Republicans or "against" Democrats.[141]

When looked at through partisan lenses, interest group attacks appear more prominent. The organizations that back Republicans attack the opposition much more frequently than the organizations that support the Democrats. In House and Senate races during the 1980s and 1990s, groups that backed the Democratic candidates spent forty-five cents against the Republican opposition for every dollar they spent in favor of the Democratic candidate. Groups that backed the Republican candidates, on the other hand, spent sixty cents against the Democratic opposition for every dollar they spent in favor of the Republicans.

In presidential elections, things looked worse for the Democratic candidates. Much worse. Not only did Republican-leaning groups overwhelm the Democrats with independent expenditures, but the Republican groups have been much more negative. For every dollar spent in support of a Republican presidential candidate during the 1980s and 1990s, groups spent seventy cents against the Democrats. Groups that backed the Democrats, by contrast, spent only twelve cents against Republican candidates for every dollar they spent promoting Democrats.

Interest groups seem to be keying off of the same ideological forces that shape candidate advertising. Negative messages appeal disproportionately to Republicans and Independents, while positive messages are more powerful for Democrats. Conservative interest groups should be able to exploit this difference just as effectively as Republican candidates can. Liberal interest groups, on the other hand, may find themselves in the same bind as Democratic candidates. Their aim is to rally liberal voters behind a cause or a candidate. The best way to do so is to promote particular ideas and politicians, but in doing so liberal groups may lose of some their appeal among moderate and more conservative voters.

Monied interests are a convenient target for critics of American campaigns, but they really deserve little blame for the spread of negative campaigning. While there is a decided partisan bias to interest group attacks, independent campaign expenditures still go primarily to promote specific policies, ideologies, and ideas rather than to destroy people who are disliked. This is not to say that independent expenditures are wholly salutary. Highly negative independent campaigns punctuate the landscape of recent elections, especially at the presidential level. The prospect of interest group attacks, moreover, can have a chilling effect on public policy. Most candidates assiduously avoid hot-button issues like gun control and abortion. And the multi-million-dollar advertising campaign of the insurance industry in opposition to President Clinton's health care initiative is widely credited with having grounded that policy effort. In addition, the messages of advertisements like Willie Horton or those aired by NCPAC in the early 1980s can take on lives of their own. They force candidates to address issues that they would not ordinarily discuss, and they automatically attract coverage by newspapers and television news.

THE MEDIA

Political consultants have long exploited the willingness of television stations to replay advertisements. Consider the infamous "Daisy" commercial. On September 7, 1964, Lyndon Johnson's presidential campaign launched "Peace, Little Girl." The advertisement shows a sweet young girl plucking the petals from a daisy and counting from one to nine. Then, a male announcer counts down from ten. With each successive number the camera jumps to a closer shot of the child's face. At zero, a nuclear blast fills the screen, and President Johnson says: "These are the stakes—to make a world in which all of God's children can live, or to go into the dark. We must either love each other, or we must die."

The commercial aired just once, but it caused an instant furor. NBC, the network on which the commercial aired, was flooded with phone calls and letters. Senator Goldwater requested equal time from NBC to clarify his positions on the tactical use of nuclear warheads. Out of shock and voyeurism, television news programs on all three networks featured the commercial and the resulting controversy. Bill Moyers, President Johnson's press secretary, reported to the president a week after the spot aired:

[W]HILE WE PAID FOR THE AD ONLY ONCE ON NBC LAST MONDAY NIGHT, ABC AND CBS BOTH RAN IT ON THEIR NEWS SHOWS FRIDAY. SO WE GOT IT SHOWN ON ALL THREE NETWORKS FOR THE PRICE OF ONE. THIS PARTICULAR AD WAS DESIGNED TO RUN ONLY ONE TIME.[142]

Three decades later, campaign commercials remain very much in the media spotlight. Advertisements have become a regular feature on the news, and candidates play that fact for all its worth. Newspapers and television news programs that give even the most superficial attention to the campaign cannot avoid reporting on the candidates' paid messages.

Political advertisements also make the nightly news because they are perfect news stories. Reporters need low-cost, high-impact stories that can be compressed into a half-hour newscast. Most aspects of political campaigns are time-consuming to cover and don't make for good TV. Speeches, press releases, and debates cannot compete with the images of urban violence, medical emergencies, and natural disasters. In contrast to the standard campaign fare, thirty-second spot ads contain great soundbites, arresting visuals, and sensational attacks, all in a package that fits easily into the two-minute format of television news or the fast format that many newspapers have copied from USA Today. Campaign advertisements are made for TV. They're made for TV news.

Negative advertisements make particularly tasty morsels for the media. For journalists, it is a no-lose situation when candidates attack one another. Allegations of dishonesty and incompetence lay the seeds of controversy and scandal. Even if the charges prove to be false, reporters can always rail against the candidate who aired the attack for slandering his or her opponent and engaging in sleazy campaigning. The fight itself often becomes the story.[143]

Political consultants cater to the incentives facing newsrooms. Campaign managers produce materials that journalists can easily use. That strategy worked in 1964, and it has been further refined. Copies of advertisements are regularly sent to television news stations and newspaper op-ed page editors even before the spots air. Sometimes campaigns do not even bother to purchase air time; they simply rely on local television stations to show the commercials for them.

Consultants also dovetail their advertisements with the candidates' speeches and staged events. One technique is "the message of the day." Running a spot on crime and visiting a ward of AIDS babies on the same day only produces confusion. Running a spot on crime and giving a speech in front of 100 uniformed policemen whose union has endorsed the candidate enables the campaign to set the public agenda. The advertisement can ride the wave of favorable news about the endorsement. What is more, by focusing on a single issue, the campaign can lead the press to focus on that issue as well. A story about the endorsement makes a natural lead-in for a story about the concerns raised in the advertisement.

And nothing seems to provoke the press like a stinging attack. Commenting on the 1988 election, Roger Ailes surmised that the news media "either want mistakes, pictures or attacks and we [the Bush campaign] were giving them pretty good pictures and pretty good lead stories and we were sticking to our theme of the day. . . . We were disciplined, giving them the soundbites and feed that they wanted. It wasn't that they were rolling over for us. It was that we were basically programming something that they would air."[144]

Even obscure campaigns on tight budgets use attack advertisements to get free press. Herbert London, the 1994 candidate for comptroller in New York state, provides just one of the most recent examples.

"Kill the Jews?" began a London advertisement. The ad identified Mr. London as the "Jewish candidate" and went on to portray Carl McCall, an African-American, as an opponent of the state of Israel and an extreme radical. The spot never appeared on television, but it was released to the news media, it was played on WNBC-TV, and it was discussed in articles in the *New York Times*.

Another London commercial appeared in the *Jewish Press* and played up the same themes. A photo shows a smiling Mr. London beneath the heading "Kosher," while a photo of an unsmiling Mr. McCall appears beneath the heading "Non-Kosher." The ad then lists quotes that were designed to upset Jewish voters and were attributed to Jesse Jackson, David Dinkins, and other black leaders. The small print in the ad is a disclaimer that the quotes are "fictitious." The ad prompted protests from Democratic and black political leaders. Even better, from London's point of view, this ad in a small-circulation newspaper suddenly became big news in the *New York Times*.[145]

For London, the bad press was worth it. The Comptroller's election received just five feature stories in the *New York Times*, three of them on London's advertising. None of the stories about the ads discussed McCall's candidacy, only the charges of anti-Semitism raised by

London. Even if the stories were critical, London succeeded in getting his basic message spread more widely for free and he got the press's discussion of the campaign defined on his own terms.[146]

All of this works to the advantage of the candidates. Turning advertisements into news stories allows candidates to set the campaign agenda and magnifies the effects of the ads considerably. Coverage of particular issues boosts the candidates and parties who are already associated with those issues in the voters' minds.[147] Of course, news coverage of the advertisements recycles the sponsoring candidates' messages, providing them with valuable prime time, free of charge. Media guru Roger Ailes described this as the best of all worlds: "You get a 30 or 40 percent bump out of getting [an ad] on the news. You get more viewers, you get more credibility, you get it in your framework."[148]

Ad-news also serves the interests of individual journalists. They get their bylines, and editors get a cheap, high-impact story. This sort of reporting, however, compromises the quality of campaign journalism. The image of the press as a whole suffers. Campaign news is a function of what the candidates say and do. As candidates have come to rely more heavily on negative advertisements, the message of the media has become more negative as well. Not surprisingly, voters increasingly give election coverage poor marks. In 1994, for example, the *Times Mirror* survey of the electorate gave the media a C grade. The problem is not lack of substance, but the negativity of the message that the media convey. Seventy percent of the voters in the 1994 survey said they had learned enough to make a reasoned decision, but a majority also complained about the negativity of the news. In states where the campaigns were highly negative, people rated the media especially badly.[149] The problem is that voters get a stiff dose of vinegar from the press, because that is what the campaigns have fed them.

Journalists, of course, are aware that coverage of campaign advertisements, especially the negative ones, compromises the overall quality of election coverage. Following the 1988 election, reporters and editors were deeply critical of the machinations of the Bush campaign and their own complicity in the "Willie Horton" saga. How could they be so readily manipulated by one campaign? What perverse incentives led sensible, experienced reporters to cave into television's single-minded quest for good visuals and good leads?

In the wake of 1988, a number of journalists decided to fight back. Several editorials floated proposals for new kinds of press coverage that would allow reporters and editors to prevent and even counteract future manipulations of the press by the campaigns. All came to the same conclusion: the media should act as referees. Distinguished journalists including David Broder and Ken Bode suggested that the press should evaluate campaign advertisements on a regular basis and condemn those that distorted or blurred the record. The views of Broder, Bode, and others had a significant impact in newsrooms across the country. A new genre of campaign journalism, devoted to monitoring campaign advertising, was born.[150]

By 1992, "truth-box" or "ad-watch" journalism had come into its own. The *Los Angeles Times*, for instance, published more than twenty ad-watch stories focusing on the two races for U.S. Senate in California. Ad-watches appeared regularly on national and local newscasts. The producers of CNN's "Inside Politics" program assigned a senior correspondent, Brooks Jackson, to the task of inspecting and analyzing advertisements aired by the presidential candidates. Today, ad-watches are standard fare in print and broadcast outlets at both national and local levels.[151]

Ad-watches represent an important shift in campaign journalism. They give reporters and editors a tool with which to assert their independence and to rebuild the integrity of their media. Now, journalists subject the candidates' messages to critical analysis and, thereby, alter the incentives facing the candidates. If ad-watches live up to their promise, they will make voters generally less susceptible to campaign advertising and less supportive of candidates who engage in deceptive advertising.

The media's foray into truth in political advertising also presents an important test of the role that journalists play in campaigns. Are journalists inadvertent boosters for whomever they happen to cover, or can they serve as the referees in increasingly hostile campaigns? Can they defuse the effects of unfair advertising or do they only magnify the effects?

Since ad-watch journalism is relatively new, little evidence has been collected concerning the effects of these reports on public opinion.[152] We conducted three experiments using actual ad-watch stories from the 1992 presidential election campaign. The methods used in these experiments are similar to those of other experiments discussed in this book. Each experiment involved two videotapes of a newscast. The presentations were identical except that one of the newscasts contained an ad-watch story; the other contained a nonpolitical (personal interest) filler story. Two of the ad-watch stories analyzed advertisements run by the Clinton campaign; one examined an advertisement run by the Bush campaign. One of the Clinton spots described his accomplishments as Governor of Arkansas, emphasizing the state's economic growth and welfare and educational reforms. The other Clinton advertisement attacked Bush's record on the economy. This commercial juxtaposed statements by Bush claiming that the economy was growing with gloomy economic statistics. The Bush advertisement denigrated the so-called Arkansas miracle by noting that Clinton had repeatedly raised taxes and increased government spending.

The ad-watches were actual news stories done by CNN's Brooks Jackson. Each story first replayed the particular commercial, then questioned its facts and assumptions, and offered contrary information. Whenever a false or misleading statement was encountered, the label MISLEADING or FALSE, in bold, red, capital letters, was slapped on the advertisement. Each story concluded by rating the advertisement as either inaccurate or misleading. In the case of the Bush attack ad, Jackson noted that Bush himself had raised taxes and increased government spending. In analyzing the Clinton negative spot, the report pointed out that the economic statistics had been taken out of context and presented out of order. And about the Clinton promotional ad, the ad-watch compared Arkansas to the nation and demonstrated that on some fronts the state did well, but on others it lagged well behind. In sum, these were actual ad-watch stories; they were representative of the genre; and they accented the misrepresentations and falsehoods in the candidates' advertisements.

If ad-watches have their intended effect, then viewers should be less favorably disposed toward and less likely to vote for the candidate whose advertisement is criticized. We considered two different measures of our viewers' preferences.[153] As with our advertising experiments, we asked viewers to rate the candidates according to several traits—intelligence, integrity, diligence, and compassion. Respondents were asked to determine which of the traits described the candidates. From these judgments, we calculated the strength of a candidate's traits relative to his or her opponent. The net trait rating ranged from 1 (complete support for the candidate whose ad is featured in the ad-watch) to -1 (complete support for the opponent). We also examined voting preferences. Specifically, we considered the margin (electoral lead) of the candidate who sponsored the ad shown in the ad-watch. To examine the effects of the ad-watches we compared those viewers who saw the story against those who saw no ad-watch (the control group).

Table 6.3 shows how respondents rated the candidates in reaction to ad-watch news stories. The first column of Table 6.3 presents the net trait ratings; the second column contains the voting preferences. The rows of the table show the experimental conditions. There are three groups of rows, one for each experiment, and an additional row showing the pooled effects of the ad-watches (the average over all three experiments). Experiment 1 corresponds to the ad-watch about the positive Clinton commercial; Experiment 2, to the Clinton advertisement attacking Bush; Experiment 3, to the Bush advertisement attacking Clinton. Within each experiment we present the net trait ratings and vote preferences of the group of viewers who saw the ad-watch (Ad-watch), the group of viewers who saw no ad-watch (Control), and the difference between these two groups, which is the "effect" of the ad-watch. The pooled effects are shown at the bottom of the table. Below each average effect we present the margin of error.[154]

The ad-watch stories clearly backfired. The candidates whose advertisements were criticized gained support on both measures. Clinton scored 6- and 14-point gains in his net trait ratings in Experiments 1 and 2, respectively. Bush registered an 8-point jump in his net trait ratings in Experiment 3. Clinton's electoral margin rose 6 points in Experiment 1 and 8 points in Experiment 2. Bush's margin leapt 27 points in Experiment 3. Overall, there was a 9-point increase (with a margin of error of plus or minus 5 points) in the net trait rating of the candidate whose advertising was featured in the ad-watches and a 14-point increase (with a margin of error of plus or minus 8 points) in that candidate's electoral margin.[155] In addition, the ad-watches aimed

TABLE 6.3

Effects of Ad-Watch Stories on Assessments of the Candidates

	Net Trait Ratings of the Candidate Whose Ad Was Featured	Vote Margin of the Candidate Whose Ad Was Featured
Experiment 1		
Ad-Watch	.175	.417
Control	.118	.357
Difference (effect)	.050	.060
Experiment 2		
Ad-Watch	.238	.342
Control	.103	.267
Difference (effect)	.135	.075
Experiment 3		
Ad-Watch	−.024	−.163
Control	−.103	−.433
Difference (effect)	.079	.270
Pooled effect	.090	.135
Margin of error[a]	±.050	±.080

[a] 95 percent confidence interval.

at the negative commercials seem to benefit the candidates somewhat more. Clinton got a slightly bigger boost from the ad-watch about his negative advertisement than from the ad-watch about his positive advertisement, and the message of the Bush attack clearly got through the truth-box filter. In short, just as with the ads themselves, negativity wins in campaign reporting, and the referees can't stop it.

The ad-watch stories had a further effect on participatory attitudes of the electorate. As with negative advertising, ad-watches primarily turned off the nonpartisan voters. The stories in our experiments produced no significant changes in the intentions to vote and the feelings of political efficacy of Republican and Democratic viewers. Nonpartisan viewers, however, registered a significant increase in their sense of alienation and cynicism. Thirty-eight percent of the Independents in the control group reported high levels of efficacy and confidence in government; only 29 percent of the Independents who saw the ad-watch did.[156] As with negative advertising, hostile news coverage of the campaigns erodes the participatory ethos of the Independent voters still further and widens the gap between the highly motivated partisan voters and the increasingly alienated and increasingly numerous nonpartisans.

There are a variety of reasons that these ad-watch stories failed. First, by repeating the advertisement itself, the ad-watch may strengthen recall of the advertisement, thus making favorable information about the candidate and unfavorable information about the opponent more accessible in memory. The CNN stories used in our study, which we believe are representative of the genre, repeated the theme of the advertisement several times, often replaying the relevant segments from the advertisements.

Second, the ad-watch frames the issues in the terms used by the candidates, further reinforcing the sponsoring candidate's messages. When CNN documented the misleading chronology provided in the Clinton advertisement that attacked Bush's economic performance, the report focused viewers' attention on the recession and repeatedly showed President Bush making Polyannish statements about the economy. Similarly, the ad-watch on Bush's advertisement fixated on the "tax and spend" label applied to Clinton. This style of reporting prompts viewers to judge the candidates according to the criteria provided by the advertisements, which gives the sponsor of the advertisement a significant edge.

Finally, the audience may consider the ad-watch an unfair attack by the media and side with the candidate whose advertisement is scrutinized. By singling out a particular candidate for criticism, ad-watch reports run the risk of violating the basic journalistic norm of fairness. Paradoxically, ad-watches may reduce the credibility of the press and elicit sympathy for the scrutinized candidates.

Whatever the reasons for their failure, the results of our experiments are very discouraging. To date, the most careful attempts to cover advertisements while maintaining professional standards of neutrality and fair play seem to have backfired. Even stories that pick apart a candidate's advertising can be good news for that candidate. The consequence is that ad-news chiefly magnifies the effects of candidates' commercials, providing politicians additional incentives to attack one another.

Our findings are by no means the last word on ad-watch journalism. This form of campaign coverage is still in its infancy, and our experiments may have detected the flaws with current practices as much as with the genre itself. The challenge facing reporters and editors is to develop methods of covering advertising that do not inadvertently benefit one candidate or the other. To facilitate their roles as monitors, journalists might change the ad-watch story format along the following lines:

1. *Avoid repetition of the advertisement.* Ad-watches typically replay the advertisement, sometimes straight-up, sometimes set-off in a box. While the advertisement's visuals make the story more attractive, refraining from showing the actual advertisements will minimize the danger of recycling the candidate's message.

2. *Develop two-sided ad-watches.* Almost all ad-watches single out just one candidate for scrutiny. As a result, the candidate's agenda becomes the media's agenda. To prevent this, reporters should produce ad-watches that focus on a common theme on which both candidates in a race have advertised.

3. *Use nonpartisan sources.* Ad-watches often include soundbites from representatives of the campaigns. This provides the candidates additional free air time and an opportunity to spin the news. Experts on the issues addressed in the advertisements may offer more balanced commentary on the subject matter.

Whether these suggestions will actually improve matters is an open question. Our results counsel caution. Attempts to police the airwaves can backfire just as surely as they can succeed.

CONCLUSIONS

American political campaigns focus excessively on the foibles of individual politicians and the failings of our government. Some voters (in our experiments Republicans and Independents) find attack advertisements to be more informative and persuasive than positive messages. But even these people are turned off by the pugilism of contemporary campaigns.

The reasons for the excesses are clear. Each player in the campaign game acts, reasonably enough, to defend his or her own interests. Candidates, groups, and journalists all have strong incentives to emphasize the negatives. Candidates attack each other because that is the best way to maximize their own support, while guarding against the possibility of attacks from the opposition. Groups jump into the fray to push their own political agenda into the legislative arena, though they do so with positive messages more commonly than is thought. Journalists replay political commercials, especially negative ones, because advertisements make for simple, sensational news stories. Candidates, in turn, produce negative messages to attract free media from reporters, who are drawn to the punch and counterpunch of the campaign.

All of this, however, does not absolve the electorate. The incentives to run negative advertisements or to replay them on the news originate with the viewing public. Candidates' campaign strategies are driven by voters' reactions to competing messages; since every candidate in our experiments looked comparatively weak ignoring an attack, candidates have little choice. Candidates have only one means of fending off an attack, and that is to attack. Similarly, the perverse effects of campaign reporting stem from the way people watch television news. Reporters may well attempt to act as referees, but viewers absorb not the journalists' skepticism but the very messages from which reporters are trying to protect them.

In short, we are drawn to political campaigns as spectators to a fight, and we egg the combatants on.

7

CONCLUSION

Political advertising is not the bogeyman that its critics have often portrayed it to be. As we have shown in several chapters of this book, television actually fosters the democratic ideals of an informed and reasoning electorate. Campaign commercials, which are now the dominant means of political communication in the United States, instruct people about the candidates' abilities, personalities, and ideas, and they strongly reinforce voters' partisan loyalties. Unfortunately, however, advertising is increasingly at odds with another democratic value—an active and efficacious citizenry. Negative campaigning transforms elections into an entertaining spectator sport. A healthy democracy, though, requires more than citizen spectators. We need citizen participants.

The legitimacy of particular policies and of government generally depends on elections being an expression of the popular will. If people feel distant from the electoral process, they can take no pride in the successes of the government, and they can avoid responsibility for the problems facing the nation. Similarly, high levels of electoral participation are essential for guaranteeing that government represents the public as a whole. If those dissatisfied with the political process choose to stay home, then elections will not register their dissent, and politicians have every incentive to stay the course. The most effective way that people can vent dissatisfaction is through the vote.

More and more Americans don't vote. Only half the eligible electorate turns out for presidential elections; only a third show up for midterm congressional elections. Those who do vote represent in-creasingly extreme partisan groups within the electorate. Campaign advertising has contributed significantly to the disappearance of the nonpartisan voter and the polarization of elections.

Like party loyalty, political participation is a consequence of the electoral process. Political campaigns can instill the sense that voting is a duty, that an individual's vote matters, and that elected officials are responsive to the wishes of the electorate. Or, campaigns can breed cynicism and alienation.

In an earlier era, mobilization was the name of the game. The party machines of old lived and died by their ability to get their own voters to the polls. It was a labor-intensive enterprise that produced many electoral irregularities, such as the vote of the dead in Chicago and widespread vote buying.[157] The practice of vote buying, in fact, was so widespread that one woman testified in court that she "thought it was the law to pay us fer our votes."[158] But for all its irregularities, fierce party competition pushed *up* voter turnout. A century ago, when party organizations were at the peak of their game, 70 to 80 percent of the eligible electorate voted.[159]

Political parties still play a vital role in American elections, but cam-paigns are now run by and for individual candidates, who rely heavily on the techniques of mass marketing. Unfortunately, television adver-tising has divorced voter mobilization from the goal of winning elections. While it makes campaigns more efficient (and less corrupt), it leaves candidates little incentive to stimulate high levels of partici-pation. Since broadcast advertisements reach friend and foe alike, candidates must focus on the techniques and strategies of persuasion. Increasingly, that means going on the attack and shrinking the size of the market. In the end, politicians are just as happy and some are even more likely to win with very low turnout as they are to win with very high turnout.[160]

High levels of citizen involvement and political participation have thus become collective goods, and like all collective goods, they will be underproduced. Collective goods, such as common grazing lands and waterways, public parks and roads, and clean air, have two important features. First, everyone enjoys the benefits; second, no one experi-ences the direct consequence of his/her own actions or his/her own use of the good. The result, wrote Thomas Schelling, is that "people so impinge on each other in pursuing their own interests that collectively they might be better off if they could be restrained, but no one gains individually by self restraint."[161]

Modern political campaigns present us with just such a tragedy of the political commons. We all benefit from a citizenry that feels a strong duty to vote and voice its preferences about government, but television advertising removes the incentives for candidates, journalists, and groups to foster public spiritedness. Candidates care only about their market shares, not about the total turnout. Reporters care only about getting their bylines, not about whether their stories foster faith in the political system. Interest groups care only about making an impact on government policy, not about whether that policy carries the public's blessing. Those who produce the main messages of political campaigns simply have no reason to make the people feel that the outcome of the elections is just.

This is not to say that television advertising cannot inspire participation and confidence in government. Candidates' positive campaign commercials bring people to the polls, just as attack ads turn them away. Many politicians do offer positive images of themselves and of government, and the candidates are not alone. Party committees and civic groups often take to the airwaves urging people to turn out and vote. Also, several recent lobbying campaigns have successfully used television advertising and other new technologies to rally people behind particular causes and encourage them to contact their representatives.[162]

But against the trickle of ads urging people to vote rushes a flood of negative campaign commercials that erode the participatory ethos. Candidate after candidate has turned to negative advertising, and once the gates of negative campaigning are opened, they are difficult to close. The best way to answer an attack is with another attack, and journalists, who thrive on political conflict, echo the negativity of the campaigns in their own increasingly critical and cynical reporting.

Whatever its causes, negative politics generates disillusionment and distrust among the public. Attack advertisements resonate with the popular beliefs that government fails, that elected officials are out of touch and quite corrupt, and that voting is a hollow act. The end result: lower turnout and lower trust in government, regardless of which party rules.

The marginal voter—the Independent—feels the pinch of negative advertisements most sharply. Attack ads produce the highest drop in political efficacy and in intentions to participate among nonpartisans. Most of these people have shed their traditional party attachments not because they feel ambivalent about which of the two parties they should support, but because they dislike politics in general. The hostile tenor of campaign advertising further reinforces their contempt for candidates, parties, and government. As a result, negative campaigning divides the American electorate into a voting public of party loyalists and a nonvoting public of apathetics.

With each election this schism widens. Though their growth has been glacial, Independents are now the single largest of the "partisan" groups in the electorate—36 percent, according to the Gallup poll.[163] They tend not to vote, and regardless of which party is in the majority, they do not feel that the government represents their ideas and interests. Each succeeding election raises their frustration higher yet. Our evidence is that the political campaigns deserve much of the blame for the Independents' retreat from the polls. Positive campaign advertising generally fails to reach Independents. Nonpartisans do not find the typical political commercial compelling or persuasive, and they are only further angered, frustrated, and alienated by negative campaigning. The current climate of attack politics strengthens their resolve to remain Independents, but weakens their electoral voice.

As a consequence, electoral politics are becoming less representative. Elected officials respond mainly to the opinions of those who vote, which is increasingly a partisan and ideologically extreme crowd. Contemporary campaigning discourages nonpartisans from expressing their interests and frustrations at the polls; it thus obstructs politicians from hearing their anger.

Bad campaigns make for bad government. The shrillness and hostility of campaigns infect the day-to-day politics of legislatures. The making of sausage and of legislation, goes an old saw, are best left behind closed doors. Political advertising opens up those doors and shines the harshest of light on the proceedings. Politicians have always shied away from decisions that are difficult to explain to the folks back home, but fear of attack ads makes elected officials especially skittish about casting controversial votes.

The 1994 Massachusetts Senate race exemplified the ease with which candidates can exploit peculiarities in each other's voting records. Mitt Romney, the Republican challenger, assailed Senator Edward Kennedy as soft on crime because Kennedy voted against an amendment in the Senate Judiciary Committee that would have made it easier for juveniles to be tried as adults. According to Kennedy, the amendment would almost certainly have killed the Crime Bill, and that was the reason for his nay vote in the committee. The message that got through to the voters, though, was that Kennedy was "soft" on crime. Kennedy eventually turned the 1994 election around, but only after the toughest and most expensive campaign of his career.

Stories like Kennedy's are all too common. They heighten the representatives' fears that their votes might be easily distorted in a thirty-second spot. This, in turn, makes the task of building legislative coalitions, especially bipartisan agreements, more difficult. Senator Howard Baker complained:

TIME AFTER TIME WHEN I WAS LEADER IN THE SENATE AND TRYING TO ROUND UP VOTES ON CONTROVERSIAL ISSUES, I WOULD HAVE SENATORS SAY TO ME, "HOWARD I WOULD LIKE TO VOTE WITH YOU BUT THEY WOULD KILL ME WITH NEGATIVE ADS NEXT TIME I RUN."[164]

The need to generate materials for negative commercials also produces an ugly blame game in Washington. Posturing for their next campaigns, elected officials sometimes introduce legislation designed to embarrass the opposition. This sort of behavior has heightened the gridlock in Washington over the past decade. Before his retirement, Senator John Danforth of Missouri blamed negative campaigning for the "increased mood of defensiveness or testiness, and a breakdown in the comity and collegiality that we need to function as a deliberative body."[165]

Campaign finance is a case in point. Public support for reform of campaign fund-raising and spending practices runs high, while Democratic and Republican office holders like the system the way it is. But that hasn't prevented Congress from using the issue as a political football. In 1992, the Democratic Congress passed a campaign finance bill primarily to get President Bush and the Republicans in Congress on record against it.[166] Similarly, in the waning months of the 1994 session of Congress, Senate Republicans killed Clinton's lobbying reform bill, knowing that the Democrats would be blamed for not making good on their promises to clean up Washington. Now that the Republicans hold a majority in Congress, they have the opportunity to mirror the Democrats of Bush's term, by daring Clinton to veto very popular reform legislation. Such actions make for good political strategies, but often produce incoherent public policies, or none at all.

The election of Republican majorities to the House and Senate will not end the hostilities in Washington, just as the Democrats' brief stint of unified government did not. The Democrats have every incentive to attack, block, and embarrass the majority; and the Republicans have every incentive to continue their assault on the White House. Attacking, moreover, resonates with the Republicans' antigovernment ideology. Whether those convictions square with their new majority status remains to be seen. Regardless, no end is in sight of the political hostility that has gripped Washington for the better part of a decade. Out of the nastiness and gridlock will come still more negative campaigns and still greater public frustration and alienation.

How do we short-circuit this cycle of negativity?

The usual remedy in our society for injurious or dangerous political speech is simple: more speech. Our institutions are founded on the belief that truth comes out only through the multitude of tongues. "The ultimate good desired," wrote Justice Oliver Wendell Holmes in the classic formulation of this doctrine, "is better reached by free trade in ideas. . . . [T]he best test of truth is the power of the thought to get itself accepted in the competition of the market."[167] Typically, the United States government has left the political marketplace alone. If candidates feel they have been slandered or libeled, they may, and sometimes do, sue one another.[168] But unbridled campaign discourse is almost a sacred right.

To this end, the government could expand competitive markets for political speech by guaranteeing that those attacked in political advertisements have a reasonable opportunity to respond, regardless of their own financial resources. There is precedent in the law governing the broadcast media requiring that people who are targets of personal attacks in news and editorial programs should be given equal time. Also, the Federal Communications Commission could stimulate more speech by enforcing the lowest unit rate rule. The Federal Election Campaign Act allows candidates to purchase airtime at the lowest price for a specific time and type of broadcast advertising. The FCC rarely enforces the rule, and recent audits reveal that candidates often pay the *highest* prices.[169] By lowering the cost of campaign advertising, the lowest unit rate rule would make it more feasible for candidates to respond to political attacks.

More speech, however, may only make matters worse. Equal or cheaper time to respond to attacks may simply multiply the number of negative advertisements. Candidates will be sorely tempted to use the time to punch back, rather than to defend themselves or to offer new ideas.

The government could also try to regulate political speech. In other countries, such as Great Britain, candidates are forbidden to advertise on the airwaves; only the party committees are allowed to do so. The British rules stems explicitly from a desire not to have "American style" political campaigns.[170] In the United States, the federal government currently restricts advertising by companies marketing products that have antisocial and personally harmful effects. Tobacco and alcohol advertisements, for example, have been banned from certain venues altogether and are required to include mandated health warnings in their messages and on their product labels. While similar labels for politicians border on silliness, the Federal Communications Commission does have some leeway in regulating political advertising. It requires, for instance, that each campaign commercial clearly identify the committee or person who paid for the spot and show a photo of the sponsoring candidate. But caution is warranted: political speech is at the core of the values protected by the First Amendment. Further direct regulation of political speech is probably impossible as a matter of law and undesirable as a matter of policy.

A more realistic approach involves changing the incentives that candidates face. Both the government and the market can raise the cost of airing negative campaign commercials.

One way that government can raise the stakes is by erecting legal

remedies for candidates who are unfairly attacked. Although candidates can sue for damages, the civil proceedings often last longer than
the campaign season and, thus, provide no relief when it is needed. In
the realm of product advertising, government arbitration has stream-
lined the legal procedures for companies and consumers. The Federal
Trade Commission and the state attorneys general provide grievance
mechanisms for disgruntled consumers and competitors. A similar
dispute resolution mechanism for candidates and voters may offer
some relief from negative political advertisements.

In addition, the government could allow nongovernmental agencies
to establish and enforce standards for political advertising. In product
advertising, every ad must be approved by censors at the three major
networks, who watch for unfair comparisons or false claims. About
one-third of the ads submitted each year require further revision or sub-
stantiation of their claims.[171] No such rules apply to political advertisements since communications law exempts political advertising from
censorship by broadcasters. According to many observers, lack of
screening makes political advertising fundamentally corrupt. Malcolm
MacDougall, chairman of MacDougall, Co., a product advertising
agency whose clients have included Gerald Ford in 1976 and Michael
Dukakis in 1988, highlighted the gap between political and product advertising:

> Suppose I'm Lipton and I find out that once, way back in 1948, a watch
> strap fell into a can of Campbell's soup in a factory in the South some-
> where. It was found and no one was hurt and it never happened again.
> If I said all that in an ad, no one would pay any attention. But suppose I
> ran an ad with eerie music in the background and I had some poor
> woman screaming as she discovers the watch strap and I had a grotesque
> close-up of the Campbell soup container and my tag line said: "Do you
> want a soup like this? Or do you want Lipton? We check every can." It
> would be pretty damn effective. But of course there's no way I could get
> it past the network censors.[172]

Network screening of political advertisements would force many
candidates to tone down their attacks, and possibly take the edge off
negative ads altogether. A review process with clear guidelines would
also preempt many hostile and distorting advertisements. In the ex-

treme, such standards are already in force. Since 1990, the FCC has allowed radio and television stations the right to refuse advertisements from any candidate wishing to purchase airtime. Before 1990, communications law forced stations to accept advertisements from any political candidate. The FCC struck down that requirement, citing the large number of television and radio channels now available. Some radio stations have already taken the lead in censoring political advertising by simply refusing any campaign commercials. It remains to be seen, though, whether broadcasters will actively screen commercials based on their content, tenor, or truthfulness.

Truth in political advertising, whether enforced by the courts, the government, or the broadcasters, has some practical downsides. Truth standards are very difficult to apply fairly. The agencies that oversee elections are often highly partisan themselves, and judgments about the truthfulness of political commercials seem inherently subjective. Such standards may also have a chilling effect on political advertising. If the enforcement and penalties are strict enough to have much bite (say forfeiture of office), candidates may eschew the risks of scrutiny and choose less effective means of communication, like mass mailings. Even if a workable truth standard could be invented and enforced, it remains to be seen whether it would really clean up the airwaves. Network screening and truth standards have not prevented product advertisers from criticizing their competitors. In fact, as we pointed out in Chapter 4, product advertising has seen an explosion of negative advertising similar to that in the political arena.

The most promising way for government to raise the costs to candidates of airing political attacks involves regulation of the price of advertising. We seek more positive speech, not just more speech overall. One way to obtain that is to impose a double standard on advertising rates under which only positive campaign commercials would be entitled to the lowest unit rate; television stations could charge any rate for negative commercials. This measure would give candidates enormous incentives to promote themselves, without also producing a disincentive to advertise or raising the morass of constitutional questions posed by direct restrictions.

The marketplace offers further opportunities for changing the candidates' incentives. One area is the consulting profession. Political consultants advise candidates as to which messages to air and craft the candidates' advertisements. Like other professions, political consultants should develop standards for ethical behavior and professional review. For two decades, the product advertising industry has had a panel—the National Advertising Division of the Better Business Bureau—that handles complaints about product advertisements and censures the makers of deceptive commercials. In 76 of the 104 cases that the board reviewed in 1989, it negotiated voluntary agreements with the advertisers to modify or discontinue the offending ads.[173] There is growing pressure on the American Association of Political Consultants (AAPC) to take similar steps. Criticism from product advertisers, noises about advertising reform in Congress, and growing unease about negative campaigns have opened discussions within the AAPC to develop an ethics panel. The AAPC does have a code of ethics and it does have an ethics committee within the organization, but these serve largely symbolic roles. As yet political consultants have no self-regulating mechanism in place. But the growing criticism of political consultants, especially from leaders of the commercial advertising business, might push political consultants in this direction.

A second area for market form is campaign reporting. Journalists have shown great willingness to police the airwaves in recent years. Their valiant efforts, such as ad-watches, have so far been disappointing and even counterproductive. In our study, ad-watches actually *benefit* the candidates whose messages are scrutinized in the media. Not surprisingly, candidates do everything possible to attract such coverage. It is, of course, possible to improve the genre along the lines suggested in Chapter 5. Such changes are worth a try, but likely amount to tinkering. The fundamental flaw with this sort of campaign coverage is that it replays the candidates' messages and allows the candidates to set the media's agenda.

What is more, the negativity of the news only further contributes to the withdrawal of the electorate. By constantly questioning the sincerity and motives of politicians, journalists add to Americans' cynicism about their own government.[174] In short, the outpouring of interpretive news coverage in recent years, of which ad-watches are one manifestation, is part of the problem more than it is part of the solution.

A tactical retreat is in order. Journalists should leave advertisements alone; editors should encourage reporters to get back to the beat. Although advertisements make quick and dirty stories, the more useful function of the media is to report the events of the campaigns and the ideas and policies of the candidates. This may seem like drudgery, but it allows people to see a side of the politicians that they normally would not. Covering the ads merely repeats messages that the voters have already heard.

All of these reforms have a certain degree of plausibility, since they give individual candidates stronger incentives to run positive campaigns. Each, though, also has drawbacks. Some offend civil libertarians and may not pass constitutional muster. Others raise objections from those concerned with the competitiveness of elections. As with campaign finance reform, broadcast advertising reform may inadvertently work to the benefit of those in office at the expense of challengers. And, of course, all of these solutions face the same practical obstacle that the politicians, journalists, and consultants involved in the process have little incentive to regulate themselves, just as they have no incentive to refrain from airing attack ads.

The greatest objection, though, is that none of these proposals make participation a primary concern of American political campaigns. Candidates are still as likely to win by shrinking the electorate as they are to win by enlarging it. This is the tragedy of the political commons, and it is the heart of the problem posed by television advertising.

The best insurance for more positive campaigns has nothing to do with advertising. And that is a rebirth of party campaign organizations. Political parties, like individual politicians, care first and foremost about winning. The constraints facing the parties, though, are quite different from those on candidates. The parties' interests lie in mobilizing voters as well as persuading them.

Strong parties make for more responsible campaigns for a number of reasons. First and foremost, a party-centered campaign must sell the entire ticket, not just a particular name. Since money spent to boost turnout benefits all of the party's candidates on the ticket, any one candidate has an incentive to free-ride on the others' efforts at getting out the vote. Left to their own devices, individual candidates will focus on persuading voters and let the other candidates in their party worry about turnout. Unfortunately, this means that in a candidate-centered world no one will bear the burden of inspiring one's own partisans to get to the polls. In a party-centered system, no such perverse incentive exists. The parties care equally about persuading people to support the party and mobilizing supporters to vote. Second, party-centered campaigns remove the incentive to air personal attacks. When the opposition is a collectivity (e.g., the Democratic Party), attacks on the personalities or legislative decisions of individual politicians have much less bite. A voter in California really doesn't care how Ted Kennedy voted in the Judiciary Committee on an amendment to a crime bill. Party advertisements, instead, must deal with the overall strengths and weaknesses of the competing policies and ideologies. Finally, while a party's main goal is winning a majority of seats, the party's leaders and organizers also have a stake in the health of the institutions of government. They, after all, are one of those institutions, and if the people's faith in them slips, they are likely to fall from power.

Stronger party organizations would certainly lessen the attack dog mentality of American political campaigns. Americans, though, have never embraced strong parties. Forty years ago the American Political Science Association published a lengthy blueprint for revitalizing the American parties.[175] In the intervening years, electoral and legislative reforms have further weakened the organizations to the point that they have become virtually irrelevant to the conduct of political campaigns. Most notably, primary elections have wrested control of the nominating procedure from party leaders, placing it in the hands of the candidates and the voters, and campaign finance regulations have seriously impaired the ability of parties to fund candidates. Today, all party committees combined account for only about 5 percent of the total campaign budget of a typical congressional candidate. Worse still, the tide of antiparty reforms has not yet ebbed. "Soft money," campaign funds that are funneled from the national party organizations to the state parties and then to the candidates, continues to be a sore point for reformers, who wish to close loopholes in existing laws, at any expense.

Such regulations strike us as wrong-headed, not because they benefit one party or the other, but because they hurt both. Stemming the flow of soft money would likely gut the parties' campaign organizations. Instead, campaign finance laws should be changed so as to fortify party organizations. Specifically, we favor raising the limits on the total amount that party committees can give directly to candidates. Doing so would likely give the parties greater control over their candidates' campaign messages and would make candidates more responsive to the parties' platforms. We also think that the government should provide public funds not to individual candidates, but to the Democratic and Republican National Committees. A certain fraction of public funding for parties should also be earmarked for get-out-the-vote activities. Public financing of the parties would enable their campaign organizations to engage in activities that benefit the party as a whole, but that are currently underfunded because the parties have to compete with the candidates for money.[176]

Our point, of course, is not so much that campaign messages in the television era need to be more partisan. Rather, political parties have strong incentives to cultivate an active electorate, but the organizational weakness of the American parties renders them incapable of taking responsibility for the alienating consequences of individual candidates' campaigns.

The American public, for its part, has lost patience with attack politics. Despite rhetoric of change and hope mouthed by Republicans and Democrats alike, negative campaigning continues apace and the public grows increasingly impatient for a new kind of political message. At the second presidential debate in 1992, a woman rose to ask a question of President Bush and instead scolded Bush, Clinton, and Perot for the negative tenor of their advertisements and of the first debate. To the roaring applause of the audience, she asked them not to repeat the hostilities of previous encounters and to present their own solutions to the nation's problems.

H. Ross Perot and other independent candidates are the ultimate beneficiaries of such anger. Perot won the support of one in five voters in 1992, more votes than any independent candidate since 1912. Independents have also recently captured governor's offices in Alaska, Connecticut, and Maine as voters in those states have sought refuge from the partisan rancor. And recent polls find outright majorities favoring a new, third party in the United States that would oppose the Republicans and Democrats in state and national elections.[177]

The growing support for independent candidacies and the growing frustration with negative campaigning present both a threat and an opportunity for the parties. The threat is that if negative campaigning continues to alienate people, especially nonpartisans, then the parties will lose their legitimate claim to represent the majority will, and any policies that they enact while in government will be viewed as a minority's interests imposed on the majority. The seriousness of the threat, though, opens the doors for party renewal. Over the last twenty years, Democrats and Republicans could assail one another and remain secure in the belief that come the next election the Democrats would retain control of the House of Representatives and the Republicans would win the presidency. But the electorate has now become volatile. They turned Bush out of office in 1992, despite record public approval ratings a year earlier; they handed the Democrats their walking papers in 1994, after four decades of being the majority party; and every indication is that the public will keep the Republican majorities in the House and Senate on very short leashes. Facing the wrath of a frustrated and volatile electorate, the parties' leaders now have strong incentives to cooperate and reinvent the rules of political campaigning so as to foster more positive and responsible electoral behavior. Either that, or let negative candidate-centered campaigns drive one or both of the parties into extinction.

APPENDIX A
LIST OF EXPERIMENTS

Date	Race	Candidates	Design	Manipulation	Content of Experimental Ad(s)
8/90	Governor	Dianne Feinstein, Pete Wilson	1A	Advertising tone, issue content	Environment+[-]: "When federal bureaucrats asked for permission to drill for oil off the coast of California, ——— said yes [no]." Crime+[-]: "As Mayor of ———, major crime rates rose [fell] seven percent."
10/90	Governor	Dianne Feinstein, Pete Wilson	2A	Advertising tone	DF+: "Her leadership triumphed over the fiscal crisis of Prop. 13. Voted the nation's most effective mayor, the only Democrat for the death penalty. . . ." DF-: "In six years, Pete Wilson has written one substantive bill that became law. He voted against cracking down on toxic polluters and voted to cut social security 17 times. . . ." PW+: "Pete Wilson didn't take the pay raise that Congress voted. He gave his to fight AIDS and Alzheimer's disease. . . . He knows what's important and he's there for California."

| 5/92 | U.S. Senator primary | 1A | Barbara Boxer, Mel Levine, Leo McCarthy, Gray Davis, Dianne Feinstein, William Dannemeyer, John Seymour | Advertising tone, image content | PW-: "Dianne Feinstein denies leaving San Francisco with a deficit, but the *LA Times* reported a deficit of 180 million. The *Sacramento Bee* said Feinstein left SF in a financial mess. . . ." Competence+[-]: "——— sponsored [blocked funding for] government job training programs, cracked down [went easy] on corporate polluters, and fought for [opposed] legislation to protect our civil rights." |
| | | | Barbara Boxer, Mel Levine, Leo McCarthy, Gray Davis, Dianne Feinstein, William Dannemeyer, John Seymour | Advertising tone, image content | Integrity+[-]: "——— proposed [opposed] new government ethics rules, rejected [accepted] large donations from special interests, and supported [opposed] tough penalties on S&L crooks." |

Date	Race	Candidates	Design	Manipulation	Content of Experimental Ad(s)
7/92	U.S. Senator	Barbara Boxer, Bruce Herschensohn, Dianne Feinstein, John Seymour	1A	Issue content	Crime: "April 29. Los Angeles burns. Gang and lawlessness have ruled our cities for too long. As U.S. Senator, ____ will fight for better police protection, tougher sentencing, and strengthening our justice system." Unemployment: "April 29. Los Angeles burns. 40,000 people out of work. As U.S. Senator, ____ will fight to create new jobs, to keep companies in California, and to revitalize American industry."
7/92	U.S. Senator	John Seymour	1A	Ad-watch reporting	JS-: "Dianne Feinstein consistently supports higher taxes. She boasted of cutting prison terms to their lowest levels ever. . . . She won't support term limits for politicians like herself."
8/92	U.S. Senator	Barbara Boxer, Bruce Herschensohn, Dianne Feinstein, John Seymour	1A	Advertising tone	Women's Issues+: "October 11, 1991. Anita Hill testifies before the Senate Judiciary Committee. The Senators reject Hill's testimony. ____ believes that sexual harassment is a real problem and that it is time to stand up for the rights of women."

				Women's Issues-: "October 11, 1991. Anita Hill testifies before the Senate Judiciary Committee. The Senators reject Hill's testimony. —— doesn't believe that sexual harassment is a real problem and has opposed laws that stand up for women."
8/92	President	Bill Clinton	1A	Advertising tone	Women's Issues+: "October 11, 1991. Anita Hill testifies before the Senate Judiciary Committee. The Senators reject Hill's testimony. Bill Clinton believes that sexual harassment is a real problem and that it is time to stand up for the rights of women."
					Women's Issues-: "October 11, 1991. Anita Hill testifies before the Senate Judiciary Committee. The Senators reject Hill's testimony. George Bush doesn't believe that sexual harassment is a real problem and has opposed laws that stand up for women."

Date	Race	Candidates	Design	Manipulation	Content of Experimental Ad(s)
9/92	U.S. Senator	Barbara Boxer, Bruce Herschensohn, Dianne Feinstein, John Seymour	1A	Advertising tone	Unemployment+[-]: "Since 1990, California has lost more than two million jobs. ——— will work [has done nothing] to bring jobs back to our state. As a U.S. Senator ——— will introduce [opposes] legislation to increase job training programs. . . ."
9/92	President	Bill Clinton	1A	Ad-watch reporting	BC+: "Bill Clinton has an economic plan..."
9/92	U.S. Senator	Barbara Boxer, Bruce Herschensohn	2A	Advertising tone	BB+: "Why are we spending $150 billion a year to defend Europe and Japan? . . . It's time to take care of our own."
					BB-: "Bruce Herschensohn opposes social security, wants to eliminate your home mortgage tax deduction. . . ."
					BH+: "While we lose jobs, Congress takes a pay hike. Let's have real reform and get things done."
					BH-: "Boxer bounced 143 checks and spent thousands of taxpayer dollars for VIP travel on Air Force jets. . . ."

9/92	U.S. Senator	Dianne Feinstein, John Seymour	2A	Advertising tone	DF+: "California's next Senator has to fight for jobs and economic growth here at home."
					DF-: "John Seymour has done nothing to bring jobs back to our state."
					JS+: "I'm going to fight to ensure that they don't pull the rug out from underneath our defense industry."
					JS-: "Feinstein raised taxes and the budget deficit while Mayor of San Francisco."
10/92	President	Bill Clinton, George Bush	1A	Ad-watch reporting	GB-: "To pay for his increased spending in Arkansas, Bill Clinton raised state taxes, and not just on the rich. . . ."
					BC: "America's jobless rate is at a three year high. . . . If George Bush doesn't understand the problem, how can he fix it?"

Date	Race	Candidates	Design	Manipulation	Content of Experimental Ad(s)
10/92	U.S. Senator	Barbara Boxer, Bruce Herschensohn	2A	Advertising tone	BB+: "I'm pro-environment, pro-jobs, pro-choice. . . ." BB-: "Bruce Herschensohn is anti-choice, . . . wants to abolish the Department of Education, . . . is that what you want? BH+: "Worked in the Nixon White House and Reagan transition team. . . . While we lose jobs, Congress takes a pay raise. . . ." BH-: "Boxer bounced 143 checks and voted to hide it . . . bills taxpayers for limosine rides. . . ."
10/92	President	George Bush, Bill Clinton	2A	Performance vs. character and advertising tone	GB/Character+: "I hope as President that I've earned your trust . . . a lot of being President is about character and trust. . . ." GB/Character-: "He said he was never drafted and then admitted he was drafted. . . . For Bill Clinton, it's a question of avoiding the truth."

GB/Performance+: "Here's what I'm fighting for . . . open markets, lower government spending, competition ready for the 21st century."

GB/Performance-: "Bill Clinton says he'll only tax the rich, but here's what Clinton Economics could mean to you."

BC/Character+: "I was born in a little town called Hope . . . as President, I could help to change all of our people's lives. . . ."

BC/Character-: "George Bush is running attack ads. George Bush is trying to scare you away from Bill Clinton. . . ."

BC/Performance+: "Twelve years battling the odds in one of our nation's poorest states. Arkansas now leads the nation in job growth. . . ."

BC/Performance-: "Americas jobless rate is at a three year high. . . . If George Bush doesn't understand the problem, how can he solve it?"

Date	Race	Candidates	Design	Manipulation	Content of Experimental Ad(s)
5/93	Mayor of L.A.	Michael Woo, Richard Riordan	1A	Advertising tone	RR+: "Dick Riordan has created thousands of jobs . . . championed term limits, created computer labs that teach 350,00 kids. . . ."
					RR−: "Mike Woo. Eight years on the LA City Council, eight years of decline: Now Councilman Woo wants to be mayor. Does he really deserve the position?"
					MW+: "Mike Woo knows what it takes to clean up government. He stands for campaign finance reform and will push for term limits."
					MW−: "Dick Riordan says he supports campaign finance reform, but is spending millions of his own dollars to run for mayor. Dick Riordan says he knows how to bring jobs to Los Angeles, but his business deals cost our people jobs. . . ."

1A One Ad Study; 2A Two Ad Study; + Positive Ad; − Negative Ad.

APPENDIX B
DATA ANALYSIS

This appendix describes our procedures for estimating the effects of advertising discussed in Chapters 3 through 6. Before presenting the details of measurement and analysis, we briefly consider the strengths of randomized experiments and their connection to the analytical methods employed here.

It is certainly possible to answer many of the questions posed in this book without ever doing a randomized experiment. Social and natural scientists have learned much of what they know from simple observation. Survey researchers have concluded that advertising plays some role in voting behavior and that the effects of campaign messages interact with voters' partisan predispositions. The magnitude of these effects has remained a nagging, unanswered question. Observers of the contemporary political scene have also speculated that negative campaigns turn people off, but again, a definitive answer is lacking. Like many natural phenomena, the effects of political campaigns cannot be understood by simply watching politicians, voters, and consultants in the wild. One must identify some relevant causal mechanisms and assess how well they work in the absence of many other forces that affect the behavior we see on election day.

Experiments have two advantages that allow us to speak with greater certainty about the size and nature of the effects of campaign advertising. First, and foremost, experiments involve a degree of control that is unavailable in other methods, including surveys, focus groups, and analysis of aggregate data, such as campaign expenditures. Experiments allow us to determine who sees a particular type of advertisement and to contrast those people with those who view a different sort of advertisement or no advertisement at all. We designed the experiments in this study so that the only differences between any two groups of viewers concerned one particular aspect of the campaign commercial—either the tone, the sponsor, or the subject matter. There is no confounding of the video of the ad or the context in which it is seen with the message itself.

Second, random assignment of people to videotapes allows us to derive accurate (unbiased) estimates of the reactions of individuals to particular aspects of advertisements. A simple example clarifies the importance of randomization. We want to see the effect of exposure to an advertisement on vote intentions one-half hour after the viewing. There are two people: one will see the commercial, the other will not. The effect of the commercial is the difference in the individuals' attitudes when they have seen the commercial and when they have not. We cannot, of course, both show a person a commercial and not show a person a commercial. If we show a person a videotape with the commercial first and then the same videotape without the commercial, the viewer will likely be alerted to the nature of the experimental manipulation and try to answer the questions in a way that the person thinks would satisfy the interviewers. Also, there may be some residual effect of the ad left over from the first showing.

Each person, then, is to be shown a different videotape, and the difference between the opinions of the person shown the ad and the person shown no ad is an estimate of the effect of advertising exposure. Is there a way to assign people to videotapes that will provide an especially good estimate? We could assign people arbitrarily. For example, the first person to come in the door could get the advertisement. Arbitrary assignments, such as this one, are subject to biases of which the experimenters may be unaware. Perhaps the first person to arrive at the lab is especially attentive and motivated, while the tardy person is not. These characteristics of the individuals may temper reactions to the experiment.

Random assignment of people to videotapes protects against biases due to idiosyncracies of the individuals. On average, randomized experiments will produce the right answer. Here's why. Suppose we randomly assign people to tapes by flipping a coin. If the coin lands heads, then person 1 sees the ad and person 2 sees no ad. If it is tails, then person 1 sees no ad and person 2 sees the ad. Our (statistical) expectation prior to running such an experiment is that the result will be an average of the two possible outcomes, which is identical to the average of the results had we been able to show each person both the tape with the ad and the tape without the ad.

Mathematically, let Y_i be the opinion of person i (either 1 or 2). Denote with a superscript which videotape the individual saw, either 0 (no ad) or 1 (ad). If we could show both people the tape with the ad and the tape without the ad, then the causal effect would be the average of the effect for each person. Specifically, the causal effect would be $[(Y_1^1 - Y_1^0) + (Y_2^1 - Y_2^0)]/2$. We can only estimate this quantity, and our estimate is the observed difference between the responses of *different* individuals to *different* tapes. With probability 0.5 we observe the opinions of each individual when person 1 sees the ad and person 2 does not: $Y_1^1 - Y_2^0$. And with probability .5 we observe the opposite: $Y_2^1 - Y_1^0$. The mathematical expectation is the weighted average between these two cases, where the weights are the probabilities. So the expected value of our estimate is $[.5 (Y_1^1 - Y_2^0) + .5 (Y_2^1 - Y_1^0)]$. Grouping the Y's according to subscripts (individuals) reveals that the expected value of our estimate is exactly equal to the causal effect, defined above. (For a fuller mathematical treatment of the importance and benefits of randomization see Donald Rubin, "Estimating Causal Effects in Randomized and Non-randomized Experiments," *Journal of Educational Psychology* 66 (1974): 683–704.)

A critical reader should not be satisfied with just one coin toss and one observation of the effect of the experimental manipulation. After the experiment is run, the idiosyncracies of the individuals may still affect their reactions. Randomization does not remove the unique characteristics of the subjects; rather, it transforms those factors into random errors in the responses, which we can then treat statistically. The estimate based on a single coin toss is not biased—it is just very noisy, and this noise can be reduced by conducting the experimental manipulation on many people. If we repeat the procedures above many times, then the average of the individuals' responses will be less susceptible to the unique characteristics of any one case. The precision of the experimental estimate grows at a rate of the square root of the number of people divided by the number of experimental conditions. For a simple experiment, such as the one used as an example here, having 100 people participate will produce very sharp estimates. For more complicated experiments involving many factors, much larger samples are required. To guarantee accurate estimates of the effects within each experiment required at least 240 persons per experiment. Pooling all experiments produced a total sample for the single-ad experiments of 2,250 persons.

The logic behind randomization suggests that the effects of the advertisements can be estimated by comparing the means of the response variables across different experimental groups. For example, the effect of advertising tone on turnout can be measured as simply the percent intending to vote among those who saw a positive advertisement minus the percent intending to vote among those who saw a negative advertisement. Often, though, it is better to compare the adjusted means of different groups, where the adjustment controls for other factors, such as party identification, gender, race, age, and past voting behavior, measured *before* the videotapes were viewed. Most of our results take the second form: they are the effects of the advertisements holding all other factors constant.

We prefer the estimates that include controls for other factors for three reasons. First, randomization does not always work. Random assignment of treatments provides a general safeguard against biases but it is not foolproof. By chance, too many people of a particular type may end up in one of the treatment groups, which might skew the results. One statistical test to see if such problems might exist is an F-test to see if the control variables are independent of the treatment variables. In our experiments, this test led us to accept the hypothesis that the assignment of the treatments was independent of the characteristics of the participants. Controlling for characteristics of individual viewers provides further protection against biases.

Second, control variables improve the precision of the estimated effect of the experiments. Randomization forces the nontreatment variables to be random error, but the noise from these errors can be quite high. Controls reduce the variability, thereby improving the precision of the estimated effects.

Finally, the nontreatment factors can interact with the experimental effects. Advertising, for example, largely works to reinforce party identification. Control variables allow us to determine how characteristics of individuals shape their receptiveness to the messages contained in thirty-second political ads.

The remainder of this appendix presents the results of the data analyses used to support the arguments made in Chapters 4, 5, and 6. Since Chapter 3 dealt only with unadjusted means to measure information gains, the results presented in the text need no further elaboration or statistical support. Section 1 of this appendix describes the variables used in Chapters 3 through 6. Section 2 and 3 present the regression analyses for the experiments discussed in Chapters 4 and 5, respectively. Section 4 presents the analysis of aggregate turnout data from Chapter 5. Section 5 deals with the data discussed in Chapter 6.

1. MEASUREMENT

We distinguish three types of variables in our analysis: stimuli, responses, and controls. The stimuli, or treatment variables, correspond to the experimental factors contained in our advertisements, e.g., sponsor, tone, content. The responses, or dependent variables, concern information or opinionation, voting preferences (likes and dislikes, trait ratings, issue opinions, and vote preferences), and participatory attitudes (intentions to vote and political efficacy). The controls, or independent variables, measured demographic and political characteristics of the viewers (such as gender, race, and partisanship) and aspects of the context of the experiment that could not be controlled (such as year of the experiment).

Stimuli

Our experiments manipulated three factors: the sponsor, tone, and content of the advertisements. Chapter 2 and Appendix A explain how these manipulations were actually performed.

In our analyses, the treatments were typically coded as dummy variables in the regression equations. The experimental stimuli tapped discrete, rather than continuous, variables. A person saw either a political ad or a filler (product) ad; or a person saw an ad from a Republican candidate or a Democrat; or a person saw an ad about one issue or another. The only factor that could be conceived of as a continuous variable was tone: commercials can mix the positive messages about one candidate with the negatives of the other. We chose to model the pure forms of negative and positive commercials. Advertising tone, then, is also a discrete variable.

At times we treat some of the treatment variables as trichotomies. First, in our discussion of persuasion, we code the variable that indicates the Source to take +1 if the sponsor is a Democrat, 0 if no advertisement, and −1 if the sponsor is a Republican. The dependent variable is coded similarly, +1 if a respondent intends to vote for the Democrat, −1 if a respondent intends to vote for the Republican, and 0 otherwise. In the regressions, the coefficient on Source measures the effect of an advertisement on intentions to vote for the source. The trichotomy restricts the effect to be symmetric for Republicans and Democrats. In our discussion of participation, we assign treatments with negative ads a −1, treatments with positive ads a +1, and treatments with no political ad a 0. The dependent variable equals +1 if the respondent intends to vote and 0 otherwise. The trichotomy restricts the effects of advertising tone on turnout to be symmetric—positive ads stimulate turnout by the same amount that negative ads depress it.

Responses

Three categories of dependent variables were examined: opinionation or information, voting preferences, and participatory attitudes. All of the response variables were measured in the posttest questionnaire, after subjects had seen the advertisements.

Chapter 3 examined what people learn from advertisements. Our measures of learning drew on a variety of questions. First, we gauged whether people developed any opinions at all. In each of the campaigns under investigation, our posttest questionnaire asked participants to place the candidates on the "target" issues—the issues on which they advertised. Our measure of issue information is simply a count of the number of "correct" responses to these questions. The specific questions and the identification of "correct" responses are described below.

In the 1990 gubernatorial study, participants rated both candidates' positions on the death penalty and governmental protection of the environment on a five-point scale. Participants who rated the candidates correctly (i.e., Wilson and Feinstein as proponents of the death penalty and as advocates of governmental activism in the area of the environment) were considered informed. In the two-advertisement study, the candidates discussed crime and abortion. In addition to the question on the death penalty, participants rated Feinstein and Wilson as either prolife or prochoice. For both candidates, the latter response was scored as correct.

In the 1992 Senate studies, we coded the issue evaluation that was appropriate to the content of the ad. Depending on the study, the candidates' advertisements offered positions on government jobs programs, urban crime, and women's issues. Participants were asked to indicate how well a set of terms and phrases described the candidates running for U.S. Senate. The phrases included "supports government jobs programs," "soft on crime," "will fight for women's issues," and "prochoice." When the candidates advertised on the issue of crime, responses of "not so well" and "not well at all" (with respect to being soft on crime) were considered correct; when they discussed unemployment, participants who rated the sponsor as a supporter of jobs programs were considered informed; and when the subject of the advertisement was women's issues, the correct response was the average of the "prochoice" and "will fight for women's issues" ratings. For participants in the control group, the issue information score was defined as the average percent of correct responses pooled across all three issues.

In the presidential study, we focused on only one of the candidates (Bill Clinton) and the advertisement described Clinton's prochoice stance and his responsiveness to the political interests of women. Accordingly, participants who rated Clinton as prochoice were classified as informed. In the two-advertisement study, Bush and Clinton discussed the economy and taxes. We asked participants to rate both candidates in terms of their support for government jobs programs (Clinton was in favor of such programs, Bush was opposed). We also asked participants to place the two candidates on a liberal-conservative scale. Participants who rated Clinton as liberal and Bush as conservative were considered informed.

Our second measure of learning draws on open-ended likes and dislikes. Respondents were asked to list things that they liked and disliked about the candidates. Each separate item was recorded. We separated the likes and dislikes into two categories—those that referred to issues (directly or indirectly) and those that referred to alternative considerations (such as the candidates' personalities). For each participant, we then divided the number of references to issues by the total number of references.

Chapter 4 examines the effects of advertisements on voting preferences. Preferences have both a behavioral and an attitudinal component. Our analysis emphasizes the effects of advertising on behavior. We used a standard survey question to tap voting preferences.

LOOKING AHEAD TO NOVEMBER, FOR WHOM DO YOU INTEND TO VOTE IN THE COMING ELECTION?

Respondents could choose one of the candidates listed, they could write in a candidate, they could answer that they were not yet sure, or they could specify that they did not intend to vote. Since advertisements could affect the number voting for the source or the number voting for the opponent, we coded voting preferences in a trichotomy that equaled +1 if the respondent intended to vote for the Democratic candidate, −1 if the respondent intended to vote for the Republican candidate, and 0 otherwise.

Our analysis of attitudes examined the individuals' assessments of the candidates' personal traits and their overall impressions of the candidates. Social psychological research has found that personality ratings are an extremely important component of the vote.[178] We used a standard question in this area of research.

NOW WE ARE INTERESTED IN YOUR OPINIONS ABOUT THE CANDIDATES RUNNING FOR PRESIDENT AND U.S. SENATOR. PLEASE INDICATE HOW WELL

YOU THINK EACH OF THE FOLLOWING TERMS OR PHRASES DESCRIBES EACH CANDIDATE. IF YOU AREN'T SURE OR CAN'T SAY, CIRCLE "9."

The four traits were "Intelligent," "Dishonest," "Compassionate," and "Inexperienced." Using these questions, we computed the total number of positive ratings for the sponsor and the total number of positive ratings for the opponent. We then computed the difference to arrive at the "net trait rating."

Our final measure of preference draws on open-ended likes and dislikes. Respondents were asked to freely list things that they liked and disliked about the candidates. Each separate item was recorded in our data set. For each candidate we computed the total number of likes minus the total number of dislikes. We then calculated the difference between the competing candidates' likes and dislikes to measure each respondent's overall evaluation of the candidates.

Chapter 5 examines the effects of advertising, especially negative advertising, on participation. As with preferences, participation has a behavioral component—turnout—and an attitudinal component—efficacy.

Intentions to turn out to vote were measured with a pair of questions. We asked people, first, if they were registered to vote and, then, if they intended to vote in the coming elections. The registration question was included as a means of sorting out people who lied about their intentions. Turnout rates in survey items are notorious for their inflation. In the National Election Study, participation rates are often fifteen to twenty points higher than the actual turnout rate. About half of the exaggeration in reported turnout is due to people stating that they voted, when in fact they had not.[179]

Six separate questions were used to measure efficacy. We asked respondents to state the extent to which they agreed or disagreed with each of the following statements.

1. GENERALLY SPEAKING, THOSE WHO GET ELECTED TO PUBLIC OFFICE KEEP IN TOUCH WITH THE PEOPLE IN THEIR CONSTITUENCIES.

2. IN THIS COUNTRY, POLITICS WORKS FOR THE BENEFITS OF A FEW SPECIAL INTERESTS RATHER THAN THE PUBLIC GOOD.

3. MOST POLITICIANS ARE WILLING TO TACKLE THE REAL PROBLEMS FACING AMERICA.

4. HAVING ELECTIONS MAKES GOVERNMENT RESPONSIVE TO THE VIEWS OF THE PEOPLE.

5. SOMETIMES POLITICS AND GOVERNMENT SEEM SO COMPLICATED THAT PEOPLE LIKE ME CAN'T REALLY UNDERSTAND WHAT'S GOING ON.

6. PEOPLE LIKE ME HAVE NO SAY ABOUT WHAT GOVERNMENT DOES.

We analyzed the effects of the advertisements on each of these items separately. A simple tally of the number of questions on which each participant gave a positive evaluation of the political process offers a crude measure of an individual's overall sense of efficacy.

Efficacy, of course, has many aspects. We distinguished two: the individual's confidence or trust in the governmental process and the individual's self-confidence in his or her ability to influence that process. Many people retain their faith in American government, even though they feel that their vote does not really count. Others feel cynical about the process and personally alienated. Our measure of confidence in government or "external efficacy" was the average of questions 1 through 4. Our measure of an individual's political self-confidence or "internal efficacy" was the average of questions 5 and 6.

Control Variables

A third set of variables are used as controls. These factors include characteristics of the voters and the experiments. All control variables were measured in the pretest questionnaire, before subjects had seen an experimental advertisement. Because they are relegated to the pretest these variables can affect reactions to the advertisements, but they cannot be affected by the advertisements.

The most important class of controls are characteristics of individual respondents. Several of the controls deal explicitly with political behavior and attitudes. We asked people whether and for whom they voted in the 1988 presidential election and in the 1990 California gubernatorial election. We asked respondents to indicate their partisan leanings. "Generally speaking, do you think of yourself as a Republican, a Democrat, an Independent, or what?" We asked people to place themselves on a seven-point ideology scale ranging from "Strongly Liberal" to "Strongly Conservative." We asked people to identify their own positions on such issues as the death penalty and abortion.

In addition, respondents answered several questions that tapped their levels of interest and information about politics. As an objective measure, we asked respondents to identify six important political figures (Supreme Court Justice Sandra Day O'Conner, Los Angeles Police Chief Willie Williams, Governor Pete Wilson, then-House majority whip Richard Gephardt, California Insurance Commissioner John Garamendi, and Los Angeles County Supervisor Gloria Molina). As a subjective measure, we asked

SOME PEOPLE SEEM TO FOLLOW WHAT IS GOING ON IN GOVERNMENT MOST OF THE TIME, WHETHER THERE'S AN ELECTION OR NOT; OTHERS AREN'T THAT INTERESTED. WOULD YOU SAY THAT YOU FOLLOW WHAT'S GOING ON IN GOVERNMENT MOST OF THE TIME, SOME OF THE TIME, ONLY NOW AND THEN, OR HARDLY AT ALL?

People who said "only now and then" or "hardly at all" were treated as low-interest voters; those who said "some of the time" were treated as moderate-interest voters; and those who said "most of the time" were treated as high-interest voters. The sample split fairly evenly across these three categories, with the modal response being "some of the time."

Beyond these explicitly political variables, we ascertained several demographic factors often correlated with political opinions: gender, age, race, education, and occupation. We also inquired how much television the respondent watched daily, whether the respondent watched the national news, and whether he or she watched the local news or read a newspaper or magazine. These media use questions are often used by survey researchers as surrogates for exposure to campaign advertising or news. Importantly, our analyses showed that these media use measures were unimportant.

In interpreting and extrapolating from our analyses it is important to know exactly what the variables look like. Table B1.1 presents the descriptive statistics of the treatment, control, and response variables in our one-ad studies.

Regression Estimates and Interpretations

The effect of an experimental factor is the difference between the mean of a dependent variable when the feature is present and the mean when the feature is not present. We estimated these means controlling for other factors using linear regressions. Three progressively more complicated models were estimated.

In the first type of regression model we entered the experimental factors as separate independent variables in order to estimate the overall effect of a stimulus. The following regression, taken from Table B 2.4, provides an instructive example.

$$\text{Preference} = .10 + .08 \text{ Sponsor} + .18 \text{ Party Id} + \text{ other variables}$$

Preference equals +1 if Democratic, −1 if Republican, and 0 if undecided; Sponsor equals +1 if Democratic sponsor, −1 if Republican sponsor, and 0 if no ad; Party equals +1 if the respondent is a Democrat, 0 if an Independent, and −1 if a Republican. For simplicity, we suppress the other variables in this model; the term "other variables" holds their place.

The intercept of .10 means that when there is no advertising, the Democratic lead is 10 percentage points. The coefficient of .18 on Party means that when the voter is a Democrat, the Democratic candidate's lead is 18 percentage points higher than the baseline of 10 points (i.e., 28 points in the absence of advertising). The effect of Party Identification is constrained to be symmetric, so when the voter is a Republican, the Democratic candidate's lead is 18 points lower; i.e., there is an 8-point Republican lead.

The coefficient on Sponsor (.08) measures the increase in the sponsoring candidate's lead produced by exposure to a thirty-second spot. As with Party Identification, the trichotomous specification of Source makes the effects of advertising exposure on the Democratic candidate's lead symmetric. When no political advertisement is seen, Sponsor equals 0, so the lead of the Democratic candidates in the con-

TABLE B1.1
Descriptive Statistics for One-Ad Studies

Treatment variables

Sponsor of experimental ad		Percent of cases
	Democratic candidate	50
	Republican candidate	38
	No candidate (control)	12
Tone of experimental ad		
	Negative	40
	Positive	48
	Neutral (control)	12

Response variables

Vote preference		
	Democrat	46
	Republican	18
	Not sure	36
Intentions to vote		
	Yes	63
	No	36
Recall experimental ad (excludes control group)		
	Yes	54
	No	46
Overall efficacy rating		
	Range = 0–1	Median = .20
	Mean = .29	Standard deviation = .27

Control variables

Party identification		
	Democrat	47
	Independent	30
	Republican	23
Interest in politics		
	High	29
	Moderate	43
	Low	38
Gender		
	Female	54
	Male	46
Education		
	Completed college	41
	Some college	42
	High school degree or less	17
Race		
	Caucasian	54
	African-American	25
	Other	21
Age		
	Range = 18–89	Median = 34
	Average = 37	Standard deviation = 14.5

Number of participants = 2252

---

trol group is just the baseline. When the sponsor of the political advertisement is a Democrat, the Democratic candidate's lead grows 8
percentage points, from 10 to 18 points. When the sponsor of the political advertisement is a Republican, the Democratic candidate's lead
falls 8 percentage points, from 10 to 2 points.

The second regression model introduces interactions between a treatment variable and the control variables. The interaction between Sponsor and Party is presented in full in Table B 2.4. In addition to the
indicator for Sponsor, we have created two new variables. One interacts
Sponsor with a dummy variable that indicates whether a viewer is a
member of the same party as the sponsor. The other interacts Sponsor
with a dummy variable that indicates whether a viewer is of the opposite
party as the sponsor. The variable Sponsor now corresponds to the effect
of advertising exposure among nonpartisan voters. The variable "Sponsor*Same" captures the effect of advertising exposure among viewers
who have the same party identification as the sponsor. The variable
"Sponsor*Opposite" measures the effect of advertising exposure among
viewers who have the opposite party identification as the sponsor.

$$\text{Vote} = .10 + .02 \text{ Sponsor} + .12 \text{ Sponsor}*\text{Same}$$
$$+ .03 \text{ Sponsor}*\text{Opposite} + .15 \text{ Party}$$

From these data we can reconstruct the effects of advertising exposure on each partisan group. Among Independents, an advertisement
raises support for the sponsor by 2 percentage points. Among people
of the same party as the sponsor, an advertisement raises support for
the sponsor by 14 percentage points (2 points from main Sponsor
effect plus 12 points from the interaction of Sponsor and Same Party).
Among people of the opposite party as the sponsor, an advertisement
raises support for the sponsor by 5 percentage points (2 points from
main Sponsor effect plus 3 points from the interaction of Sponsor and
Opposite Party).

A third, and somewhat different, regression specification was used
to estimate priming effects. The earlier regressions treat the vote decision as a black box. Advertisements go in; votes come out. In fact,
advertisements affect many intermediate factors that affect voting decisions—assessments of the candidates' personalities, evaluations of
the candidates' issue positions, certainty about one's beliefs, and so

on. The priming regressions examine how much weight voters give to the various factors and whether advertising exposure significantly changes the weight of specific factors.

Imagine conducting two separate regressions of voting preferences on all factors that may go into voting preferences, such as ideology, party, assessments of the candidates' personalities, and issues. One of the regressions is estimated for the subset of the participants who saw no advertisement; the other is estimated for the subset who saw an advertisement. The subscript denotes the group: 1 = advertisement, 0 = no advertisement. For simplicity of presentation assume that there are just two assessments that influence preferences, X and Z. The weights of X and Z in the vote are the constants b and c. The two regressions are

$$\text{Preference}_0 = a_0 + b_0 X + c_0 Z$$
$$\text{Preference}_1 = a_1 + b_1 X + c_1 Z$$

The difference between these two regressions captures the priming effect. The direct effect of the advertisement on preferences is $a_1 - a_0$. The priming effects are the changes in the weights of X and Z due to the advertisement, i.e., $b_1 - b_0$ and $c_1 - c_0$.

Rather than estimate two separate regressions, we used dummy variables (variables consisting of two categories scored 1 and 0) and interactions to set up a single equation that captured the direct and priming effects. The dummy variable indicated exposure to an advertisement; its coefficient captured the direct effect of advertising on preferences, $a_1 - a_0$. The evaluations of traits and of issues were entered as separate variables and interacted with the dummy variable that indicated the treatment. The coefficients on the evaluations measured the weight of these variables among viewers who saw no advertisements. The coefficients on the interactions between the evaluations and the treatment indicators measured the priming effects. Specifically, these coefficients measure how much advertising exposure changed the weight of particular evaluations. Statistical tests (t-tests) on the coefficients of these interactions can be used to assess the significance of priming effects.

One methodological subtlety arises in this specification. Should the evaluations be measured in the posttest or in the pretest? The somewhat counterintuitive answer is the posttest. The reason is that if the pretest measure of these evaluations is used and if the treatment variable affects evaluation itself as well as the weight of the evaluation, then the coefficient on the interaction will include both the change in the evaluation and the priming effect.

One final concern with these regressions is our use of the *linear* model when the dependent variable is discrete rather than continuous. If the discrete variables are nearly uniform (i.e., an equal split of the observations across categories), then the potential biases are necessarily small. However, if the dependent variable is highly skewed, then linear regression may incorrectly estimate the value of the coefficient. We explored more complicated models, such as ordered probits and logits, and found that these nonlinearities are of little concern. Though the more sophisticated models improved the estimates of the effects of some of the controls, the t-values of the advertising effects in the linear and in the nonlinear models were virtually identical across almost all of our analyses. Since the nonlinear model muddies the interpretation of the analyses considerably, we opted for the more accessible model.

2. DATA ANALYSIS FOR CHAPTER 4

Chapter 4 employs all three types of regression analyses discussed earlier: direct effects, interactions, and priming. We present the analyses behind the figures and tables in Chapter 4 in that order.

Direct Effects

The regressions shown in Table B2.1a produced the effects presented in Table 4.1. Table B2.1a corresponds to the regression estimates for the general election studies. In these regressions, the dependent variable is vote preference (=1 if the respondent intended to vote Democratic, −1 if the respondent intended to vote Republican, and 0 if the respondent was undecided). The Advertising Exposure variable equaled +1 when the advertisement was sponsored by a Democrat, −1 when the advertisement was aired by a Republican, and 0 if no advertisement was seen. The control variables for party identification and past vote were coded similarly. Table B2.1b shows the estimated effects for the primary elections. Here we present the unadjusted means

TABLE B2.1a
Regression Estimates of Effect of Advertising Exposure on Vote Preference: General Election Studies

Independent Variable	1990 Governor		1992 Senate: Riots		1992 Senate: Gender		1992 Senate: Jobs		1993 Mayor	
	ß	(S.E.)	ß	(S.E.)	ß	(S.E.)	ß	(S.E.)	ß	(S.E.)
Constant	.065	(.060)	.204	(.059)	.252	(.046)	.033	(.088)	.033	(.045)
Sponsor	.074	(.041)	.058	(.042)	.115	(.034)	.055	(.040)	.068	(.043)
Vote 1988	.256	(.061)	.168	(.057)	.187	(.033)	.300	(.074)	.659	(.042)
Party ID	.315	(.062)	.275	(.056)	.110	(.029)	.207	(.060)	.112	(.045)
Female	.165	(.080)	.045	(.046)	.006	(.040)	.143	(.078)	.117	(.063)
R^2	.35		.19		.30		.32		.68	
N	240		329		400		295		233	

TABLE B2.1B

Estimates of the Effect of Advertisements on Vote Preference: 1992 Senate Primaries

(A)
Republican Race

Sponsoring Candidate's Lead over Opponent(s)

	Treatment Group (*N*)	Baseline Group (*N*)	Effect
Sponsor			
Dannemeyer	−.017 (59)	−.018 (277)	.001
Seymour	.094 (53)	.018 (277)	.076

(B)
Democratic 2-Way Race

Sponsoring Candidate's Lead over Opponent(s)

	Treatment Group (*N*)	Baseline Group (*N*)	Effect
Sponsor			
Davis	−.014 (67)	−.108 (465)	.094
Feinstein	.286 (70)	.108 (465)	.178

(C)
Democratic 3-Way Race

Sponsoring Candidate's Lead over Opponent(s)

	Treatment Group (*N*)	Baseline Group (*N*)	Effect
Sponsor			
Boxer	−.030 (101)	−.028 (287)	.002
Levine	−.075 (107)	−.154 (287)	.079
McCarthy	.020 (107)	−.088 (287)	.108

Average effect = .076
Pooled within standard error = .032

because none of the control variables attained conventional levels of statistical significance.

We arrived at pooled estimates using a similar regression procedure for all the general election studies combined. Since this regression was also used to test for the significance of the partisan reinforcement effect, we present the results in Table B2.4.

Table B2.2 provides the estimates of the direct effect of advertising tone on support for the sponsor in both the general election and primary experiments. The tone variable was coded +1 for negative advertising and 0 for positive advertising. The control group was omitted from this analysis since we were interested in measuring the persuasiveness of negative versus positive advertising. The vote choice variable was intention to vote for the sponsor of the advertisement. This variable was created simply by multiplying the preference variable (+1 = Democratic, 0 = undecided, −1 = Republican) by the Sponsor variable (+1 = Democrat, 0 = no ad, −1 = Republican). Vote for the sponsor, therefore, equaled +1 if the participant intended to vote for the sponsor, −1 if the participant intended to vote for the opponent, and 0 if the participant chose neither candidate.

Table B2.2a presents the means, corresponding to the values in Table 4.2. Included are F-tests from the analysis of variance showing the strength of the effect of tone on preference. Table B2.2b presents the regression estimates of the effect of advertising tone, controlling for other factors. The effects are slightly smaller than the comparison of the raw means, but still significant, and the difference between the primary and general election studies remains strong.

To test the symmetry of positive versus negative effects we estimated these regressions with the control groups and used a dichotomous variable to indicate exposure to positive advertising and a separate dichotomous variable to indicate exposure to negative advertising. The F-statistic comparing the restricted and unrestricted models was 2.2, which was not large enough to reject the symmetry restriction.

Interactions

There were three types of interactive effects: Sponsor times Interest, Sponsor times Party, and Sponsor times Party times Interest. Interest

TABLE B2.2A

Effects of Advertising Tone on Vote Preference

Tone	Primary Election Experiment		General Election Experiments	
	Sponsor's Lead (N)		Sponsor's Lead (N)	
Positive	.074	(229)	.095	(692)
Negative	−.020	(345)	.190	(384)
F	3.6 ($p = .06$)		3.7 ($p = .05$)	

TABLE B2.2B

Regression Estimates of the Effects of Tone on Preference

Independent Variable	Primary Election Experiment		General Election Experiments	
	ß (S.E.)		ß (S.E.)	
Constant	.044	(.120)	−.275	(.057)
Negative ad	−.089	(.050)	.069	(.039)
Pretest preference	—		.311	(.029)
Same gender	.136	(.051)	.120	(.037)
Follow govt. affairs	−.019	(.028)	.028	(.022)
Independent	−.021	(.036)	−.082	(.041)
Female sponsor	−.149	(.058)	—	
Democrat sponsor	—		.476	(.040)
3-way primary: 1990 general	−.168	(.060)	−.019	(.047)
Rep. primary: 1993 general	−.180	(.078)	−.023	(.062)
R^2	.04		.41	
N	573		1061	

was measured as three separate dummy variables—one indicating the low-interest viewers, one indicating the moderate-interest viewers, and one indicating the high-interest viewers. An alternative measure is a numerical scale—say 1, 2, 3—but the variable is too subjectively defined to assume that the difference in interest and information between high and moderate is the same as the difference between moderate and low.

Table B2.3 presents regression estimates of the interaction between Sponsor and level of interest. These estimates were not discussed in the text but provide a useful baseline against which to contrast the effects in Table B2.5. In addition, they provide some confirmation of the nonlinear models of information and persuasion independently developed by William McGuire in the 1960s and by John Zaller in the 1980s.[180] McGuire and Zaller describe a quadratic relationship between political preferences and informativeness. They attribute this to the interaction between two factors: *exposure* to information, which we control experimentally, and *acceptance* of the messages. One impli-

TABLE B2.3

Interactive Effects of Interest in Politics and Advertising Exposure on Vote Preference: General Election

Independent Variable	ß	Standard Error
Constant	.100	.029
Sponsor * Low Interest	.078	.038
Sponsor * Moderate Interest	.112	.030
Sponsor * High Interest	.040	.029
Party identification	.181	.022
Gender	.116	.029
1988 turnout	.116	.030
1988 presidential vote	.340	.022
R^2 = .29		
N = 1716		

cation of the pattern of results in Tables B2.3–B2.5 is that partisan predisposition and level of interest may interact even after someone has been *exposed* to a message.

Partisan reinforcement was measured by interacting party identification of the viewer with the party of the sponsor. As described in the examples in section 1, we constructed dummy variables to indicate whether a viewer was of the same or the opposite party of the sponsor and we interacted those variables with the treatment variable, Sponsor. The relevant regressions are shown in Table B2.4. The first column presents the estimated effect of Sponsor without any interactions,

TABLE B2.4

Effects of Party and Advertising Exposure on Vote Preference: General Election Studies

	(1)		(2)	
Independent Variable	ß (S.E.)		ß (S.E.)	
Constant	.100	(.029)	.102	(.029)
Advertising effects				
Sponsor	.077	(.012)	.023	(.034)
Sponsor * Same Party	—		.119	(.054)
Sponsor * Opposite Party	—		.028	(.055)
Control variables				
Party ID	.182	(.022)	.152	(.031)
Past Vote	.339	(.022)	.341	(.022)
Past turnout	.115	(.030)	.113	(.029)
Gender	.115	(.029)	.114	(.030)
R^2	.28		.30	
N	1716		1716	

Same party and opposite party are dummy variables.
F-statistic for difference between the regressions is 3.9, $p < .05$

pooling across all studies. In contrast to this baseline, the second column presents the estimated effect of Sponsor interacted with the indicators Same Party and Opposite Party. As discussed earlier, Sponsor measures the effect of advertising among Independents, and Same Party and Opposite Party measure the deviations of those two groups from the Independents. To reconstruct the adjusted means for Same and Opposite party identifiers simply add the deviations to the baseline Sponsor effect.

Table B2.5 contains three separate regressions, one for each level of interest in politics, and was used to construct Figures 4.2 and 4.3. Each regression reproduces the specification in column 2 of Table B2.4 for those people identified as having a specified level of interest in politics, either low, moderate, or high interest.

Of all the control variables, only 1988 presidential vote remained stable across levels of interest. Moving from low to high levels of interest, the strength of Party Identification and Gender grew as predictors of the vote, while the importance of 1988 Turnout diminished as an indicator of preference.

The party identification numbers are especially important: the degree of party loyalty grows with the level of interest in politics. Figure 4.2 presents the unadjusted means for these groups. The adjusted means can be examined from Table B2.5, and follow the same pattern as the unadjusted means. In the absence of advertising, Party ID among low-interest voters has a coefficient of .02 and a standard error of .07, a statistically trivial effect on voting preferences. Among the moderate-interest voters, the effect of Party is .12, with a standard error of .05; this effect is highly significant. The effect of Party ID among the high-interest voters was double that of the moderate-interest voters—a coefficient of .24 with a standard error of .05.

Table B2.5 also shows that advertising exposure has the strongest reinforcing effects among the low-interest partisans, but exhibits no significant converting effects among nonpartisans and voters of the opposite party. The main effects of Sponsor are statistically insignificant in all three levels of interest. Though they have bigger magnitude than the main Sponsor effect, the interactions between Sponsor and Opposite party are statistically insignificant as well. The interactions between Sponsor and Same Party are substantively and statistically

TABLE B2.5

Effects of Experimental Ads on Vote Preference Across Levels of Interest in Politics and Categories of Party Identification: General Election Studies

	Interest in Politics		
	Low	Medium	High
Independent Variable	ß (S.E.)	ß (S.E.)	ß (S.E.)
Constant	.149 (.053)	.051 (.046)	.168 (.052)
Advertising effects			
Sponsor	−.027 (.057)	.057 (.046)	.043 (.060)
Sponsor * Same Party	.266 (.094)	.107 (.079)	.027 (.089)
Sponsor * Opposite Party	.076 (.099)	.053 (.080)	−.058 (.091)
Control variables			
Party ID	.020 (.067)	.122 (.047)	.243 (.054)
Past Vote	.300 (.046)	.298 (.037)	.365 (.036)
Past turnout	.183 (.055)	.181 (.048)	.124 (.048)
Gender	.010 (.058)	.181 (.048)	.124 (.048)
R^2	.21	.28	.40
N	391	669	656

significant among the low- and moderate-interest voters. The effect of Sponsor among people of the same party as the sponsor grows from 3 percentage points among the high-interest viewers, to 11 percentage points among the moderate-interest viewers, to 27 percentage points among the lowest-interest voters.

The pattern of coefficients in Table B2.5 suggests another way to look at the interactions between party, interest, and advertising. Rather than estimate the strength of reinforcement and conversion for each level of interest, we could have estimated the effect of interest on persuasion for each partisan group. In other words, we could have estimated Table B2.5 using the specification in Table B2.3; the treatment variables would have been interactions between Sponsor and the indicators for Low, Moderate, and High interest. The adjusted means from the estimates would have been the same as the estimates we have offered. One could imagine drawing a line for the relationship between interest and effect of advertising exposure within each partisan group. The strength of this line would measure how interest strengthens or weakens the persuasive effects of advertising. The estimates of these lines in our data were +.02 among nonpartisans, −.06 among viewers of the opposite party, and −.12 among viewers of the same party. Only the third slope is statistically significant, indicating that the effect of interest on persuasion is statistically important only among people of the same party as the sponsor. Among these partisans, the ads reinforce their political predispositions, and every unit decrease in interest (from High to Moderate or Moderate to Low) increases their loyalty by 12 percentage points. Though statistically insignificant, the negative slope of members of the opposite party suggests that interest has a similar effect among these viewers: the higher the interest of opposition partisans, the more resistant they are to the message. The positive slope among Independents suggests that the higher-interest nonpartisans are somewhat receptive to advertising, but the low-interest nonpartisans generally find the medium a turnoff.

A third variety of interactions examined in our regression analyses concerns the extent to which advertising shapes what people think that the election is about. Two separate analyses undergird our discussion of priming. The first was an estimate of priming without regard to the viewers' predispositions; the second looks at the effects of partisan priming. As described in section 1, priming was measured by regressing vote preferences on evaluations of the candidates on specific issues and the interaction of those evaluations with an indicator for advertising exposure. To show the robustness of the effects three different dependent variables were employed: vote preference, net likes and dislikes, and net trait ratings.

Table B2.6 shows the simple priming effects of issue advertising. Across all three dependent measures, the interactions between exposure to advertising and the relevant issue were statistically significant in the unemployment and crime treatments but not the women's issue treatments.

Table B2.7 shows that party affiliation mediates priming effects. Here we have introduced a main effect for issue content, which measures the extent to which a candidate benefits from issue ownership, and have interacted the advertising term with party identification. Among viewers of the party who owned the issue, priming effects were exceedingly strong. Among all other groups, the priming effects were insignificant. We have suppressed the control variables for sake of space; these are available from the authors upon request.

Footnote 67 (Chapter 4), provides corroborating evidence of the overall notion of partisan reinforcement. We regressed the Democratic candidate's share of the vote in the 1990 U.S. House elections on the 1988 presidential vote (as a measure of partisanship), campaign spending (as a measure of advertising exposure), and the interaction between the two. The independent variables are DUKAKIS VOTE and BUSH VOTE (the percent of the total vote won by each of these candidates), DEM SPEND and REP SPEND (the total expenditures of the Democratic and Republican candidates, respectively, measured in logarithms), DUK*DS and BUSH*RS (the interactions between Dukakis vote and Democratic expenditures and Bush vote and Republican expenditures), AGE of the incumbent, a dummy variable I for Incumbent, a Dummy variable D for Democratic-held seat, and an interaction I*D between the two. Table B2.8 shows the regression results. The spending variables have the proper sign—more spending helps. The interactions on the spending variables also have the sign predicted by our experiments. The more Democratic the district, the higher the effect of the Democratic candidate's expenditures; the more Republican the district, the higher the effect of the Republican candidate's expenditures. The effects are symmetric, though only the coefficient on Republican spending is statistically significant, and it is significant at the .01 level.

One final analysis in Chapter 4 concerns the interaction between negative advertising and partisanship of the viewers. Table B2.9 demonstrates the extent to which negative advertising plays on partisan predispositions of the voters. The regression in this table is similar to

TABLE B2.6

Priming Effects of Advertising Exposure: Crime, Jobs, and Women's Issues Ads

Independent Variable	Vote Preference ß (S.E.)		Likes & Dislikes ß (S.E.)		Trait Ratings ß (S.E.)	
Constant	−.029	(.024)	.022	(.019)	.046	(.024)
Abortion						
Own position on abortion	.374	(.040)	.812	(.111)	.136	(.024)
Own position Gender ad	−.053	(.070)	.128	(.144)	.038	(.041)
Crime						
Own position on death penalty	.185	(.036)	.470	(.101)	.108	(.010)
Own position Crime ad	.176	(.071)	.240	(.175)	.062	(.032)
Jobs						
Own position on gov't jobs	.096	(.028)	.255	(.078)	.057	(.014)
Own position Jobs ad	.138	(.072)	.296	(.201)	.048	(.038)
Gender	.109	(.031)	n.s.		.063	(.018)
Education	.059	(.030)	.206	(.088)	.067	(.018)
Same party	.270	(.036)	.591	(.100)	.104	(.020)
R^2	.21		.15		.14	
N	1213		1212		1213	

TABLE B2.7

Regression Estimates of Priming Interacted with Party

Independent Variable	Vote		Likes & Dislikes		Traits	
	ß	(S.E.)	ß	(S.E.)	ß	(S.E.)
Sponsor	.040	(.022)	.123	(.050)	.377	(.059)
Issue	.021	(.022)	.237	(.060)	.080	(.051)
Party ID	.235	(.032)	.041	(.072)	.046	(.078)
Sponsor * Issue	.052	(.022)	.062	(.052)	.082	(.058)
Sponsor * Party	.076	(.027)	.205	(.062)	.414	(.071)
Issue * Party	−.020	(.026)	.106	(.061)	−.142	(.071)
Sponsor * Party * Issue	−.034	(.029)	.175	(.062)	.113	(.071)
Controls suppressed						
R^2	.33		.19		.12	
N	1071		1071		1071	

Note: Regression uses same controls as in Table B2.7, but we have suppressed them to consolidate the table. Full results available on request.

that in Table B2.2, except that we pool the primary and general elections. Separate fixed effects are estimated for each experiment, but are not presented in the table. The dependent variable equals +1 if the respondent intends to vote for the sponsor of the ad, −1 if the respondent intends to vote for the opponent(s), and 0 if the respondent is undecided or does not intend to vote. Exposure to the negative (as opposed to the positive) version of an advertisement is indicated by the dummy variable Negative Ad. The variable Party Id is a trichotomy that equals +1 for Democrats, 0 for Independents, and −1 for Republicans. The first specification in Table B2.9 presents estimates of the direct effect of negative versus positive advertising and the interaction between the trichotomous party variable and exposure to a negative advertisement. The main effect here estimates the effect of negative

TABLE B2.8
Campaign Spending and Partisan Reinforcement:
1990 U.S. House Elections

Dependent Variable: Democrat's Share of Vote		

Independent Variable	ß	Standard Error
Constant	5.41	83.24
Incumbent seat	−5.35	3.01
Democratic seat	4.52	4.17
Democratic and incumbent seat	8.48	4.31
South	5.04	1.32
Percent voting for Dukakis in 1988	.277	.868
Percent voting for Bush in 1988	.544	.837
Republican spending (in logs)	−.914	.477
Democratic spending (in logs)	1.232	.718
Percent Bush * Log Republican Spending	−.026	.010
Percent Dukakis * Log Democratic Spending	.022	.018

R^2 = .81
N = 434

advertising overall, and the interaction the (symmetric) deviation of Republicans and Democrats from that baseline. The second specification estimates the effects of negative advertising for Democrats, Republicans, and Independents. Separately.

The first specification shows a strong main effect of negative advertising on the persuasiveness of campaign advertising, as well as a strong interaction between negativity and partisanship. The second specification confirms that the effect is symmetric. Democrats find positive ads slightly more persuasive than negative ones; Independents find negative ads somewhat persuasive; and Republicans are the most receptive to negative advertising.

TABLE B2.9

Persuasiveness of Negative versus Positive Ads by Party (Excluding Control Groups)

Independent Variable	(1)		(2)	
	ß (S.E.)		ß (S.E.)	
Constant	.100	(.029)	.102	(.029)
Advertising effects				
Negative ad	.099	(.044)	—	
Negative * Party ID	−.122	(.052)	—	
Negative * Democrat	—		−.029	(.057)
Negative * Independent	—		.116	(.080)
Negative * Republican	—		.204	(.089)
Control variables				
Democratic sponsor	.447	(.046)	.377	(.059)
Same party	.251	(.062)	.190	(.031)
Past vote	.386	(.033)	.382	(.033)
Past turnout	.053	(.044)	.056	(.046)
Same gender	.074	(.053)	.079	(.053)
Democrat	−.029	(.067)	−.021	(.066)
Republican	.191	(.076)	.159	(.060)
R^2	.28		.30	
N	1716		1716	

Party ID coded 1 = Democrat, 0 = Independent, −1 = Republican.
F-statistic for difference between the regressions is 2.9, $p > .1$.

The results in Table B2.9 are the product of a more extensive analysis of interactions between party of the sponsor, tone of the ad, partisanship of the viewers, and type of election (primary or general). Our data show no evidence that these other interactions are statistically important. In other words, the discrepant effects of negative ads between the primary and the general elections evident in Table B2.2 results not from the party labels of the sponsors or the distinctive nature of the two elections, but from the greater receptiveness of more liberal viewers (who were overrepresented in our primary election study) to positive messages.

3. DATA ANALYSIS FOR CHAPTER 5

Chapter 5 considered the effects of advertising on the participatory ethos of the electorate. Here we present the experimental results; the next section details the analysis of aggregate turnout data and campaign tone.

Table B3.1 shows the effect of advertising exposure on participatory attitudes. The table contains regression results for three dependent variables—intentions to vote (TURNOUT), confidence in the electoral process (EXTERNAL EFFICACY), and political self-confidence (INTERNAL EFFICACY). The treatment variables are exposure to one advertisement and exposure to two advertisements. In addition, we have included control variables for the particular electoral context (presidential, gubernatorial, and senatorial general election), with the constant capturing the Senate primary, and we have included various demographic and political variables that research on participation has previously shown to be important.

The tone of the experiment was coded as a trichotomy (+1 for positive advertising, 0 for no advertisement, and −1 for negative advertisements). The coefficient on this variable restricts the effects of negative and positive advertisements to be symmetric. The coefficient of +.023, for example, means that the average turnout in the positive advertising conditions was 2.3 percentage points higher than the turnout in the no-advertising conditions and that turnout in the negative advertising conditions was 2.3 percentage points lower than turnout in the no-advertising conditions. Accordingly, the total turnout difference between the positive and negative conditions was 4.6 percentage points.

Two questions can be raised about this specification. First, were the effects of advertising tone symmetric? Second, was the pooling of all

TABLE B3.1

Effect of Advertising Tone on Participatory Attitudes

Independent Variable	Turnout		External Efficacy		Internal Efficacy	
	ß	(S.E.)	ß	(S.E.)	ß	(S.E.)
Constant	.432	(.031)	.268	(.017)	.346	(.033)
Advertising tone[a]	.023	(.009)	.014	(.006)	.026	(.013)
Interest	.073	(.014)	.004	(.007)	.102	(.018)
Gender	.026	(.018)	−.060	(.012)	.050	(.023)
Education	.017	(.018)	.024	(.012)	.051	(.024)
Age	.036	(.012)	.017	(.007)	−.047	(.016)
Race	.077	(.019)	.059	(.012)	.011	(.025)
Newspaper reader	.048	(.014)	.009	(.008)	.027	(.018)
Information	.067	(.013)	−.009	(.007)	.038	(.015)
Partisanship	.112	(.024)	.079	(.013)	.057	(.026)
R^2	.20		.09		.15	
N	2216		2216		790	

[a] +1 = positive ad; 0 = no ad; −1 = negative ad.

the experiments justified? We reestimated the regressions with separate indicators corresponding to exposure to positive and negative advertising and found that the differences were uniform, thus validating the assumption of symmetry. In the case of voting intentions, for instance, the coefficient for exposure to positive advertising was 2.8 and the coefficient for exposure to negative advertising was −2.1. F-tests showed that the symmetry restriction was warranted for all three dependent variables.

The decision to pool was more of a judgment call. We reran the regressions shown in Table B3.1, this time interacting the tone variable with an indicator for high- and low-salience campaigns. Of the five campaigns under examination, the Senate primaries and the Los Angeles mayoral election were considered low-salience races, and the 1990 gubernatorial and the 1992 presidential and senatorial general elections were rated as high-salience campaigns. The regressions for all three dependent variables revealed the same pattern. Advertising tone exerted greater effects on participation in low-salience elections. The salience-based difference in the effects of tone on turnout was not significant, and given our emphasis on this indicator, we decided to pool the data.[181]

At the close of Chapter 5, we considered how party identification mediated the effects of advertising tone on mobilization. For both electoral confidence and political self-confidence, the interaction between partisanship and tone was nonsignificant. This is consistent with our argument that negative advertising produces across-the-board decreases in public spiritedness. We did detect a significant interaction, however, on intentions to vote. These regressions are presented in Table B3.2.

4. AGGREGATE DATA ON CAMPAIGN TONE AND TURNOUT

Aggregate turnout figures and demographics for each state came from two separate sources. First, we used the turnout and demographic figures reported by Michael Barone and Grant Ujifusa, *The Almanac of American Politics, 1994*, Washington, DC: The National Journal, 1993. Second, we relied on the Census mailback and undercount rates reported in U.S. Bureau of the Census, *Content Reinterview Study: Accuracy of Data for Selected Population and House Characteristics as Measured by Reinterview*, PHC90-E2, Washington, DC: U.S. Government Printing Office, 1993. Controlling for literacy and factors related to the ability to fill out the census forms, these variables measure the "civic culture" of the state.

To measure the tone of the 1992 general elections campaigns, we relied on newspaper reporting of the races as contained in the NEXIS and DATATIMES databases. These databases provided full-text reproductions of articles about the thirty-four Senate races from more than thirty major daily newspapers and five politically oriented magazines (such as the *Cook Political Report, Roll Call*, and the *Hotline*). A

TABLE B3.2

Effects of Advertising Tone and Partisanship on Participatory Attitudes

Independent Variable	Vote Intentions		External		Internal	
	ß	(S.E.)	ß	(S.E.)	ß	(S.E.)
Constant	.492	(.025)	.257	(.017)	.375	(.032)
Negative	−.013	(.011)	−.016	(.007)	−.017	(.015)
Negative * Party	−.034	(.021)	.008	(.014)	−.029	(.028)
Education	.017	(.019)	.022	(.012)	.062	(.025)
Gender	.027	(.019)	−.056	(.012)	−.025	(.025)
Age	.036	(.012)	.016	(.007)	−.042	(.016)
Party	−.320	(.024)	−.077	(.013)	−.065	(.026)
Race (white)	.078	(.019)	.058	(.012)	.020	(.025)
Interest	.073	(.014)	−.001	(.009)	.123	(.017)
Print use	.049	(.014)	.015	(.009)	.017	(.032)
Information	.067	(.013)	.006	(.008)	.003	(.021)
R^2	.191		.060		.11	
N	2216		2216		798	

separate search was conducted for all thirty-four senatorial campaigns. The search retrieved all articles about a given campaign printed after the primary election and before the general election. When the search produced more than 150 articles, as was the case with seven races, then the search was limited explicitly to campaign advertising.

Each article was read by a graduate student coder who specifically looked for discussion of campaign tone. Descriptions of the campaigns as nasty, dirty, or vicious and that provided examples of attacks from each of the candidates were classified as instances of negative campaigning. The coder followed a strict scheme to place each race into one of three campaign tone categories. If a majority of the tone-related references to a campaign were negative (regardless of the source of the attacks), the overall campaign was coded as negative. If at least three articles mentioned that one of the candidates deliberately refrained from making a negative response to an opponent's attacks and no later article contradicted this information, then the race was coded as mixed. If the news coverage discussed the positivity of the race or made no mention of campaign tone, the race was coded as positive.

Independent of the classification based on newspaper reports, we asked two national political consultants (David Hill, a Republican, and Mark Mellman, a Democrat) to rate each of the campaigns as negative, mixed, or positive. The consultants agreed with our classification in all but one case, Kentucky, which they called mixed instead of negative. We deferred to their expertise. Our findings are unchanged if Kentucky is excluded from the analysis.

Based on the newspaper reports, the races classified as positive included Alaska, Hawaii, Idaho, Iowa, Kansas, Maryland, Nevada, North Dakota, South Dakota, Utah, Vermont, and Wisconsin. Races considered mixed were Alabama, Arizona, Florida, Illinois, Missouri, and Oklahoma. The races classified as negative included Arkansas, California (both races), Colorado, Connecticut, Georgia, Indiana, Kentucky, Louisiana, New Hampshire, New York, North Carolina, Ohio, Oregon, Pennsylvania, South Carolina, and Washington.

As in our experimental data, campaign tone was coded as a trichotomy: $+1$ for positive campaigns, 0 for mixed campaigns, and -1 for negative campaigns. The regression coefficients capture both the mobilizing effects of positive campaigns and the demobilizing effects of negative campaigns, and the trichotomy restricts the effects to be symmetric. An F-test revealed that we could not reject the hypothesis of symmetry against the alternative hypothesis that the negative and positive campaigns have differential effects on turnout.

Turnout was measured two ways. First, we computed the percent of the voting-age population that voted in each Senate election, i.e., total number of votes for Senate divided by voting-age population. Second, we calculated the ballot rolloff from the presidential vote. In 1992, the presidential election was at the top of the ticket. The Senate races came next on the ballot. The rolloff is the number of people who voted in one race but not the other. Usually, more people vote for President than vote for candidates lower on the ballot, though occasionally more people vote for the Senate than for the top of the ticket. To measure rolloff, controlling for differences in population, we computed the percent rolloff from the presidential vote, i.e., Percent Rolloff = The Difference between the Total Number of votes for President and the Total Number of Votes for Senator divided by the Total Number of Votes for President.

As a first measure of the effect of tone on electoral participation we examined the simple means of the turnout and rolloff measures in each of the categories of campaign tone. Positive Senate campaigns had average turnout rates of 57.0 percentage points and rolloff rates of 3.3 points. Mixed-tone Senate campaigns had average turnout rates of 52.4 percentage points and rolloff rates of 6.0 points. Negative Senate campaigns had average turnout rates of 49.7 percentage points and rolloff rates of 5.7 points. The F-statistics (from a one-way analysis of variance) measuring the statistical significance of the difference among these means were 4.0 for turnout (p-value = .03) and 2.7 for rolloff (p-value = .07).

Of course, many other factors affect turnout. Table B4.1 presents the regressions of Turnout and Rolloff on Campaign Tone and other factors commonly thought to affect electoral participation. These other factors include the total amount of money spent by both candidates as a measure of campaign volume, the median age, income, and education of the state population, the census mailback rate as a measure of civic culture, and the absolute value of the democratic candidate's share of the vote from 50 percent as a measure of the closeness of the race.

The effects of Campaign Tone on Turnout and Rolloff are significant at the .05 level. The difference in turnout between the positive and the negative races was 4.6 percentage points; the difference in rolloff was 2.8 points.

A further regression was performed on these data to predict the incidence of negative campaigning. The results of this regression are discussed in footnote 113 (Chapter 5). The dependent variable was

TABLE B4.1

Regression Estimates of the Effect of Tone on Turnout and Rolloff in the 1992 Senate Elections

Independent Variable	Turnout[a] ß (S.E.)		Rolloff[b] ß (S.E.)	
Constant	−.294	(.171)	.157	(.173)
Campaign tone[c]	.021	(.006)	−.012	(.006)
1988 turnout	.550	(.101)	.046	(.102)
Per capita income	.010	(.027)	.048	(.027)
Mailback rate	.337	(.149)	−.058	(.151)
Southern state	.048	(.015)	−.014	(.015)
% college-educated	.120	(.099)	−.215	(.100)
Log challenger $	.001	(.005)	−.011	(.005)
Log incumbent $	.013	(.007)	−.004	(.007)
Open seat	.011	(.012)	−.009	(.012)
(Non)closeness	−.053	(.046)	.058	(.046)
R^2	.94		.64	
N	34		34	

Note: Entries are multiple regression coefficients with standard errors in parentheses.

[a] Total votes for Senate voting-age population.

[b] (Total votes for President − total votes for Senate) / (total votes for President).

[c] 1 = positive tone; 0 = mixed tone; −1 = negative tone.

the trichotomy for tone; i.e., +1 = positive, 0 = mixed, and −1 = negative. The independent variables were CLOSENESS (absolute value of the Democrat's percent of the two-party vote minus .5), a dummy variable for SOUTH, a dummy variable for OPEN, the census MAILBACK rate, and the VOLUME of the campaign (logarithm of the total spending of the incumbent and the challenger parties' candidates per capita). The results of the ordinary least squares regression are shown in Table B4.2.

5. DATA ANALYSIS FOR CHAPTER 6

The data analysis contained in Chapter 6 is considerably simpler than that in Chapters 4 and 5. The presentation of voting preferences in the two-ad studies consists of simple means. Controlling for other factors had little effect on the results. Readers interested in regression analyses of the preference data in the two-ad studies are encouraged to consult our paper "Television Advertising and Campaign Strategy," presented at the 1991 meeting of the American Association for Public Opinion Research.

The data on interest group campaigning come from the Federal Elections Commission's annual reports of Independent Expenditures. The FEC provides very explicit instructions to political action commit-

TABLE B4.2

Predictors of the Tone of the 1992 Senate Campaigns

Independent Variable	ß	Standard Error
Constant	−6.055	2.312
Closeness	8.188	1.618
South	−0.134	0.262
Open	0.171	0.253
Mailback	0.527	2.655
Volume	0.652	0.143

$R^2 = .54$
$N = 34$

tees (which they now call separate and segregated funds, or SSFs) on what qualifies as an independent expenditure and how their reports should be made. According to the FEC,

> An independent expenditure is an expenditure for a communication *expressly advocating* the election or defeat of a *clearly identified* candidate that is NOT made with the cooperation or prior consent of, or in consultation with, or at the request or suggestion of any *candidate's campaign*. . . .
>
> When an expenditure is made under the circumstances described below [in cooperation with a campaign], it results in an in-kind contribution rather than an independent expenditure and therefore counts against the SSF's [$5,000 annual] contribution limit for the candidate.[182]

The emphasis is the FEC's.

To further clarify what counts as an independent expenditure, the FEC offers the following example.

> An SSF purchases a newspaper advertisement supporting Candidate Smith without ever contacting him or any of his campaign staff. The purchase is considered an independent expenditure. If, however, before purchasing the ad, the SSF asks Candidate Smith or his campaign staff how the SSF can help the campaign or when Smith wants the ad to appear, the SSF makes an in-kind contribution on behalf of Candidate Smith. Or, if the SSF buys a campaign advertisement using text actually prepared by the Smith campaign, the SSF makes an in-kind contribution.[183]

Any organization that spends more than $200 independently on a campaign must file a detailed report of their expenditures (Schedule E. Itemized Independent Expenditures). The detailed report specifies the full name, mailing address, and ZIP code of each payee,[185] the purpose of the expenditure, the date of the expenditure, the amount of the expenditure, the name of the federal candidate supported or opposed by the expenditure and the office sought, and whether the expenditure was to "Support" or "Oppose" the candidate listed. To measure positive- and negative-interest group expenditures, we summed independent expenditures to "Support" and to "Oppose."

In our discussion of the media in Chapter 6, we estimated the effects of ad-watches on vote preferences using a regression similar to that in Table B 2.1. The numbers presented in Table 6.3 are simple means, rather than adjusted means. The results are essentially the same in the regressions. Table B 5.1 presents regression estimates of the effects of the ad-watches, controlling for other factors. For this analysis all three ad-watch experiments are pooled into a common data set. The dependent variable in the regression is Vote Preference, coded the same as above. The treatment variable ADWATCH equals +1 if the ad-watch was about a Clinton Advertisement and −1 if the ad-watch was about a Bush advertisement. As with Sponsor in our advertising experiments, a positive coefficient on ADWATCH means that the story gives the candidate whose ad is discussed a significant boost in support, and a negative coefficient means that on average these stories hurt that candidates. We also estimated the effects of the ad-watch stories about the Clinton and Bush ads separately; an F-test

TABLE B5.1

Effect of Ad-Watch Stories on Vote Preferences

Dependent Variable: Democrat's Share of Vote		
Independent Variable	ß	Standard Error
Constant	.091	.072
Ad-watch	.131	.057
Party ID	.473	.058
Vote in 1988	.177	.082
Turnout in 1988	.084	.051
Gender	.193	.051
R^2 = .42		
N = 330		

revealed that the effects could be treated symmetrically. The control variables are the same as those in Chapter 4.

Exposure to an ad-watch story raised the support for the candidate whose ad was examined by 13.1 percentage points. With a standard error of 5.2 percentage points, this coefficient has a t-statistic of 2.51, which has a p-value smaller than .01.

APPENDIX C
GAMES AND
CAMPAIGN STRATEGY

Our two-advertisement experiments were designed as tools for thinking about campaign strategy, as well as models of the effects of "saturation advertising." The idea behind the experimental setup is that campaigns can be treated as games in which the candidates are the players. Each candidate runs one advertisement, and it can be positive, negative, or some mixture of the two. The candidate's problem is that the consequences of his or her advertising choices may depend on the strategies pursued by the opposition. Game theory offers practitioners and academic researchers a rigorous method for thinking about this problem.

Here we present the bare bones of the game theory used in Chapter 6. For an elaboration of the basic principles and consideration of several important games (such as the Prisoner's Dilemma and the Battle of the Sexes) the reader is encouraged to consult R. Duncan Luce and Howard Raiffa *Games and Decisions* (New York: Wiley, 1957).

The elements of any game are the players, their payoffs, the alternative actions, and the strategies. Each candidate is a player, and the payoffs are the candidates' chances of winning the election. The form of the payoffs in this case the game is *zero-sum*: one candidate's gain is necessarily the other's loss. (The Prisoner's Dilemma is an example of a non-zero-sum game.) Candidates are assumed to maximize their probabilities of winning. Each candidate can take one of two actions: run a positive advertisement or run a negative advertisement. The probabilities of winning (the payoffs) depend on the tone of both candidates' advertisements. Strategies are combinations of actions that may be used in the game. Candidates can use the simple strategies of attack or promote, or they can mix, attacking a certain fraction of the time. If the game continues for many periods, candidates may want to use conditional strategies, tying their current decisions to the observed behavior of the competitor.

One final element is the order of play. Order can have significant effects on the results. If a candidate gets to move first, then he or she may be able to force the opposition into a particularly bad situation. Order can also matter if the candidates have imperfect information about each other or incomplete information about the situation. Since the order of play is not prescribed by any campaign rules (as it is in legislation), it is not analyzed here.

If order of play is irrelevant, a game can be represented in a two-by-two matrix, known as the normal form. (If order matters, then a game should be represented in a tree, known as the extensive form.) The rows of the matrix correspond to the possible actions of one player; the columns correspond to the possible actions of the other player. Each cell of the table contains two numbers, which are the payoffs of each player if that cell occurs. The first number is the payoff for the row player; the second, the payoff for the column player.

Table 6.1 exhibits the normal form of the advertising game between Senate candidates Barbara Boxer and Bruce Herschensohn. The game is zero-sum since the candidates care only about their probabilities of winning, and an increase in the chance that candidate A wins necessarily lowers the chance that candidate B wins. Hence, we can summarize the payoffs with a single number, one candidate's lead over the other. The cells show Boxer's lead over Herschensohn in each of the conditions. When both candidates promote themselves, Boxer's lead is 33 points. When Boxer promotes and Herschensohn attacks, her lead is 0 points. When Boxer attacks and Herschensohn promotes, her lead is 27 points. When both candidates attack, her lead is 24 points.

Based on these payoffs, we can develop a set of predictions about the campaign. The central concept of game theory is the Nash Equilibrium. A Nash equilibrium is any pair of strategies (one for each candidate) from which neither candidate would unilaterally deviate. In Table 6.1, for example, negative-negative is a Nash Equilibrium. If Herschensohn switches to promoting from attacking, given that Boxer attacks, his payoff declines from −24 points down to −27 points. If Boxer switches to promoting from negative-negative, her payoff declines from a +24 points lead to 0 points.

The Nash Equilibrium is prescriptive. It reveals what candidates *should* do if they seek a particular goal in a given setting. This concept is also descriptive. Political and economic agents who do not behave as the theory predicts are at a long-range disadvantage. Firms that offer prices that are too high or too low are undercut by the opposition and are not in business for long. Candidates who promote when they should attack or attack when they should promote will have lower probabilities of winning office than otherwise and will not be in politics for long.

One way to find a Nash Equilibrium is to rule out choices that leave one candidate worse off than some other choice, regardless of the action of his or her adversary. In the terminology of game theory, candidates begin by eliminating dominated strategies. If no single strategy is superior to all others after the dominated strategies of both candidates are ruled out, the candidates are left with a small number of advertisements to choose among. The best each can do is use a combination of these undominated spots, known as a mixed strategy. If, for instance, two choices are undominated, then the candidate will use one some fraction of the time and the second the rest of the time. Since the payoffs are actually estimated payoffs, we will consider a payoff to be greater than another if it is statistically larger in a one-tailed test.

Applying this reasoning to Table 6.1 produces negative-negative as an equilibrium. First, consider Herschensohn's reasoning. From his perspective, lower numbers are superior. If Boxer promotes, he does much better if he goes negative rather than positive (0 versus 33-point deficit). If Boxer attacks, he does somewhat better attacking (24- versus 27-point deficit). Herschensohn, then, will attack no matter what Boxer does. Now consider Boxer's reasoning. Given that Herschensohn will definitely attack, she does much better attacking as well (24- versus 0-point lead). The Nash Equilibrium, then, is attack-attack.

The two-ad experiments presented here represent just the tip of the iceberg in the study of campaign strategy. To date, theoretical and empirical work on campaign strategy has been sparse. Our own studies have ignored the content of advertising and the order of play. And more work needs to be done to determine the origins of the finding that candidates are weakest when they promote while the opposition attacks.[185]

Combining game theory and experiments, however, offers a promising framework for understanding campaigns. Two-ad experiments show the interactive effects of competing campaign messages. Game theory provides a simple set of tools for interpreting those results and transforming them into practical campaign advice.

NOTES

CHAPTER 1

1. The FCC recorded campaign spending on broadcasting throughout the 1960s. Their figures reveal that television advertising grew from 9 percent of the typical congressional campaign's budget in 1960 to 16 percent in 1968.
2. Austin Ranney, *Curing the Mischiefs of Faction* (Berkeley: University of California Press, 1975). Nelson W. Polsby, *The Consequences of Party Reform* (New York: Oxford University Press, 1983).
3. The Gallup Poll regularly measures party identification. The number of nonpartisans has steadily trended upward since the 1940s. In 1940, less than 20 percent identified themselves as Independents; today more than 35 percent do. For a complete trend from 1940 to 1994 see "Public opinion roundup," *The American Enterprise* (March/April 1994): 86.
4. The rate of third-party challenges in Congress does not seem unusually high today, compared to historical figures. Steven J. Rosenstone, Roy Behr, and Ed Lazarus, *Third Parties in America* (Princeton, NJ: Princeton University Press, 1984). Bruce Cain, John Ferejohn, and Morris Fiorina, *The Personal Vote* (Cambridge, MA: Harvard University Press, 1988).
5. Expenditures on broadcast advertising far exceed expenditures on get-out-the-vote activities, direct mail, and other forms of voter contact. In 1992, for example, House and Senate candidates spent slightly more than $190 million on television advertising. Such expenditures accounted for 52 percent of all funds spent in the Senate elections and 34 percent of all money spent in contested House elections. Dwight Morris and Murielle E. Gamache, *Handbook of Campaign Spending* (Washington DC: Congressional Quarterly, 1994).

215

6. Feinstein's standing in the California Poll, conducted by the Field Organization, climbed from eighteen points down to five points up. Field Poll, *Release # 1521* (13 February 1990).

7. Quoted in David R. Runkel, ed., *Campaign for President: The Managers Look at 1988* (Dover, MA: Auburn House, 1989), p. 164.

CHAPTER 2

8. Edward Tufte, *Political Control of the Economy* (Princeton, NJ: Princeton University Press, 1978). Steven Rosenstone, *Forecasting Presidential Elections* (New Haven, CT: Yale University Press, 1985). Michael Lewis-Beck and Thomas Rice, *Forecasting Elections* (Washington, DC: Congressional Quarterly, 1992).

9. Thomas Patterson and Robert McClure, *The Unseeing Eye: the Myth of Television Power in National Elections* (New York: G.P. Putnam, 1976).

10. Importantly, the informative and persuasive effects of the advertisements seem unrelated to answers to the recall question. The rates of false recall and of forgetting in our experiments suggest that survey research that uses recall questions underestimates the magnitude of the effect of advertising exposure. Elsewhere, we have shown that the faulty memories of survey respondents bias estimates of the effects of advertising exposure toward zero. Stephen Ansolabehere and Shanto Iyengar, "Messages Forgotten," manuscript, MIT Department of Political Science, 1995.

11. This confidence is subject, of course, to the laws of probability.

12. Carl I. Hovland, "Reconciling Conflicting Results Obtained from Experimental and Survey Studies on Attitude Change," *American Psychologist* 14/1 (January 1959):8–17.

13. In California, during the final days of a campaign, it is not uncommon for a thirty-minute newscast to include ten or more campaign spots.

14. In addition to minimizing the visual differences in the advertisement, we also used identical "logos," in which the sponsoring candidate's name appeared in large red letters against a brown backdrop.

15. For the Feinstein versus Seymour Senate race, we used an ad-watch report that was originally broadcast by television station KCAL.

16. Using a weighted average of Los Angeles and Orange counties as the baseline, the demographics of this group broadly reflect the Los Angeles area, which has a median age of thirty-one, is fifty-one percent male, has 47 percent Democratic party registration, and is 47 percent white. Our pool of participants deviated from the local community in two respects: college education (24 percent in the two counties) and African-Americans (12 percent).

17. Random assignment of subjects to experimental conditions was used throughout.

18. The newscast was described to participants as having been selected at random from all local newscasts broadcast during the past week.
19. The Republican race excluded was the primary for the "long" seat, which was contested by Congressman Tom Campbell and television commentator Bruce Herschensohn.
20. Seymour was somewhat ahead of his time. Two years later, the immigration issue proved crucial in the gubernatorial campaign between Pete Wilson and Kathleen Brown.
21. "Herschensohn Halves Boxer's Lead," *Congressional Quarterly Weekly Reports* (24 October 1992):3345.
22. Of course, Ross Perot was also a major advertiser. His "infomercials" dealt mainly with the state of the economy and the decline of America as a superpower. Perot's advertising tended to avoid directly criticizing Bush or Clinton, but in one instance, he did disparage Clinton's experience as Governor of Arkansas as insufficient to cope with the problems facing the nation.

CHAPTER 3

23. The list of damning facts about the ignorance of the public is long. For instance, in 1989, only 68 percent of the public knew that the Democratic party had a majority of seats in the House of Representatives and only 75 percent could correctly identify the name of their state's governor. Only half of the public can *recall* (without any prompting) the names of their representatives in the U.S. House and Senate. Only a quarter can recall the names of challengers. Thomas Mann, *Unsafe at Any Margin: Interpreting Congressional Elections* (Washington, DC: American Enterprise Institute, 1977). Gary Jacobson, *Congressional Elections*, 3rd Ed. (Boston: Scott-Foresman, Little Brown, 1990).
24. Thomas Patterson and Robert McClure, *The Unseeing Eye: The Myth of Television Power in National Elections* (New York: G.P. Putnam, 1976). More recent survey research has found mixed evidence of learning. Consider the following two examples. Surveys using the same techniques as Patterson and McClure in California and North Carolina in 1992 found that people who reported that they had seen or read about the campaign in the news were more informed, while those who reported exposure to an advertisement were not. Steven H. Chaffee, Xinshu Zhao, and Glenn Leshner, "Political Knowledge and the Campaign Media of 1992," *Communication Research* 21 (1994): 305–24. Surveys in the 1990 Indiana Senate race found exactly the opposite pattern. David Weaver and Dan Drew, "Voter Learning in the 1990 Off-Year Election: Did the Media Matter?" *Journalism Quarterly* 70 (1993): 356–68. The equivocal nature of these results, of course, is likely due to the inadequacies of surveys as

instruments for measuring media exposure, as we discussed in Chapter 2.

25. For example, studies of the 1980 presidential campaign show that voter opinionation about the candidates' personal traits (including "moral," "inspiring," and "knowledgeable") exceeded voter awareness of the candidates' issue positions and that the effects of the campaign were more pronounced for traits than issues (see Scott Keeter and Cliff Zukin, *Uninformed Choice: The Failure of the Nominating System* [New York: Praeger, 1983], Chapter 5.) Similar results have been obtained in the case of the 1988 campaign (see Henry Brady and Richard Johnston, "What's the Primary Message?" in Gary R. Orren and Nelson W. Polsby, eds., *Media and Momentum* (Chatham, NJ: Chatham House Publishers, 1987).

26. For a close analysis of the advertising in the Helms and Gant race see Montague Kern, "The Advertising-Driven 'New' Mass Media Election and the Rhetoric of Policy Issues: The 1990 Gant Helms Race," in Robert J. Spitzer, ed., *Media and Public Policy* (Westport, CT: Praeger, 1993).

27. Darrell West, *Air Wars: Television Advertising in Election Campaigns, 1952–1992* (Washington, DC: Congressional Quarterly Press, 1994). Additional research on the policy content of contemporary campaign advertising is offered by Lynda Lee Kaid, "Political Advertising in the 1992 Campaign," in Robert Denton, Jr., ed., *The 1992 Presidential Election: A Communication Perspective* (Westport, CT: Praeger, 1994).

28. In our one-advertisement design, as described in Chapter 2, the identical advertisement is broadcast on behalf of both the candidates contesting a particular election. In the 1992 Senate races, therefore, depending on the experimental condition to which participants had been assigned, this particular advertisement was presented on behalf of Dianne Feinstein, Barbara Boxer, John Seymour, or Bruce Herschensohn. The question used to measure information asked participants to rate how well the phrase "supports government jobs programs" (or "soft on crime" or "prochoice") described each of the candidates. In the case of the advertisement on unemployment described above, the response categories of "extremely well" and "quite well" were treated as "correct" and all other responses were treated as "incorrect."

29. For evidence of the public's awareness of party differences, see Samuel Popkin, *The Reasoning Voter: Communication and Persuasion in Presidential Campaigns* (Chicago: University of Chicago Press, 1993); John R. Petrocik, "The Theory of Issue Ownership" (Los Angeles: University of California, unpublished manuscript, 1994).

30. We also carried out the analysis of spillover effects at the level of individual candidates. The results were parallel. Advertising from Clinton did

little to boost familiarity with Boxer or Feinstein. Advertising from Herschensohn (or Seymour) had no effects on familiarity with Bush, and so on.

31. The difference in the effects of negativity between the presidential and senatorial campaigns may, in part, reflect differences in the issue content of the advertisements. In the case of the Senate candidates, the experimental advertisements focused on the issues of crime and unemployment; for the presidential race, the advertisements concerned women's rights and sexual harassment.

32. For representative examples, see Philip E. Converse, "Information Flow and the Stability of Partisan Attitudes," *Public Opinion Quarterly* 26/4 (Winter 1962): 578–599; John R. Zaller, *The Nature and Origins of Mass Opinion* (New York: Cambridge University Press, 1994); Vincent Price and John R. Zaller, "Who Gets the News? Alternative Measures of News Reception and Their Implications for Research," *Public Opinion Quarterly* 57/2 (Summer 1993): 133–64.

33. Our measure of knowledge was based on five questions that asked participants to identify well-known public officials and public policies. Interest in politics was gauged by two questions asking participants to indicate how often they talked about politics and the frequency with which they "followed" public affairs. Print media usage was measured by comparing those who said they read a newspaper and weekly newsmagazine regularly with those who did so less often. Finally, our indicator of voting history was based on participants' reported vote in the 1988 presidential election. The exact wording of these questions is given in Appendix B.

34. The sharp divergence in the effects of advertising among more and less attentive voters means that the effects of advertising on learning are contingent upon voter attentiveness. In technical terms, we detected very strong interaction effects between our indicators of attentiveness to the campaign and the level of exposure to advertising. In each of the graphs shown in Figure 3.4, the interaction effect is significant at the $p < 0.05$ level.

35. The analysis of partisan and gender differences in learning is possible only in the one-advertisement studies where participants watched either a Republican or a Democratic sponsor.

36. This impressive swing produces a marked interaction effect between the party of the candidate and the party identification of the viewer ($F < .001$).

37. In statistical terms, these differences were highly significant ($p < .001$).

38. This difference in the gender-based swing in information cannot be attributed to chance fluctuations. The interaction between the gender of

the candidate and the gender of the voter was statistically significant at the .001 level.

39. This analysis, by necessity, is limited to voters who have at least one item of issue information. That is, voters who know nothing about either of the candidates are excluded.

40. The example is cited in Edwin Diamond and Stephen Bates, *The Spot: The Rise of Political Advertising on Television* (Cambridge, MA: MIT Press, 1992), pp. 377–78.

41. Thomas Patterson and Robert McClure, op cit., p. 110.

CHAPTER 4

42. Thomas Mann, *Unsafe at Any Margin: Interpreting Congressional Elections* (Washington, D.C.: American Enterprise Institute, 1977).

43. Kathleen Hall Jamieson, *Dirty Politics* (New York: Oxford University Press, 1991). Jack Germond and Jules Witcover, *Whose Bold Stripes and Bright Stars?* (New York: Warner Books, 1989). Evidence of the polarizing effects of the Bush and Dukakis campaigns among specific groups such as blacks and Republicans is found in Andrew Gelman and Gary King, "Why Are American Presidential Election Polls So Variable When Votes Are So Predictable?" *British Journal of Political Science* 23 (1993): 403–53. These authors analyze polling data from the 1988 presidential election campaign and find that the effect of the presidential election campaign was to drive blacks and women firmly into the Democratic camp and suburban voters firmly into the Republican camp. Large movements in the preferences of these groups corresponded temporally with the introduction of the Bush campaign ads, the conventions, and the debates.

44. This definition of manipulation is closely related to Robert Dahl's famous formulation of influence and power. Person A has influence over person B if in the absence of person B's action person A would have behaved differently. See Robert Dahl, *Dilemmas of Pluralist Democracy* (New Haven, CT: Yale University Press, 1982), Chapter 2; Robert Dahl, *A Preface to Democratic Theory* (Chicago: University of Chicago Press, 1956, 1965).

45. Bernard Berelson, *et al.*, *Voting* (Chicago: University of Chicago Press, 1954). Recent academic writing has further explored the psychological principles that underlie this reinforcing effect.

46. Gelman and King, op. cit. See Samuel Popkin, *The Reasoning Voter* (Chicago: University of Chicago Press, 1991); Paul Sniderman, Richard Brody, and Philip Tetlock, *Reasoning and Choice* (New York: Cambridge University Press, 1991); Richard Johnston, Andre Blais, Henry E. Brady,

and Jean Crete, *Letting the People Decide: Dynamics of the Canadian Election* (Stanford, CA: Stanford University Press, 1992).

47. Tony Schwartz, *The Responsive Chord* (Garden City, NY: Anchor Press, 1973). Earl Shorris, "A Nation of Salesmen," *Harper's* (October 1994).

48. John Cooper, quoted in Shorris, p. 46.

49. This is the "causal effect" of seeing a single experimental advertisement. For a fuller discussion of causality and its connection to randomized experiments, see Donald T. Campbell and Julian Stanley, *Experimental and Quasiexperimental Designs for Research* (Chicago: Rand-McNally, 1966). A more complicated question involves the effect of the campaign as a whole. How do viewers react to competing messages and to the statements of the media and other players? These subtleties are considered in Chapter 6.

50. One interpretation of the confidence interval 7.7 plus or minus 3.8 is that, if these experiments were repeated many times and if the variability is due solely to sampling, then in 95 percent of replications the observed effects would lie between 4.9 percentage points and 11.6.

51. Omitting the Women's Issue experiment, which may be an outlier, produces an average effect of 6.9 with a margin of error of plus or minus 2.1 points.

52. For a full discussion of the statistical significance of the results in particular studies see Appendix B. Other, less direct, measures of preference offered even stronger evidence of the persuasive effects of the experimental advertisements. Using the likes and dislikes questions described in Chapter 3, we constructed a "net likes" index, which equals the difference between the likes of the sponsor minus the dislikes of the sponsor and the likes of the opponent minus the dislikes of the opponent (i.e., Likes of Sponsor − Dislikes of Sponsor) − (Likes of Opponent − Dislikes of Opponent)). This scale ranges from +3 to −3. In our experiments, exposure to advertising significantly raised the "net likes" of the sponsoring candidates by .31. With a standard error of .13, this effect is highly significant.

53. These figures are based on electoral returns from 1988 to 1992. In 1994, turnover of seats was higher still and the number of seats won by seven points or less jumped dramatically.

54. For a review of the importance of these traits in evaluations of politicians see D. R. Kinder and D. O. Sears, "Public Opinion and Political Action," in G. Lindzey and E. Aronson, eds., *The Handbook of Social Psychology* (New York: Random House, 1985).

55. We computed the total number of positive issue and personality ratings for each candidate and determined the margin by which the sponsor's score exceeded the opponent's.

56. The difference was significant at the .001 level.
57. A regression of vote intentions on trait rating and other factors showed that a 1-point increase in our 3-point trait rating translates into a 15-percentage-point improvement in the sponsoring candidate's vote margin in one of the primaries and a 23-percentage-point increase in the other two primaries. See Appendix B for actual regression results.
58. The standard error for this effect is 1.3. With a t-statistic of 3.57, the difference of 4.8 points is significantly bigger than zero at the .001 level.
59. The weight of trait ratings in the voting decision rose fully 10 percentage points (with a standard error of 3 points) in response to our primary election advertisements. This increase in the weight of the trait ratings indirectly led to a 1.4-percentage-point increase in the sponsoring candidate's vote margin.
60. The unemployment advertisement raised the weight of jobs programs in voters' preferences from .1 to .24, and the crime advertisement raised the weight of the death penalty from .19 to .37. With t-statistics of 2.01 and 1.95, both increase are significantly bigger than 0 at the .05 level. The effects on net-likes and dislikes and on net trait ratings are more significant still. These results are presented fully in Appendix B.
61. Maurice Duverger, *Political Parties* (London: Methuen, 1954).
62. At the time of this writing, the most recent Gallup Opinion Polls show that 36 percent of the public identify themselves as Independents, 34 percent as Democrats, and 30 percent as Republicans. *Gallup Opinion Monthly* (August 1994). Of course, the trend in the number of Independents is cause for concern: in the 1950s only 20 percent considered themselves to be nonpartisans. Evidence of the high loyalty among partisans and a spirited challenge to the conventional wisdom that voters have become more nonpartisan can be found in Bruce Keith, *et al.*, *The Myth of the Independent Voter* (Berkeley: University of California Press, 1992).
63. *Gallup Opinion Monthly* (November 1988).
64. Morris Fiorina, *Divided Government* (New York: Macmillan, 1992), p. 77.
65. Meanwhile, Reagan lost just 8 percent of the Republican vote to Carter in 1980 and 4 percent of the Republican vote to Mondale in 1984. Bush lost only 7 percent of the Republican vote to Dukakis.
66. *Gallup Opinion Monthly* (December 1992). For a sophisticated analysis of the 1988 election polls see Gelman and King, "Why Are American Presidential Election Polls So Variable When Votes Are So Predictable?" *British Journal of Political Science* 23/4 (1993): 409–51. Gelman and King demonstrate that over the course of the 1988 campaign early preference polls were highly volatile. As the election wore on, people came to vote in line with their partisan preferences and self-interest.

67. For early evidence on the primacy of reinforcement see Paul Lazarsfeld, *et al.*, *The People's Choice* (New York: Columbia University Press, 1950), and Berelson, *et al.*, op cit. In Britain similar forces appear to be at work. David Butler and Donald Stokes, *Political Change in Britain* (New York: St. Martin's Press, 1966).

68. Data on campaign spending and votes provide indirect evidence of party reinforcement as well. The effectiveness of campaign spending seems to vary with the partisan composition of the district. Candidates' campaign expenditures have more bang for the buck when the districts contain more of the candidates' own partisans. This evidence is discussed in Appendix B, section 2.

69. Partisanship was measured in the pretest questionnaire with the following item: "Generally speaking, do you think of yourself as a Republican, a Democrat, an independent, or what?" We coded respondents as the same party if they responded Republican and the sponsor was Republican or if they responded Democrat and the sponsor was Democrat. "Opposite party" contains the parings of Republican respondent and Democrat sponsor or Democrat respondent and Republican sponsor. Independents identified themselves as such in the original question.

70. The anova $F = 4.6$, which has a p-value of .01. To control for other factors—past voting behavior, intentions to turnout, gender, race, and the particular experiment—the analysis was also conducted with an ordered probit. The same pattern of coefficients arose. The likelihood ratio test for the identicality of the coefficients was 9.2, which has a p-value of .01. A more conservative test is the t-test of the difference between the coefficients. The difference between the probit coefficients was .255 with an approximate t-statistic of 2.050, which has a p-value of .025.

71. The difference between weak and strong Democrats is not statistically significant owing to the relatively small numbers of Bush Democrats.

72. As earlier, we exclude the primary elections, where party identifications play no role within a given race.

73. The high Democratic lead reflects the nature of the races. Boxer, Feinstein, and Clinton led their Republican opponents in California by twenty points throughout much of the campaign season. That lead plummeted only in the last month of the election season.

74. Though substantively large, this effect does not reach statistical significance owing to the small number of people in the cell.

75. See Keith, *et al.*, op cit., who present data from the National Election Study showing the overall apathy of the Independent voters. In our own data, one in three nonpartisans expressed low levels of interest in politics, compared to one in five partisans.

76. Quoted in Earl Shorris, op cit., p. 45.

77. These experiments were the 1990 gubernatorial experiment, the 1992 Senate Riots experiment, and the 1992 Senate Unemployment experiment. All three are described in Appendix A.

78. To measure the relative weight that partisans gave to particular issues, we regressed voting intentions on the individual's evaluation of the candidates on government jobs programs and on the death penalty. The evaluation equaled 1 if the voter perceived the candidate to be in favor of jobs programs or the death penalty, -1 if the voter perceived the candidate to be opposed to jobs programs or the death penalty, and 0 if the voter was uncertain where the candidates stood. We estimated these weights for Democrats, Independents, and Republicans separately. Independent of the messages in the experimental commercials, Republican voters tend to give more weight to crime and Democratic voters tend to give more weight to unemployment. The weight of jobs programs was 20 points higher among Democrats than it was among Republicans and Independents. The standard error of this effect was 9 points, so the probability that the difference in the weights arose by chance is less than .05. The weight of death penalty was 34 points higher among Republicans than it was among Democrats and Independents. The standard error of this effect was 10 points, so the probability that the difference in the weights arose by chance is less than .01.

79. Douglas A. Hibbs, *The American Political Economy* (Cambridge, MA: Harvard University Press, 1987).

80. Henry Brady and Paul Sniderman, "Attitude Attribution: The Group Basis of Political Reasoning," *American Political Science Review* 79 (1985): 1061–78.

81. Richard Fenno, *Dan Quayle: The Making of a Senator* (Washington, DC: Congressional Quarterly, 1988).

82. *Gallup Opinion Monthly* (August 1992).

83. Neither effect reaches conventional levels of statistical significance because the estimates are leveraged on subsample sizes of forty-six male Republicans and thirty-six female Republicans.

84. A regression analysis to test the joint effects of party and gender on the reactions to the women's issues advertising revealed that, controlling for past voting behavior and various demographic factors, the Boxer and Feinstein commercials produced a statistically significant increase in their vote margins only among male Democrats. Holding other things constant, the shift in male Democrats' support attributable to exposure to a women's issues advertisement was twenty-one percentage points. With a *t*-statistic of 2.189, this shift is statistically significant at the .01 level. No other subgroups showed significant movement in their support for the source.

85. Exposure to an advertisement on either crime or unemployment, on average, increased the weight of the relevant issue by .09. Among Republicans exposed to a Republican advertisement on crime, the weight of crime was .18; among Democrats exposed to a Democratic ad on unemployment, the weight of unemployment was .26. Appendix B contains complete regression results.

86. The list comes from Bruce Felknor, *Dirty Politics* (New York: W.W. Norton, 1966), p. 27. Felknor recounts tales of political slander in the United States throughout the 19th century.

87. For various accounts as to why this change has occurred, see Edwin Diamond and Stephen Bates, *The Spot*, 3rd Ed. (Cambridge, MA: MIT Press, 1992).

88. In each of the last five national elections, the *National Journal* has published articles by Jerry Hagstrom and Robert Guskind that review most of the ads aired during the elections.

89. Darrel D. Muehling, Donald E. Stem, and Peter Raven, "Comparative Advertising: Views from Advertisers, Agencies, Media, and Policy Makers," *Journal of Advertising Research* (October/November 1989): 38–48.

90. Muehling, *et al., ibid.*, p. 46.

91. Quoted in Robert Guskind and Jerry Hagstrom, "In the Gutter," *National Journal* 20 (5 November 1988): 2782.

92. Forty-one percent offered this as an explanation for their dislike of the candidate they did not vote for. *The Los Angeles Times* (June 6, 1993).

93. A statistical test revealed that the pooling of the general election studies was legitimate.

94. The *t*-statistic for the hypothesis that the sponsor's lead in the general elections was significantly higher when the experimental commercial was negative rather than positive is 1.95, which has a *p*-value of .06.

95. The *t*-statistic for this difference is 1.92, which means that the probability of observing such a difference by chance is .06 or smaller.

96. Ideology is highly correlated with party identification. Roughly one-third of the Independents did not respond to our ideology question.

97. The Democratic viewers were highly responsive to both the negatives and the positives from Democratic candidates, and slightly more responsive to the positives. They were completely unresponsive to either negative or positive messages from Republican candidates.

98. E. J. Dionne, *Why Americans Hate Politics* (New York: Simon & Schuster, 1991). In general, Republicans and Independents express lower levels of confidence in Congress and in their own representatives in Congress, and they express higher levels of distrust of Washington than do Democrats. *The Gallup Poll Monthly* (February 1994).

99. Martin Wattenberg, *The Decline of American Political Parties, 1952–1980* (Cambridge, MA: Harvard University Press, 1984), p. 102. For more impressionistic evidence see Morris Fiorina, "The Decline of Collective Responsibility," *Daedalus* 109 (1980): 25–74.

100. According to our estimates, advertising exposure increases the sponsor's lead among his or her own partisans by fourteen percentage points, but advertising increases the sponsor's lead among nonpartisans by only three percentage points. Extrapolating to campaigns' spending decisions, these estimates imply that candidates must raise and spend four times the amount to persuade Independent voters that they would spend to reinforce their own supporters.

CHAPTER 5

101. Ken Bode, "Pull the Plug: Empower the Voters," *The Quill* (1992): 10–14; E. J. Dionne, Jr., *Why Americans Hate Politics* (New York: Simon & Schuster, 1991); Jay Rosen and Paul Taylor, *The New News and the Old News: Press and Politics in the 1990s* (Washington, DC: Brookings Institute, 1992).

102. Robert Guskind, "Airborne Attacks," *National Journal* (31 October 1992): 2482. Thomas Neale, *Negative Campaigning in National Politics: An Overview*, Report No. 91–775 GOV (Washington, DC: Congressional Research Service. A focus group study of the 1990 North Carolina Senate race concluded that exposure to attacks and counterattacks in that race increased voter cynicism. Montague Kern and Marion Just, "The Focus Group Method, Political Advertising, Campaign News, and the Construction of Candidate Images," *Political Communication* 5 (1995): 25–49.

103. Robert Putnam, "Bowling Alone: Democracy in America at the End of the Twentieth Century," mimeo (Cambridge, MA: Harvard University, August 1994).

104. Herbert Krugman, "The Impact of Television Advertising: Learning without Thought," *Public Opinion Quarterly* 29 (1965): 349–56. Steve Curwood, "Does Television Stifle Thought?" *Boston Globe* (5 August 1990): 57, 61.

105. We carried out a parallel analysis of adverting tone in the two-advertisement studies. We grouped participants into three categories— those exposed to no negative advertising, those exposed to one negative advertisement, and, finally, those who watched a negative advertisement from each of the competing candidates. The pattern of differences was generally consistent with those detected in the one-advertisement studies, although they were of much smaller magnitude.

In the case of voting intention, for instance, there was a 3 percent drop (from 73 to 70) from the most positive to the most negative levels of advertising, an insignificant difference. Confidence in elections and campaigns was also unaffected by advertising tone, but the participants' political self-confidence was substantially weakened by negative campaigning. The average score on the self-confidence index fell .71 to .48 from the least to most negative conditions, a statistically significant difference at the .10 level. We do not want to make much of these patterns since the two-advertisement design cannot hold other things constant, as we discuss in Chapter 6.

106. In the political science literature, this concept is generally termed "external efficacy," meaning that it measures the individual's beliefs in the responsiveness of electoral institutions and processes. External efficacy is to be distinguished from "internal efficacy," which reflects the individual's beliefs in his own capacity to influence the process.

107. For wordings of specific questions see Appendix B, section 1.

108. There is weak evidence that the demobilizing effects varied across the experiments. Specifically, advertising tone had slightly bigger effects in the gubernatorial, primary, and mayoral studies than in the Senate and presidential general elections. While the difference in the effects was not statistically significant for intentions to vote, it was for the efficacy ratings. The culprit might be the salience of the campaign. The Senate and presidential races attracted more attention in the news, so people may have made up their minds to vote regardless of the messages in our experiments. Another suspect is the nature of the attacks. In both the primary and the mayoral elections, the advertisements concerned the personal character of the candidates. Character attacks may have bigger effects on participatory attitudes than issue attacks. A much more complex study would be required to resolve this question. For the sake of simplicity, we present the pooled analysis in the body of the chapter. Appendix B, section 4 contains the complete analysis.

109. The margin of error is the half-width of a 95 percent confidence interval. In lay terms, the margin of error of plus or minus, say, 1.8 points means that the chance that the true effect lies outside of this interval is less than 1 in 20.

110. The F-statistic for the effect of advertising tone was significant in all three cases—3.31, $p < .04$ for intentions to vote; 3.92, $p < .02$ for electoral cynicism; and 2.02, $p < .10$ for political self-confidence.

111. Steven Rosenstone and Mark Hansen, *Mobilization, Participation, and Democracy in America* (New York: Macmillan, 1993), Chapter 2.

112. Specifically, we estimated the effect of positive and negative advertising separately on each measure of participatory attitudes and then performed a statistical test to see if we could reject the hypothesis that the two effects were identical. We could not reject the hypothesis for any of the measures at the $p = .1$ level.

113. Regression of advertising tone on a number of variables revealed that only the closeness of the election and the volume of the race predicted the tone of the 1992 Senate elections. Every percentage point increase in the closeness of the race (decrease in the vote margin) increased the probability that the race was negative by four points. A one-dollar increase in the total spending per capita by both candidates produced an decrease in the probability that the race was negative by fourteen points. See Appendix B, section 5 for details.

114. The effect is highly significant ($p < .05$); see Appendix B.

115. See Appendix B, section 5 for details.

116. The t-statistic for the difference between positive and negative races was 2.26, significant at the .05 level.

117. In the negative and mixed campaigns combined, the total number of votes for President and for Senate in 1992 was 61,168,000 and 56,543,000, respectively, for a total rolloff of 4.52 million votes. Had the rolloff rate from the presidential vote to the senatorial vote been 3.3 percent instead of the average rate of 6.0 percent in these races, the total rolloff would have been 1.23 million votes. (Note, the average uses California twice, while the total does not double-count them; hence, the average differs from the total.) This predicted value is the total of the state-by-state deviations of actual Senate turnout from the turnout that would have occurred with 3.3 percent rolloff.

118. Albert O. Hirschmann, *Exit, Voice, and Loyalty* (Cambridge, MA: Harvard University Press, 1970).

119. Michael Basil, Caroline Schooler, and Byron Reeves, "Positive and Negative Political Advertising: Effectiveness of Advertisements and Perceptions of the Candidates," in Frank Biocca, ed., *Television and Political Advertising: Psychological Processes* (Hillsdale, NJ: Lawrence Erlbaum Associates, 1991).

120. Averaging across the different candidates, the number of negative comments about the opponent increased from .48 in the positive advertising conditions to .83 in the negative conditions. This difference was statistically significant at the .01 level.

121. This difference is highly significant statistically. The effect on the efficacy of the voter was somewhat smaller. For details see Appendix B.

122. Keith, *et al.*, op cit., 1992.

123. David Mayhew, *Congress: The Electoral Connection* (New Haven, CT: Yale University Press, 1974).

124. "Candidates Viewing Public as Too Cynical for Positive TV Ads," *Boston Globe* (10 October 1994): 8.

Chapter 6

125. Quoted in Germond and Witcover, *Whose Broad Stripes and Bright Stars?* (New York: Warner Books, 1989), p. 409.

126. Thomas Patterson, *Out of Order* (New York: Knopf, 1993).

127. Jack Germond and Jules Witcover, op. cit., discuss the 1988 campaigns broadly; Chapter 26 focuses on the general election advertising campaigns.

128. Tom Rosenstiel, *Strange Bedfellows* (New York: Hyperion Books, 1993).

129. An extension of this idea is inoculation. When researchers present people with arguments against a particular attack in advance of the attack occurring, the people who see the attack advertisement tend to be unreceptive to the message. Michael Pfau and Henry Kenski, *Attack Politics: Strategy and Defense* (New York: Praeger, 1990). As a practical matter, it is, of course, hard for candidates to inoculate voters to every possible attack, and doing so may distract them from the more important aim of communicating their own ideas.

130. The order of the advertisements was reversed in half of the subjects, so we can eliminate order effects. There does seem to be an advantage to going first. Stephen Ansolabehere and Shanto Iyengar, "Why Candidates Attack," paper presented at the annual meeting of the American Association for Public Opinion Research, Tuscon, Arizona, March 1991.

131. Summaries of the commercials are reprinted in Appendix A.

132. The 1992 Senate experiment involved only 240 people, too few to determine the role of party identification in political strategy.

133. This calculation is based on the consumer price index, which has nearly tripled since 1974. Bureau of the Census, *Statistical Abstract of the United States, 1994*, 114th Ed., Table 738.

134. *Buckley* v. *Valeo* 424 U.S. 1 (1976). For an excellent discussion of the Buckley decision and its political ramifications, see Frank J. Sorauf, *Inside Campaign Finance* (New Haven, CT: Yale University Press, 1992).

135. Quoted in Chuck Alston, "The Sky's the Limit for Free Lance Ads," *Congressional Quarterly Weekly Reports* (5 November 1988): 3187.

136. Gina Garramone, a political scientist at Michigan State University, performed an inventive experiment in which she showed subjects two

negative commercials that were identical except that one was sponsored by a candidate and one was sponsored by the National Conservative Political Action Committee (NCPAC). Respondents rated the candidate attacked in these advertisements (Senator John Melcher of Montana) significantly less favorably when the commercial was sponsored by NCPAC than when it was sponsored by Melcher's opponent. Gina Garramone, "Voter Responses to Negative Political Ads," *Journalism Quarterly* 61 (1984): 250–59.

137.   Federal Election Commission, *Candidate Index of Independent Expenditures, 1991–1992.*

138.   For a good discussion of the public policy debates over negative independent expenditures, see Thomas Neale, "Negative Campaigning in National Politics: An Overview," Congressional Research Service, Report number 91-775 GOV (18 September 1991).

139.   Section 6 of Appendix B describes the filing procedures and reports of independent expenditures.

140.   Each year in the graph actually corresponds to a two-year election cycle, so 1980 represents all expenditures in the years 1979 and 1980.

141.   Republicans hold a similar, though less dramatic, edge in direct contributions. On average, Republican incumbents receive more political action committee (PAC) money than Democratic incumbents, and Republicans running in open seats receive more PAC money than Democrats running in those seats. Frank Sorauf, *Inside Campaign Finance* (New Haven, CT: Yale University Press, 1992).

142.   Quoted in Kathleen Hall Jamieson, *Dirty Politics* (New York: Oxford University Press, 1992), p. 137.

143.   Thomas Patterson, op cit.

144.   Roger Ailes quoted in Germond and Witcover, op cit., pp. 408–9.

145.   Bob Herbert, "Mugging Carl McCall," *New York Times* (2 November 1994): A23.

146.   The accounting of the newspaper articles runs through October 10, 1994, the latest date for which the *New York Times* index was available at this writing.

147.   See Stephen Ansolabehere and Shanto Iyengar, "Riding the Wave and Claiming Ownership over Issues," *Public Opinion Quarterly* 58 (1994): 335–57 for experimental evidence. The same is also true of horserace coverage. The candidate shown to lead in the polls receives an added boost from news stories about the survey results. Stephen Ansolabehere and Shanto Iyengar, "Of Horseshoes and Horseraces," *Political Communication* 4 (1994): 413–29. A further study shows that the content of news coverage reflects candidates' advertising messages. See Marilyn Roberts and Maxwell McCombs, "Agenda Setting and Po-

litical Advertising: Origins of the News Agenda," *Political Communication* 11 (1993): 249–62.

148. David R. Runkel, ed., *Campaign for President: The Managers Look at 1988* (Dover, MA: Auburn House, 1989), p. 142.

149. "Media Earn Low Marks for Election Coverage," *Boston Globe* (November 27, 1994): A7. Times Mirror Center for the People and the Press, *News Release*, 17 February 1995.

150. The pioneering efforts at scrutinizing televised spots occurred during the 1990 Texas gubernatorial campaign between Ann Richards and Clayton Williams. KVUE, an Austin television station, broadcast a series of highly critical reports on the content of both candidates' advertisements. David Broder, "Five Ways to Put Sanity Back In Elections," *Washington Post* (January 14, 1990): B1. David Broder, "Hit the Streets. . . ," *The Quill* 80 (1992): 8–9. Ken Bode, "Pull the Plug: Empower the Voters," *The Quill* 80 (1992): 10–14.

151. Allen Otten. "TV News Drops Kid-Gloved Coverage of Election, Trading Staged Sound-Bites for Hard Analysis," *Wall Street Journal* (12 October 1992): A12. Leo Wolinsky, *et al.*, "Refereeing the TV Campaign," *Washington Journalism Review* (January/February 1991): 22–28. Lynda Kaid, *et al.*, "Television News and Presidential Campaigns: The Legitimization of Televised Political Advertising," *Social Science Quarterly* 74 (1993): 274–85.

152. The rise of ad-watch journalism has, however, created something of a cottage industry in communications research. In addition to our own work, three other projects have examined the format. Most of the findings of these other researchers corroborate our own pessimistic results. See Montague Kern, Darrell West, and Dean Alger, "Political Advertising, Ad Watches, and Televised News in the 1992 Presidential Election," paper presented at the annual meeting of the American Political Science Association, Washington, DC, September 1993. The results of that study also suggest that candidates are aided by ad-watch reports. Also, see Michael Pfau and Allan Louden, "Effectiveness of Ad-Watch Formats in Deflecting Political Attack Ads," *Communication Research* 21 (1994): 325–41. This article demonstrates that the full-screen format has significant boomerang effects. One paper, which relies on small focus groups, does show positive effects of ad-watches. Joseph N. Cappella and Kathleen Hall Jamieson, "Broadcast Adwatch Effects: A Field Experiment," *Communication Research* 21 (1994): 342–65.

153. Unlike our advertising experiments, open-ended likes and dislikes of the candidates were not ascertained in these experiments.

154. This corresponds to the half-width of a 95 percent confidence interval and equals ± 1.96 times the standard error of the estimated pooled effect.

155. Appendix B contains the complete statistical analyses.
156. The corresponding figures for partisans were 41 percent efficacy in the control group and 42 percent efficacy in the ad-watch group. Among nonpartisans the drop in turnout was less than half a percentage point, and not statistically significant.

CHAPTER 7

157. "For securing [the votes of] the more disreputable elements—the 'floaters' as they are termed—new two dollar bills have been scattered abroad with a prodigality that would seem incredible but for the magnitude of the object to be obtained." Eldon Evans, *A History of the Australian Ballot System in the United States* (Chicago: University of Chicago Press, 1917). Quoted in Alan Gerber, "The Adoption of the Secret Ballot," mimeo (Yale University, 1993). This paper gives numerous examples of vote buying, including the "prices" of immigrant votes in cities like Chicago and New York.
158. Quoted in Louise Overacker, *Money in Elections* (New York: MacMillan, 1932), p. 33.
159. Paul Kleppner, *Who Voted?* (New York: Praeger, 1982). Turnout in the South was markedly lower than in the nonsouthern states. Many southern states imposed poll taxes, literacy tests, and the white primary that kept African-Americans from voting. This in turn strengthened the Democratic party in the South, so that most elections were essentially uncontested, pushing turnout down further. V. O. Key, Jr., *Southern Politics* (New York: Knopf, 1949).
160. One conventional wisdom is that there is a Democratic slant to high-turnout elections. Several careful academic studies, however, have detected no significant partisan slant among nonvoters. Raymond Wolfinger and Steven Rosenstone, *Who Votes?* (New Haven, CT: Yale University Press, 1980).
161. Thomas C. Schelling, *Micromotives and Macrobehavior* (New York: Norton, 1978), p. 111. Garrett Hardin, "The Tragedy of the Commons," *Science* 162 (13 December 1968): 1243–48.
162. Rosenstone and Hansen, op cit., Chapter 5.
163. The Gallup Poll regularly measures the party identification of the electorate. In 1940, 18 percent used the Independent label; in 1960, 23 percent did; in 1970, 28 percent did; in 1980, 31 percent did; in 1994, 36 percent did. For a complete report of the party identification trend, see "Opinion Round Up," *American Enterprise* (March/April 1994): 86.
164. United States Congress, Senate Committee on Commerce, Science, and Transportation, *Clean Campaign Act of 1985*, Hearings on S.

1310 (Washington, DC: U.S. Government Printing Office, 1986). See also Douglas Arnold, *The Logic of Congressional Action* (New Haven, CT: Yale University Press, 1991).

165. U.S. Senate Commerce Committee hearings, op cit. Eric Uslaner, *The Decline of Comity in Congress* (Ann Arbor: University of Michigan Press, 1993).

166. *Congressional Quarterly Weekly Report* (16 November 1991): 3359.

167. *Abrams* v. *U.S.* 250 U.S. 616, 630 (1919). Though Holmes's famous defense of free speech was issued in dissent, it has since become the law of the land. In the area of elections and broadcasting, for instance, Justice Brennan wrote a half-century later: "It is the purpose of the First Amendment to preserve an uninhibited marketplace of ideas in which the truth will ultimately prevail." *Red Lion Broadcasting, Inc.*, vs. *Federal Communications Commission* 395 U.S. 367, 390.

168. For example, Ruthann Aaron sued her Republican rival, William E. Brock III, for defaming her in political advertisements and statements to the media. *Washington Post* (16 November 1994): D6.

169. Thomas B. Rosenstiel, "Candidates Rates Too High, FCC Says," *Los Angeles Times* (8 September 1990).

170. Herbert Alexander, ed., *Campaign Financing* (New York: Oxford University Press, 1995).

171. Paul Taylor, "Political Pitches Called Insult to Advertising," *Washington Post* (25 March 1990): A20.

172. Quoted in Taylor, op. cit., p. A21.

173. Taylor, op cit., p. A20.

174. This critique of the media has been expanded upon by a number of writers. See, for example, Thomas Patterson, op cit.

175. Committee on Political Parties of the American Political Science Association, *Toward a More Responsible Two-Party System* (New York: Reinhart, 1950); Austin Ranney, *Curing the Mischiefs of Faction: Party Reform in America* (Berkeley: University of California Press, 1975).

176. For a concrete proposal for party financing and a fuller discussion of its benefits, see Daniel Hays Lowenstein, "On Campaign Finance Reform: The Root of All Evil Is Deeply Rooted," *Hofstra Law Review* 18 (1989): 301–67.

177. For example, the *Time Magazine*/CNN poll conducted in January 1994 by the Yankelovich Partners shows that 54 percent favor "the formation of a third political party that would run candidates for president, Congress, and state offices against the Republican and Democratic candidates." Thirty-five percent of the respondents in that survey stated that they opposed the formation of such a party and 11 percent were

not sure. "Opinion Round Up," *American Enterprise* (March/April 1994): 86.

APPENDIX B

178. D. R. Kinder and D. O. Sears "Public Opinion and Political Action," in G. Lindzey and E. Aronson (eds.), *The Handbook of Social Psychology* (New York: Random House, 1985).
179. Stephen Ansolabehere and R. Douglas Rivers, "Correcting for Nonresponse and Misreporting in Surveys," paper presented at the annual meeting of the Political Methodology Group, June 1992.
180. William J. McGuire, "Personality and Susceptibility to Social Influence," in E. F. Borgatta and W. W. Lambert, eds., *Handbook of Personality Theory and Research* (New York: Rand-McNally, 1968); John Zaller, *The Nature and Origins of Mass Opinion* (New York: Cambridge University Press, 1992).
181. The difference in the effects of advertising tone on voters' confidence in the electoral process and their own self-confidence suggests that as the use of broadcast advertising spreads to less prominent races, the demobilizing effects of negative advertising will be strengthened.
182. Federal Elections Commission, *Campaign Guide for Corporations and Labor Unions* (Washington, DC: Government Printing Office, June 1985), p. 14.
183. *Ibid.*, p. 15.
184. The names and addresses of the recipients, donors, and groups are available as a matter of complete disclosure and, by federal law, cannot be used as a list for fund raising.

APPENDIX C

185. Stegrios Skaperdas and Bernard Grofman, "Modeling Negative Campaigning," *American Political Science Review* 89 (1995): 49–61.

INDEX